Managing the Modern Law Firm

'*Managing the Modern Law Firm* offers powerful insights into the dynamics of change in the global mega-law firms that are transforming the world of corporate legal practice. This book is unique because it brings together chapters written by the leading scholars of organizations, markets, and the legal profession, with provocative analyses written by the managing partners of these very firms. It is required reading for scholars of the legal profession, managers of law firms, and the professionals and clients whose lives are shaped by these important institutions.'
Professor Robert L. Nelson, American Bar Foundation and Northwestern University

'For law firms this is an era of radical change. A substantial number of them have quickly grown into large international organisations as they have followed their clients around the world. This book offers truly helpful insights and recommendations about how to reconcile a large international organisation with the individual freedom and inspiration professionals seek.'
Dr. Konstantin Mettenheimer, Senior Partner, Freshfields Bruckhaus Deringer

'Legal firms face severe challenges in adapting their working practices in these rapidly changing times. This lively and thorough account of those challenges will give partners—and their aspiring colleagues—plenty to think about.'
Stefan Stern, Management Columnist, *Financial Times*

'Under the pressures of globalization, lawyers and law firms must find a path between a set of sharply competing concerns: collegial partnership or competitive business; broad-guaged trustee or sharp-edged expert; individual freedom or organizational discipline; niche player or global behemoth. This book provides important insight into these and other hard questions facing the modern law firm in a fast-moving era of change.'
Ben W. Heineman, Jr., Harvard Law School; Former General Counsel, GE

'Clear, challenging and thought-provoking. A quality contribution to a topic which has had too little serious attention, despite the undoubted economic importance of the legal services sector.'
Terence Kyle, General Counsel, Nomura International plc

'The duties attaching to the partnership form of ownership and governance, venerable though that form may be, have never been free of conflict. The advent of newer forms of organization and formidable competitive challenges have aggravated and complicated those tensions. With theoretical rigor and empirical savvy, *Managing the Modern Law Firm* makes a signal contribution to the literature of the professions by indicating convincing ways of rejuvenating this embattled institution. Professionals of all kinds, and corporate managers besides, have much to learn from this book.'
Ben Gerson, Editor, *Harvard Business Review*

'The evolution of several large law firms into truly global law firms is a relatively recent development in the legal profession. Even the most successful of these firms face new challenges on a daily basis, and they have no proven model to emulate. This book provides an outstanding addition to the very limited literature studying these new, powerful, and rapidly evolving institutions.'
Robert Dell, Chairman and Managing Partner, Latham & Watkins LLP

'*Managing the Modern Law Firm* is an excellent and timely contribution to an important debate. A recurring theme in professional practices is finding the right balance between spending time in personal added-value activities which tend to be client facing and spending time in management which is so often regarded as a necessary chore. It is remarkable that with the explosive growth in knowledge-based organisations no definitive means of managing them has yet been found. This book provides the thought processes and disciplines required of the leaders of these firms as they seek to develop the management structures and processes required to take forward their individual approach to this issue.'
Richard Lapthorne, Chairman, Cable and Wireless plc

'Since being made a partner 27 years ago in Accenture (or so it was to become—a story in itself!), I have been fascinated by the complex challenges of "managing" a professional services firm. In recent years I have been increasingly interested in the parallels (and contrasts) between international law firms and both accounting and consulting firms. But there has been a real paucity of serious analysis of the critical issues. This book will make an excellent contribution to answering this need.'
Vernon Ellis, Global Chairman, Accenture

'*Managing the Modern Law Firm* is a rich and stimulating blend of practical insight, scholarly analysis, historical narrative, and solid empirical research. It is a fascinating and accessible collection, written by a formidable array of leading experts who tackle their subjects with authority and gravitas and yet with a refreshing lightness of touch.'
Professor Richard Susskind OBE, author of *The Future of Law* and *Transforming the Law*

Managing the Modern Law Firm

New Challenges, New Perspectives

Edited by
Laura Empson

OXFORD
UNIVERSITY PRESS

OXFORD
UNIVERSITY PRESS

Great Clarendon Street, Oxford ox2 6DP

Oxford University Press is a department of the University of Oxford.
It furthers the University's objective of excellence in research, scholarship,
and education by publishing worldwide in

Oxford New York

Auckland Cape Town Dar es Salaam Hong Kong Karachi
Kuala Lumpur Madrid Melbourne Mexico City Nairobi
New Delhi Shanghai Taipei Toronto

With offices in

Argentina Austria Brazil Chile Czech Republic France Greece
Guatemala Hungary Italy Japan Poland Portugal Singapore
South Korea Switzerland Thailand Turkey Ukraine Vietnam

Oxford is a registered trade mark of Oxford University Press
in the UK and in certain other countries

Published in the United States
by Oxford University Press Inc., New York

© Oxford University Press 2007

The moral rights of the authors have been asserted
Database right Oxford University Press (maker)

First published 2007

British Library Cataloguing in Publication Data
Data available

Library of Congress Cataloging in Publication Data
Data available

Typeset by SPi Publisher Services, Pondicherry, India
Printed in Great Britain
on acid-free paper by
Biddles Ltd., King's Lynn, Norfolk

ISBN 978-0-19-929674-3

1 3 5 7 9 10 8 6 4 2

For Michael and Henry

Preface

This book began with a bewildered look on a lawyer's face. A select group of academics who study professional service firms were gathered for our annual conference, which is sponsored by Clifford Chance. Stuart Popham, Senior Partner of Clifford Chance, had joined us. He questioned our evidence when it seemed unconvincing and encouraged us to extend our interpretation when we seemed too cautious. He sought to apply our abstract theoretical models to his experience of reality in the legal market. As the morning progressed, this became increasingly difficult as the papers became more explicitly 'academic'. As we academics became immersed in a particularly esoteric and heated argument about a fine-grained piece of statistical analysis, I looked up and saw the bewildered look on Stuart's face.

I was struck at that moment about the absurdity of the situation. Here was a roomful of academics who were fascinated by law firms but who were unable to communicate directly with lawyers. We had chosen an unusually intelligent group of people to be the subject of our research, people who, like us, enjoyed abstract conceptualization and intellectual arguments and whose work demanded rigorous logic and the precise use of language. Yet here we were, apparently speaking an entirely different language.

I decided to do something about this, to find a way of bringing our high quality, theoretically grounded, and empirically rigorous research on law firms to the people who were trying to manage them—to build a bridge between academics and lawyers. I was pleased to find that my academic colleagues were keen to cross that bridge and that the lawyers I knew and respected were happy to meet us half-way.

Translating our research has not been a simple task. We have been greatly assisted by many partners and professional business managers within Clifford Chance. Each of the research-based chapters has been carefully reviewed by members of Clifford Chance who have made very useful suggestions about how to revise our text. Several people in particular have made valuable contributions to the development of this book, notably: Leiv Blad, Amanda Burton, Peter Charlton, Paul Greenwood, Matthew Gorman, Kate Howles, and Jeremy Sandelson. I would also like to thank Ben Gerson of *Harvard Business Review* and Partha Bose for their comments on earlier drafts of these chapters.

Above all I would like to thank Stuart Popham, not simply for inspiring the book, but for all he has done to help create a community of scholars—through Clifford Chance's sponsorship of our conference and more generally for supporting the work of the Clifford Chance Centre for the Management of Professional Service Firms at Saïd Business School, University of Oxford. Many professional service firms talk about 'thought leadership'. The partners of Clifford Chance have put their hands in their pockets and done something about it.

Finally, I would like to thank Camilla Stack, Administrator of the Clifford Chance Centre at Oxford. She has been an invaluable help to me in preparing the manuscript of this book. Camilla has a remarkable array of talents, which include a Cambridge Classics degree, exceptional word processing skills, the ability to spot a typo at a hundred paces, a sophisticated understanding of statistical analysis as well as the rules of grammar and punctuation, and a training in human psychology. All of these talents have proven useful in the preparation of this manuscript.

Laura Empson
Oxford

Contents

List of Figures   xi
List of Tables   xii
Notes on Contributors   xiii

PROLOGUE   xvii
John J. Gabarro

1. **INTRODUCTION AND OVERVIEW**   1
Laura Empson and Stuart Popham

2. **YOUR PARTNERSHIP**
SURVIVING AND THRIVING IN A CHANGING WORLD:
THE SPECIAL NATURE OF PARTNERSHIP   10
Laura Empson

3. **YOUR PEOPLE**
VALUING DIVERSITY: SOME CAUTIONARY LESSONS FROM
THE AMERICAN EXPERIENCE   37
David B. Wilkins

4. **YOUR EXPERTISE**
DEVELOPING NEW PRACTICES: RECIPES FOR SUCCESS   64
Heidi Gardner, Timothy Morris, and Narasimhan Anand

5. **YOUR CLIENT RELATIONSHIPS AND REPUTATION**
WEIGHING THE WORTH OF SOCIAL TIES: EMBEDDEDNESS AND
THE PRICE OF LEGAL SERVICES IN THE LARGE LAW FIRM MARKET   91
Brian Uzzi, Ryon Lancaster, and Shannon Dunlap

6. **YOUR INCOME**
DETERMINING THE VALUE OF LEGAL KNOWLEDGE: BILLING AND
COMPENSATION PRACTICES IN LAW FIRMS   117
Huseyin Leblebici

Contents

7. **YOUR CAPITAL**
   BUILDING SUSTAINABLE VALUE: A CAPITAL IDEA   141
   Stephen Mayson

8. **YOUR COMPETITORS**
   MAPPING THE COMPETITIVE SPACE OF LARGE US LAW FIRMS:
   A STRATEGIC GROUP PERSPECTIVE   162
   Peter D. Sherer

9. **YOUR ETHICS**
   REDEFINING PROFESSIONALISM? THE IMPACT OF MANAGEMENT
   CHANGE   186
   Royston Greenwood

10. **YOUR CHALLENGE**
    SUSTAINING PARTNERSHIP IN THE TWENTY-FIRST CENTURY:
    THE GLOBAL LAW FIRM EXPERIENCE   196
    Tony Angel

Bibliography   218
Index   231

List of Figures

2.1. Governance of professional service firms by sector (global top 100, 2003) — 12

2.2. Resolving stakeholders' competing claims in a professional service firm — 13

2.3(a). Partnership ethos — 20

2.3(b). Dynamics of partnership — 20

4.1. Four different types of new practices, based on novelty and differentiation from core — 70

4.2. Essential ingredients for new practice creation — 74

4.3. Failures of the Turf-driven recipe — 78

4.4. Failures of the Expertise-led recipe — 82

4.5. Failures of the Support-centred recipe — 86

5.1. Number of US *Fortune 250* corporations with in-house counsel departments of more than 60 attorneys — 92

5.2. 100 largest US law firms' gross revenues, 1990–2004 — 93

5.3. Standard economic model of price setting — 95

5.4. Embedded model of price setting — 95

5.5. Embeddedness and partner billing price — 111

5.6. Embeddedness and associate billing price — 111

6.1. Source of institutionalized practices in corporate law firms — 120

6.2. Distribution of alternative fee choices in different fields of law — 127

6.3. The growth in the average size of top 250 corporate law firms in the USA — 134

List of Tables

4.1. Turf considerations, sources of expertise, and organizational
support needed for different types of new practice 72

5.1. Descriptive statistics of the mega law firms, 1989–95 99

5.2. Variables used in statistical analysis and their measurement 102

6.1. A short chronology of the changes in the compensation of
attorneys and legal fees since the Roman Empire 123

6.2. The institutional logic of law firm economics 131

6.3. Descriptions of common alternative billing practices 136

8.1. Seven-cluster analysis, 1999 171

8.2. Six-cluster analysis, 2003 173

8.3. Key differences for 2003 six-cluster analysis 175

8.4. Number of lawyers in four major US cities for early and later
internationalizers and Baker & McKenzie in 2003 178

8.5. Number of international lawyers in major international cities in
2003 for early and later internationalizers and Baker & McKenzie 179

Notes on Contributors

Narasimhan Anand is Reader in Organizational Behaviour at Tanaka Business School, Imperial College London. His current research examines the development of new practice areas in management consulting and law firms. Other research interests include the evolution of organizational fields, the production of culture, and use of social networks in organizations. He has a Ph.D. from Vanderbilt University.

Tony Angel is Managing Partner of Linklaters. He was elected to this position in 1998 and has managed the firm since then as it has developed a market-leading position in both Europe and Asia, as well as a growing US presence. He was head of the global tax practice from 1994 to 1998. He joined the firm in 1976 and worked for twenty years as a corporate tax lawyer, dealing with mergers and acquisitions, capital markets, structured and international finance, and international tax structuring. He has a law degree from Cambridge University.

Shannon Dunlap is the former Communications Assistant for the Center for Executive Women at the Kellogg School of Management. She has collaborated with professors at Kellogg in their research and writing on organizational behaviour. She is currently a graduate student at New York University.

Laura Empson is Director of the Clifford Chance Centre for the Management of Professional Service Firms and Reader at the University of Oxford's Saïd Business School, where she lectures in Organizational Behaviour and Strategy. Her research has focused on a wide range of issues in accounting, consulting, and law firms, including the organizational implications of strategic change, managing the post-merger integration process, overcoming impediments to knowledge-sharing among professionals, changing organizational and professional identities, and the governance of professional service firms. Prior to becoming an academic, Laura Empson worked for several years as an investment banker and strategy consultant and continues to act as a consultant to professional service firms. She has a Ph.D. and an MBA from London Business School.

John J. Gabarro is UPS Foundation Professor of Human Resource Management in Organizational Behavior at the Harvard Business School and a co-founder of Harvard's Leadership in Professional Service Firms Program. His current research is on the effects of product intensity of professional services on firm structure, managerial roles, and developmental processes. He has advised leading global firms in public accounting, investment banking, strategy consulting, and the law. He has a Doctorate and an MBA from Harvard Business School.

Heidi Gardner is a Ph.D. student in Organizational Behaviour at the London Business School. Her research on professional service firms examines how to organize for innovation and effective client service. Her other research focuses on group-level issues of status and conflict, knowledge creation and sharing, and multinational teams. Prior to becoming an academic she worked as a consultant with McKinsey & Company for five years. She has an M.Sc. from the London School of Economics.

Royston Greenwood holds the Telus Chair of Strategic Management and is the Associate Dean (Research) at the School of Business, University of Alberta, Canada. He is also the Director of the University of Alberta's Centre for Professional Service Management. His research on professional service firms has appeared in most of the leading academic journals in the field of management. Currently, he is studying the determinants of performance of professional service firms, and the relationships between large firms and professional associations. He has a Ph.D. from the University of Birmingham.

Ryon Lancaster is Assistant Professor of Sociology at the University of Chicago and Faculty Fellow at the American Bar Foundation. His research interests include organizational change and the economic behaviour of professional service firms. He has a Ph.D. from Northwestern University.

Huseyin Leblebici is Professor of Organizational Behaviour and the Head of the Department of Business Administration at the University of Illinois at Urbana-Champaign. His research interests are in the sociology of economic transactions, organizational design, and inter-organizational relations within the context of professional service firms. He has served on the editorial boards of many of the top academic management journals, including *Administrative Science Quarterly, Organization Science, Journal of*

Management, and Organization Studies. He has a Ph.D. and an MBA from the University of Illinois at Urbana-Champaign.

Stephen Mayson is Professor of Legal Practice at Nottingham Law School and Director of the Centre for Law Firm Management. He created the part-time MBA in legal practice at Nottingham Law School, the only MBA of this kind in the world. His research interests include the strategy, economics, ownership, and valuation of law firms. Since 1985, he has also acted as a consultant on these issues to hundreds of leading law firms and legal departments around the world. He has a Ph.D. from Nottingham Law School.

Timothy Morris is Professor of Management Studies at the University of Oxford's Saïd Business School and the founding Director of the Clifford Chance Centre for the Management of Professional Service Firms. His research interests on professional service firms focus on the ways in which they organize to innovate and on the nature and patterns of change in their management. He has acted as an advisor to leading professional service firms in many different sectors and countries. He has a Ph.D. from the London School of Economics.

Stuart Popham is Senior Partner of Clifford Chance LLP, the world's largest law firm. He was elected to this role in 2003. He chairs the firm's Partnership Council, the supervisory board of the worldwide firm, as well as being responsible for a number of client relationships. He joined Clifford Chance thirty years ago and, prior to being elected senior partner, led the Banking and Finance practice. He has a law degree from Southampton University.

Peter D. Sherer is Associate Professor at the Haskayne School of Business, University of Calgary, Canada. His research is at the intersection of strategy and human resource management and he has published a number of articles in leading management journals on the sources and consequences of organizational change. His paper on institutional change in law firms that appeared in the *Academy of Management Journal* was awarded the Best Paper of 2002 by the Academy of Management, the major professional association among academics in management. He has a Ph.D. from the University of Wisconsin, Madison.

Brian Uzzi is the Richard L. Thomas Distinguished Chair of Leadership and Professor of management and sociology at the Kellogg School of Management, Northwestern University. His research on professional service firms focuses on the adoption of the corporate model of organizing, pro bono activity and on lawyers' and law firms' networks. He has advised professional firms in the arts, law and finance and holds a PhD from the State University of New York at Stony Brook.

David B. Wilkins is the Kirkland & Ellis Professor of Law and the Director of the Program on the Legal Profession and the Center on Lawyers and the Professional Services Industry at Harvard Law School. His research on the legal profession focuses on the changing institutions, demographics, and norms of legal practice. He is the author of over fifty articles on the legal profession in leading scholarly journals and the popular press and is the co-author (along with his Harvard Law School colleague Andrew Kaufman) of one of the leading casebooks in the field. He has a JD from Harvard Law School.

Prologue

John J. Gabarro
Harvard Business School

The last ten years have been a period of extraordinary change for law firms and their markets. The landscape has altered irrevocably, as any managing partner will attest. Foremost among these changes has been the rapid growth of corporate law firms and the concomitant internationalization of their clients' needs. Both trends have been fuelled by the continued globalization of business which has created a huge amount of domestic work over the last decade as well as an increasing amount of cross-border transactions and matters of a multi-jurisdictional nature. Many corporate law firms have grown significantly in both size and revenues even as their competitive environments have become more demanding. Many regional firms have grown into strong national firms, while many national firms have become international in scope, either through mergers and acquisitions or through purposefully targeted expansions.

Indeed, the last decade has seen elite German, French, Dutch, and US firms merge with larger firms that had stronger global practices. These combinations have contributed to the emergence of the global mega firm, best personified by Clifford Chance, Linklaters, and Freshfields. These are firms with long international histories that have aimed at providing global reach while serving traditionally demanding, high-end clients. Other global mega firms include Skadden Arps, which has grown using a more geographically limited but highly focused strategy, and Baker & McKenzie and Jones Day, two firms that have long had an overseas presence but have used more steadily incremental approaches in attaining global mega firm status. Adding to the complexity of this landscape, however, is the fact that the majority of the most profitable and prestigious law firms in the world continue to be largely domestic in their focus and modest in their size.

These fundamental changes in the strategic landscape have been accompanied by significant micro-level changes in the way that law firms operate. The widespread use of information technology has enabled firms to automate and standardize many repetitive procedures and protocols. This has resulted in reduced costs and increased margins but also in the commoditization of many types of transactions and matters. Firm growth has been accompanied by extensive hiring of lateral partners, even in elite firms which have traditionally avoided this. The growth in legal markets has also resulted in longer hours and higher compensation levels for professionals, especially partners. The drive for profitability, combined with the increased volume of work, has led to an expanding use of non-equity (or salaried) partners and of paralegals for standardized transactions as well as non-partner-track 'staff attorneys' for routine, repetitive, low-margin work. The increasingly competitive nature of the legal market has also led to a much more extensive use of non-lawyer specialists to run marketing and business development functions, as well as IT and human resources. Importantly, the last decade has seen a growing use of non-lawyer 'COOs' who are charged with managing all but the fee-earning aspects of the firm. All of this relentless change has altered law firms and their landscapes in ways that are both dramatic and profound.

This book comes at a critical time in the evolution of the modern law firm. The confluence of the great change, growth, and competition described above has required firms to adapt in ways that have stretched and strained the traditional concept of a law firm—so much so, that it has left many observers feeling that the traditional law firm organization is no longer viable. Has the law firm become, as one of my colleagues put it, an anachronistic model that is creaking and groaning at the seams? Critics argue that the classic law firm organization is no longer able to deal with the sheer size and complexity that many large firms have attained. Many wonder whether it is time to abandon the old model and adopt more contemporary forms of structure and management. As one critic asked me, 'Would Jack Welch design a law firm that looked like this?'

Others, however, are appalled at the creeping (or rampant) 'corporatism' that they see as negatively affecting their firms. They point to the erosion in the feeling and voice of partnership and to bureaucratic management and control systems that consume valuable fee earners' time. They also bridle at what they view as excessive 'overhead'—specialist staff whose activities, though well intentioned, are at best remotely related to the 'real' task of serving clients. They also point out that the most profitable and prestigious law firms, regardless of size, are without exception organized as classic partnerships.

Who is right in this debate? This seems a particularly propitious moment to ask the question, as many long-held assumptions are being challenged by the demands of today's turbulent environment. Is the answer to become more corporate? Is it to retain the best of traditional forms while adopting the most effective new methods? Or should law firms stand fast and protect all that is true and right about their traditional ways of working?

Addressing these questions wisely requires some clarity on what we mean by the 'traditional model' and the 'corporate model'. Otherwise we risk creating a discourse based on stereotypes and sound bites.

The *corporate model* evolved in the early nineteenth century to manage the size, scale, and complexity of the large manufacturing businesses that emerged in the wake of the industrial revolution. Perhaps the most distinguishing structural feature of the corporate model is its emphasis on *specialization by function* with a clear separation of manufacturing, sales, marketing, and engineering into differentiated functional subunits. This specialization and differentiation of roles is what allowed large companies to deal with the multifaceted aspects of designing, producing, selling, and distributing standardized products for mass markets. To this day, the functional form of organization remains either the basic building block or the deep blueprint of most modern day corporations, regardless of whether they are organized by function, product division, strategic business unit, matrix, or some alternative form of structure. In contrast, the departmentalization of design, sales, and production functions does not exist in law firms, except, perhaps, in some support functions.

A second defining aspect of the corporate model is its clear *separation of managerial and producing roles*. When employees progress up the organizational ladder and become managers in the corporate model, they stop functioning as individual contributors. This allows them to devote all their time and efforts to planning, directing, and coordinating the work of others. This clear differentiation is essential to managing the size and complexity involved in mass production and mass distribution. Law firms, in contrast, do not have a clear demarcation between producers and managers. Their leaders are typically what Lorsch and Mathias (1987) described as 'producing managers', for example, practice leaders and office managing partners who continue to practice law even though they have leadership responsibilities.

A third salient aspect of the corporate model (and of managerial capitalism) is the *separation of the ownership and management* functions. In the corporate model, managers act on behalf of owners, not as owners. The two roles are differentiated even when individual managers are also shareholders. Yet in practice-based professions, like the law, the managers and owners (partners) are almost always the same.

Finally, in the corporate model, there is a relatively high degree of *routinization and standardization*, so that learning can largely occur in structured venues, such as formal training programmes. In contrast, most important learning in law firms occurs on the job.

The traditional law firm model differs significantly from the corporate model just described. For starters, its organizational DNA does not date back to the 1830s and the need to manage the size, scale, and complexity of mass production. Rather, its DNA goes back to the Inns of Court in London and the Craft and Trade Guilds of Europe. As a result, law firms are not organized as functionally specialized hierarchies like their corporate counterparts. Instead, their organizations can be described as being *three-tiered, stratified apprenticeships*. They are apprenticeships in that the actual practice of law is learned on the job, working on client problems under the supervision or guidance of one or more senior professionals. For example, project finance law is not learned at university; rather, it is learned on the job in a law firm such as Clifford Chance, Linklaters, or Milbank Tweed. These organizations are stratified in that status differences between junior, mid level, and senior professionals are clear and significant. The status differences between a second year associate and a senior associate or a partner, for example, are clear, with partners being in a class of their own.

The stratified apprenticeship organization of most law firms is characteristic of all practice-based professional service firms, of which the law firm is the prototype. By 'practice-based', I mean professional service firms whose services are based on the practice of a codified body of knowledge in solving client problems. Examples include the law, public accounting, actuarial consulting, strategy consulting, and architecture. Each of these professions has a codified body of knowledge that is agreed on but constantly evolving. In pure practice-based firms such as law firms, the true product is the professional service itself. Any actual products (e.g. contracts, instruments, etc.) are embodiments of the professional service (or in some cases incidental). In this regard, their services are very different from product-intensive professional services such as software development, systems integration, and other types of IT consulting where products often figure prominently in the firm's offerings.

A second important difference is that law firms are not organized into separate marketing, sales, and production functions. Rather, they are *organized by practices*, such as corporate, banking, litigation, intellectual property, etc. In fact, business development, client service, and execution (the law firm's equivalents of marketing, sales, and production), are not highly differentiated roles that reside in different departments as they do in the corporate model. Instead they reside in the firm's senior professionals who handle these different functions as highly integrated aspects of the partner role rather than delegating them to specialists in separate departments. Partner-level professionals are individually responsible for business development, client service, and execution on a client-by-client basis. Even when true functional specialties exist in practice-based firms, they are typically support groups such as human resources, finance, accounting, technology, and marketing. When a law firm has a marketing department or a business development group, its major purpose is to assist practice leaders and individual partners in spotting, researching, and developing new business opportunities. It is the partners themselves, however, who are ultimately responsible for business development and actual client contact rather than the firm's marketing specialists, who focus instead on identifying potential opportunities and in enabling line partners to gain entry into new or existing client segments.

A third fundamental difference between the practice-based professional service firm and the corporate model is the *lack of separation between producing and managerial roles*. The stratified apprenticeship is run by leaders who continue to produce as professionals. Even in large law firms, leaders at the office and practice group levels remain actively engaged in client work. The producing manager role persists because it provides the credibility needed to deal with sophisticated clients and the technical knowledge and legitimacy needed to lead other professionals.

Finally, the underlying governance model of the traditional law firm is rooted in a partnership concept, even in those rare instances in which they are legally organized as corporations. *Partners serve as both managers and owners*. The clear separation one sees in the corporate model between the management and ownership roles is either absent in the traditional law firm model or at least greatly diminished.

The basic stratified apprenticeship form of the traditional law firm has not changed in a hundred years. Even large law firms have relatively few levels between the newest professional and the firm's CEO or managing partner (as little as five or six in a firm as large as Clifford Chance). Law firms also tend to be what Karl Weick (1979) refers to as 'loosely coupled organizations'. This is because their work is typically done in small teams (or collections of small teams if the matter or deal is large or complex). These teams are seldom permanent, and with the exception of rare compliance-based matters, teams usually dissolve when the matter is completed. As new engagements are won, new teams are formed based on the types and degree of expertise needed. Their flat structures, the recombinant nature of their teams, and the relative autonomy partners enjoy in pursuing and executing new work result in a highly fluid and decoupled organization when compared with the corporate model.

For these reasons, the stratified apprenticeship model continues to characterize successful law firms as well as successful firms in other practice-based professions. The model is well suited to the expertise-based nature of their work, the episodal nature of client needs, and the type of independent-minded, challenge-seeking professionals that they attract. Practice-based firms are organizations in which the key assets are technical knowledge, client relationships, and reputation. The stratified apprenticeship form enables firms to utilize these assets much more effectively and efficiently than the pure corporate form of organization. It allows firms to develop needed expertise in its junior professionals while executing client work under the supervision of senior professionals. Their team-based work groups also provide the flexibility needed to assemble, dissolve, and reassemble teams of professionals based on individual client needs. The result is a highly efficient use of the firm's most important asset—its people. The stratified apprenticeship has persisted as the prevalent model in the law because it is efficient and effective in serving clients well.

With a clear understanding of these two models and their salient features it is easier to see why the stratified apprenticeship of the traditional law firm has been stretched and strained by the rapid growth, increased competitiveness, and greater complexity of the last decade. It is because the stratified apprenticeship form of organization, despite its many advantages, is limited in its capacity to deal with size, scale, and complexity. Recall that the functional form of organization, the building block of the corporate model, was invented by British entrepreneurs to cope with the consequences of mass production. The functional form of organization replaced the apprenticeships of the trades and crafts and the business partnerships that existed prior to the Industrial Revolution because they were unsuited to managing the challenges of size, scale, and complexity.

The crux of the dilemma is that corporate forms of organization are better suited for dealing with size, scale, and complexity of the modern law firm than the traditional model. Yet, we know that in order to be effective 'on the ground'—where professionals actually serve clients and deliver service—the stratified apprenticeship, led by producing managers, is the most effective means of organizing, especially if a firm is practice-based as law firms are. The challenge, then, for law firms as they grow larger or more complex, is how to use aspects of the corporate model to deal with greater scale and complexity without disassembling or negatively affecting the basic structure of the stratified apprenticeship.

What this means is that as law firms become large and/or global, they have to develop into what Tushman and O'Reilly (2002) described as 'ambidextrous organizations'. In other words, they have to manage themselves on the ground using most aspects of the stratified apprenticeship model while simultaneously managing themselves at the firm-wide level using aspects of the corporate model.

It is not easy to develop the skills and structure needed to manage yourself in different ways simultaneously at the firm-wide level and the practice level, as evidenced by the fact that there are so few world-class law firms that are either large or truly global, or both. There are two main reasons why achieving this is so difficult. First, lawyers may be highly resistant to this kind of change. As I have shown, the corporate model and traditional law firm model are fundamentally different from each other and, in many respects, at odds with each other. These differences often result in professionals on the ground viewing *any* functional staff roles or non-producing managers at the firm-wide level as dangerous signs of bureaucracy, useless overhead or intrusions of an alien 'corporate' culture. In the extreme case, partners may demonize any change that feels like creeping corporatism, regardless of its merit.

Second, lawyers' fear of bureaucratization may be well founded. The corporate-like structure and systems (which are needed at the firm-wide level to deal with scale and complexity) may begin to get replicated at the practice level. This may result in practice groups becoming more effective because they gain better control and accountability; but, if these systems and structures are replicated thoughtlessly, they may consume valuable time, thereby making the stratified apprenticeship less effective in meeting client needs. When this occurs, the firm becomes less competitive at the local and practice group levels.

So, how can law firms retain the best of the traditional ways of organizing, whilst developing more effective methods of managing scale and complexity? How can they adapt models of management developed in the nineteenth century to cope with the challenges of managing lawyers in the twenty-first century? Law firms around the world are struggling to find an answer to these fundamental questions.

This book does not set out to offer simple (or simplistic) solutions. Instead it provides a subtle and systematic analysis of the key issues that confront the modern law firm. Based on theoretically grounded and empirically rigorous research on law firms, it sheds light on the complex challenges which the managers of law firms must confront on a daily basis. It is a timely and important contribution to the debates which characterize the evolution of the modern law firm.

1

Introduction and overview

Laura Empson
Saïd Business School, University of Oxford
Stuart Popham
Clifford Chance LLP

Introduction

Some parents dream of their children becoming lawyers. None ever dream of their children becoming law firm managers. Why would anyone want to manage a law firm? Your most important assets—expertise, reputation, and client relationships—belong to highly opinionated and highly mobile individuals, who typically have a strong sense of their own worth and prize their personal autonomy. They tend to have limited time or respect for management. If you do a good job they will not give you much credit for it; if they do not like what you do, they can get rid of you very quickly.

In recent years a tough job has become even tougher, at least in those law firms which aspire to be market leaders. The competitive landscape has changed irrevocably in recent decades and models of law firm management developed in the previous century are no longer applicable in the modern world. We are at a pivotal moment in the evolution of the modern law firm as law firm managers struggle to develop new ways of organizing lawyers. There are terrible costs for those who get it wrong but for those who get it right, the rewards are enormous.

Very little guidance is available for those who have to deal with these challenges. A vast amount of management research has been published in recent decades but very little is directly relevant to law firms or professional service firms more generally (this is one of the reasons behind the establishment of the Clifford Chance Centre for the Management of

1

Professional Service Firms at Oxford). Those lawyers who do take time away from legal practice to study for an MBA will learn about how to run an airline, a fast food business, a pharmaceutical company, or a bank, but will probably never hear mention of a law firm. The typical lawyer, who never aspired to be a manager anyway, finds himself or herself thrust into a management role with no training or experience and very little useful advice. This is a particularly uncomfortable situation for lawyers as their sense of identity is strongly bound up with being valued as experts.

Thankfully, most lawyers can get by on their innate intelligence and survival instincts, which have got them out of many tricky situations with clients in the past. However, a reliance on common sense and gut instinct has serious limitations when it comes to the challenges of managing the modern law firm.

Lawyers who survive the rigours of a legal training and the intense workload required to succeed in a top law firm have an exceptional capacity to focus, to block out all distractions, and to dedicate themselves entirely to serving their clients. As they move into management roles, lawyers need to remove the blinkers that have been a source of reassurance to them in the past, and develop a new way of looking at the world around them.

The challenge of coping with day-to-day management issues leaves lawyers with very little time to reflect—to sit back and see their own experiences in perspective, to examine the implicit models of management they have developed through trial and error, to wonder about what they are missing and what else they need to learn.

This book provides an opportunity to reflect. It offers new perspectives on the challenges every law firm manager faces by presenting cutting-edge academic research on law firms. It does not present simple solutions. It is not a 'how to' book; after all, why should academics have much insight into the day-to-day issues of managing a law firm? But what academics do have is time to reflect—time to do nothing but think and think and think about the management issues which lurk uncomfortably at the back of your mind.

This book will also help professional business managers who have joined law firms from other sectors (i.e. functional specialists in areas such as human resources, marketing, and finance). It can take many months and even years to start to make sense of a law firm—there really is nothing else quite like it. This book should shed some light on the things that puzzle you.

The book introduces you to important academic concepts and presents you with new conceptual frameworks that you can apply to your own business. It helps you to put your own experience in context and reflect on what you need to do as you go forward. It also helps you to learn from the experience of professionals working in other sectors and lawyers working in other markets. You are not alone. No matter how unusual or specific your situation may be, other professionals in other sectors have gone through similar experiences before and other law firms in other countries have struggled with the same kinds of challenges you face.

A common theme runs throughout the chapters which follow: the need for change and the challenge associated with trying to change. As Jack Gabarro of Harvard Business School asks in his Prologue: how can law firms retain the best of the traditional ways of organizing whilst developing more effective methods of managing scale and complexity? Or, as Tony Angel of Linklaters asks in the concluding chapter: how can law firms develop more structured and systematic methods of management without 'selling their souls to the corporate devil'?

The chapters in this book focus on many of the things that may keep you awake at night: your partners and your people, your competitors and clients, your expertise and reputation, your income and capital, and (not to forget) your ethics. The following overview highlights some of the general themes and specific issues explored throughout the rest of this book.

Your partnership

As a large number of professional service firms abandon the partnership form of governance, Chapter 2 (by Laura Empson) asks: what should law firms do? Should UK firms avail themselves of current regulatory reforms to incorporate or go public? How can the largest national or global law firms retain the valuable characteristics of a partnership and avoid becoming corporations in all but name?

This chapter goes beyond basic legal definitions to get to the heart of what lawyers really mean when they talk about partnership. It identifies why the ethos of partnership is so extraordinarily valuable within a law firm and analyses how it is created and sustained. At the heart of any law firm lies a fundamental tension between the interests of the individual and the interests of the collective. A strong and universally recognized partnership ethos is fundamental to establishing and maintaining an

3

appropriate balance between the two. To sustain this ethos in a changing and challenging external environment, law firm managers must develop a sophisticated and subtle understanding of what exactly the partnership ethos means within their firm and how to use their systems, structures, and socialization processes to ensure that this ethos adapts and survives. In this way, managers of law firms can ensure that the partnership form of governance evolves and does not risk becoming extinct.

Your people

The previous chapter emphasizes that it is relatively easy to develop a strong and coherent partnership ethos when lawyers come from the same background and have 'grown up' together. In such an environment, socialization processes are implicit and unspoken, and there is only a limited need for formal systems for partner management. In Chapter 3, David B. Wilkins argues that, as law firms become more diverse, this implicit method of management is no longer viable. Instead law firms need to develop more explicit processes of socialization and partner management.

Law firms in the USA have been struggling with the issue of diversity for many decades. The issue is becoming increasingly important within the European context, whether diversity is defined in terms of ethnicity, gender, or geography. In many law firms, women lawyers are in the majority at entry level but are still relatively rare at partnership level. In international and global law firms the most senior management positions are still typically held by lawyers from the 'home' country. And, very recently, clients have started to ask awkward questions about the ethnic diversity of the law firms that serve them. There is much to learn from the US experience. Very little meaningful change will happen as long as the case for diversity is framed in terms of what is morally right or what is good for business. Law firms must go beyond these preoccupations to address the rigid cultural, systemic, and structural norms which inhibit their ability to respond to the changing world around them. Only then will law firms be certain of attracting and retaining the very best lawyers.

Your expertise

The previous two chapters have focused on management innovation at a cultural, structural, and systemic level. In Chapter 4, Heidi Gardner,

Timothy Morris, and Narasimhan Anand examine innovation at the practice level. They analyse ways in which new expertise is created and the role of management in facilitating (or preventing) innovation.

Fifty per cent of all new practice development initiatives are unsuccessful. These failures are expensive both in time and money and represent a major missed opportunity for many law firms. The modern law firm cannot rely simply on trial and error when it comes to something as important as the development of expertise. Gardner, Morris, and Anand explain why some initiatives fail and others succeed, identifying the key 'ingredients' that must be present for successful new practice development and the different ways in which these ingredients should be combined. Innovative individuals play a crucial role in developing new expertise but resentful colleagues can sometimes sabotage their initiatives. Managers therefore have a responsibility to identify good ideas and to create an environment in which they can flourish. The process of new practice development embodies the dynamic interplay between the individual and the collective that is characteristic of partnership and highlights the key role of management in supporting the work of individuals acting in the interests of the partnership as a whole.

Your client relationships and reputation

Expertise is clearly an important asset in a law firm but so too are client relationships and reputation. Few law firms have a clear sense of how much their relationships and reputation are really worth and how much to invest in developing them further. It is particularly difficult for law firms to determine what value clients place on reputation, or rather how much of a premium they are prepared to pay for it.

In Chapter 5, Brian Uzzi, Ryon Lancaster, and Shannon Dunlap identify the key social factors which influence pricing in the legal sector. They quantify the strength of client relationships and reputation (or status) and measure the impact of these two key variables on law firms' billing rates. Close relationships with clients translate into lower billing rates but potentially higher profit margins. Overall, it is strength of reputation which has the greater impact on billing rates. Whilst the difference in billing rates seems small when calculated on an hourly basis, it can translate into many millions of dollars across a law firm as a whole.

Your income

Even if you know how much value your clients place on you, how exactly are you supposed to charge for your services? The practice of hourly billing is condemned by lawyers and clients alike and many law firms are currently struggling to develop new methods of pricing which reflect the value of the service they offer rather than simply the time it takes them to deliver it. But there is no simple answer. Complaints about lawyers' fees have been part of the profession's history since Roman times; hourly billing was supposed to be the solution.

In Chapter 6 Huseyin Leblebici explores some of problems that billing poses for practising lawyers by studying the historical evolution of the 'billable hour' and how it shapes the lives of individual lawyers, the success of law firms, and the reputation of the legal profession. Leblebici analyses the dynamic interaction of four key elements: billing rates, compensation practices, methods of pricing, and ownership structures. He argues that these four elements are inextricably bound together in a complex and dynamic system. The billable hour is so deeply embedded in these institutionalized practices that lawyers will need to confront change at a fundamental level before new methods of charging for legal services can be adopted.

Your capital

Whilst the previous chapter focuses on current income, Chapter 7 addresses the issue of capital. Stephen Mayson asks 'what drives the value of law firms?' and advocates a shift away from an income-based, towards a value-based perspective. The key is to go beyond a simple calculation of current income to understand the sustainability of that income over the long term. The value of a law firm is bound up with three kinds of capital: human capital (i.e. key individuals in the firm), social capital (i.e. their relationships with each other and the outside world), and organizational capital (i.e. the systems, structures, and culture which make the firm as a whole more valuable than the sum of its parts—or rather its individual partners).

Organizational capital is typically undervalued within law firms, dismissed as bureaucracy or an expensive overhead. Mayson argues that organizational capital is in fact fundamental to sustaining the long-term value of the business and encourages lawyers to think about the value of their firm in this more sophisticated way—to look upon their organization with the objective eye of an external investor. This change of mindset will translate into a more disciplined approach to business management which should ultimately yield attractive returns to the owners of the firm. This is good management practice whether the firm remains a partnership or decides to bring in external capital.

Your competitors

So far, this book has encouraged law firms to think beyond their traditional models of management to develop new ways of organizing, selling, and valuing expertise. In Chapter 8, Peter D. Sherer sounds a useful note of caution.

He uses strategic group analysis to suggest different ways of looking at who your competitors are and shows how the most significant competitive threats may come from unexpected quarters. Whereas this form of analysis is long-established in a wide range of sectors, Sherer is the first to apply the concept of strategic groups to law firms. Sherer examines competitors' actions in the US market since 1999 and finds that firms tend to occupy relatively fixed positions with regard to their immediate competitors and rarely break out of their strategic groups. Those law firms who seek to innovate must confront very powerful forces of inertia. Sherer evaluates the financial consequences of various strategic actions and finds that those US firms who were the first to internationalize have experienced lower levels of profitability than those who were slower to expand internationally. The highest profits per partner are enjoyed by those US firms with a very limited international presence or who have reduced their international presence in recent years.

Your ethics

Chapter 9 offers a brief pause for thought—a chance to reflect on what may be lost in the quest to develop a new model of law firm management. Royston Greenwood asks: do ethics risk being trampled in the headlong dash towards modernization? In seeking to become more commercial do lawyers risk losing the right to call themselves professionals?

Greenwood explores the research literature on the sociology of the professions and spells out in detail what many lawyers feel instinctively: that there is an innate tension between professionalism and commercialism. He suggests that the breakdown in professional behaviour, which has characterized so many corporate scandals of recent years, is a direct consequence of increased levels of competition, size, complexity, and the associated adoption of more 'corporate' management practices within professional service firms. In order to grow their firms and achieve their commercial goals, lawyers must devolve authority to their managers and allow them to impose systems and structures which are anathema to the traditional law firm. In this context it is vital that practising lawyers and managers alike hold tight to the ethical standards and professional values which have represented the basis of lawyers' claim to professional privilege for so many decades. What shall it profit a lawyer if he or she shall gain the whole world and lose his own soul?

Your challenge

The final chapter introduces a practitioner's perspective to these academic debates. As Managing Partner of Linklaters since 1998, Tony Angel has overseen the transformation of a leading UK law firm into one of the most powerful and successful global law firms in the world. He reviews the success of the UK's magic circle law firms, such as Linklaters, Clifford Chance, and Freshfields, in expanding globally and explains how Linklaters in particular has achieved this objective.

The globalization of law firms is predicated on the assumption that clients will pay premium rates to receive a full range of integrated services across multiple jurisdictions. Delivering this exceptional level of service within such a complex organizational context requires lawyers from around the world to work closely together for the common good. But a global law firm can no longer rely upon the goodwill and implicit understanding of colleagues who have worked alongside each other all their careers. Angel argues that, far from selling your soul to the corporate devil, it becomes necessary to think far more carefully about what partnership and professionalism really mean in the context of a modern global law firm and to invest time and resources in making this a reality. He explains how this process has developed within Linklaters, how partners have come to an understanding of what needs to change in pursuit of their common vision, and what elements of the ethos of partnership and professionalism must be retained at all costs. In so doing the partners of the firm are seeking to hold fast to what is fundamentally good and valuable about partnership, whilst reinterpreting its manifestation in the context of the modern law firm.

Conclusion

For good or ill, the managers of law firms have the power to determine the future of the legal profession. Their success in creating the modern law firm will depend largely on their willingness to explore new perspectives and their courage to face up to new challenges. This book should help them to do just that. These are exciting times for law firm managers.

2

Your partnership

Surviving and thriving in a changing world: the special nature of partnership

Laura Empson
Saïd Business School, University of Oxford

The *special nature* of a partnership is that you've got a commitment and buy in that is so special. People over-achieve the whole time... they feel that being a partner is very special and very empowering. So you have these amazing people who really feel they can sort of take on the world and feel part of a club, part of a very, very, very special club. And I think in a way that's really what partnership means to me... it's quite a personal and emotional thing. (Practice Head: Law Firm)

Introduction

All around us partnerships are dying. Whilst the partnership form of governance continues to thrive in the highly regulated and protected legal profession, its survival within other professional sectors is looking increasingly precarious. The legal profession is not immune to the pressures that other professions are experiencing, as Jack Gabarro argues in the Prologue (to this book), and lawyers would be foolish to take the ongoing health of the partnership form of governance for granted.

With an endangered species of animal the plan of action is clear. We study it in detail to understand what is threatening it. We analyse how the species sustains itself (i.e. its methods of feeding, protection, and reproduction), explore alternative habitats in which it might thrive, and take steps to help it to adapt and survive. In this chapter, I set out to do much the same for partnership, by presenting the results of a major UK government-funded research study into the governance of law, accounting, and consulting firms.[1]

I begin by exploring the evidence for the decline of partnership and I identify the economic and sociological explanations for why partnership remains the optimal legal form of governance for professionals. I examine the threats to partnership which are challenging its ability to survive. I identify what exactly professionals mean by the term 'partnership' and go beyond the basic legal definition to define the ethos of partnership. I build a framework to explain how this ethos is created and sustained. I demonstrate how it is possible for valuable aspects of partnership to survive and thrive within alternative legal forms, specifically the publicly quoted corporation. I conclude by reflecting on what the managers of professional partnerships can do to help their partnerships evolve and enjoy healthy and productive futures.

Decline of partnership

Twenty years ago the partnership was the pre-eminent form of governance in most major professional sectors. Within the established professions, such as law and accounting, it was traditionally viewed as the only legitimate mode of organizing. Firms within aspiring professions, such as consulting and investment banking, often chose to organize themselves as partnerships, thus assuming the mantle of professionalism that it conveyed.

In the 1980s everything began to change. The Big Bang in 1986 ultimately wiped out most of the stockbroking partnerships in the City of London (Augur 2000) and the flotation of Goldman Sachs in 1998 signalled the end of an era in investment banking. By the start of the twenty-first century, thirty-two of the fifty largest consulting firms were publicly quoted. Only eight remained partnerships, compared with double the number ten years previously (Greenwood, Li, and Deephouse 2003). Recently, accounting firms have sought to separate and incorporate their non-audit activities (the regulatory regime in many countries still requires auditors to remain partnerships). As a result, almost fifty of the top 100 accounting firms are now organized as privately held or publicly quoted corporations (Greenwood and Empson 2003).

Law firms have been slower to change than other professional service firms (see Figure 2.1). Although UK law firms have been permitted to incorporate since 1992,[2] relatively few have exercised this option. By

11

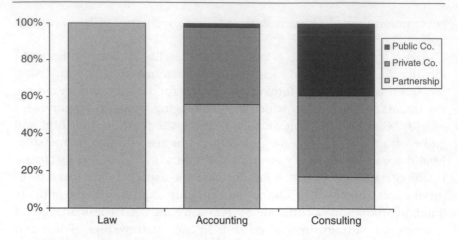

Figure 2.1 Governance of professional service firms by sector (global top 100, 2003)
Source: Adapted from Greenwood and Empson (2003).

contrast, many have converted to limited liability partnership (LLP) status after this became possible in 2001. Further change was signalled by the Clementi Review (2004) which recommended the lifting of restrictions on the ownership of law firms, making it possible for law firms to be acquired by publicly quoted companies or to go public themselves.

In the USA, partnership remains the only legitimate mode of law firm governance within all major state jurisdictions, yet there is no reason to be complacent about the future of partnership in America. For example, in 2002, Judge Posner argued that the partners of Sidley Austin Brown & Wood could be deemed to be employees (rather than self-employed) and were, therefore, eligible for protection under employment law.[3] Whilst they had shared in the profits and had unlimited personal liability for the debts of the firm, Posner argued that they had been 'at the mercy' of a small, unelected, and self-perpetuating executive committee which could 'fire them, promote them, demote them, raise their pay, lower their pay, and so forth.' These partners 'were defenceless . . . they had no voting power'. In this context, the partnership remained as a legal form but did not exist in practice in any meaningful sense. Does this matter? Should we care? The answer is unambiguously, yes.

Why partnership works

As the quotations at the start of this chapter demonstrate, lawyers get emotional about partnership. Beyond the hot emotional rhetoric,

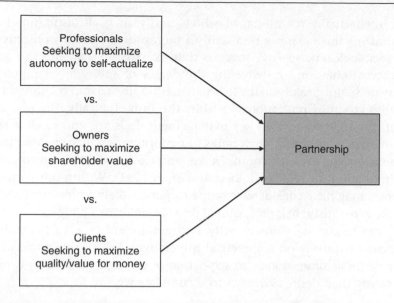

Figure 2.2   Resolving stakeholders' competing claims in a professional service firm

however, there is a fairly cool piece of logic. In the following analysis I draw together (in highly summarized and simplified form) more than fifty years of sociology and economics research into the professions and professional service firms to identify why exactly partnership works. Ultimately, partnership works for professional service firms because it is the optimal method of balancing the competing claims of three sets of stakeholders: professionals, owners, and clients (see Figure 2.2). Each of these stakeholders is discussed in turn below.

Professionals

The sociology of the professions literature emphasizes the extent to which professionals expect and enjoy high levels of personal autonomy within their working environment (Heydebrand 1973; Meiksins and Watson 1989) and the problems that can arise when this is denied them (Raelin 1985; Sorenson and Sorenson 1974). This emphasis on autonomy derives in part from the nature of professional work. In order to deliver a customised service of the appropriate quality, expert workers must be free to exercise their independent judgement. The desire for autonomy may go even further than this. Professionals seek opportunities to self-actualize (i.e. to pursue personal fulfilment) by taking on assignments which they

13

find intellectually rewarding, or which satisfy their altruistic impulses. Maximizing income is not necessarily a professional's primary objective.

A sociological perspective suggests that partnership is an effective governance mechanism for delivering the degree of autonomy required to motivate senior professionals. In a partnership, ownership is confined to an elite group of professionals within the firm. Typically, the partners retain the right to vote on key management decisions and to elect representatives from among their ranks to perform senior management roles on a fixed term basis (Dirsmith, Heian, and Covaleski 1997; Greenwood, Hinings, and Brown 1990; Tolbert and Stern 1991). Within this context, partners may have considerable scope to pursue their professional objectives (e.g. to satisfy their professional pride by delivering a superior quality of service to clients). Consequently, partners are not necessarily required to focus exclusively on commercial imperatives. Whilst this may satisfy their desire as professionals to self-actualize through their work, it may not satisfy their desire as owners to accumulate wealth.

Owners[4]

A property rights perspective emphasizes that in a professional service firm it is not clear who owns the most critical assets, the fee earners or the 'shareholders'. The key income-generating assets are expertise, client relationships, and reputation. These may be proprietary to (or at least strongly associated with) individuals and may represent a potentially significant source of power and income for these professionals. There is a clear incentive for a professional to protect rather than share these assets, thus limiting the possibility of maximizing the value of the firm. Property rights theory argues that, when the key income-generating assets are proprietary to individuals, they should share in the ownership of the firm and participate directly in decision-making. This implies a partnership form of governance (Hart and Moore 1990).

An agency theory perspective, which explores the costs associated with different governance structures, recognizes that it can be difficult and costly to apply formal controls to the monitoring of non-routine activities such as the provision of professional services (Jensen and Meckling 1976). Professionals are offering a complex and intangible service; management are unlikely to be directly involved in, or have specialist insight into, the more technical aspects of their work. The partnership form of governance emphasizes informal practices of mutual- and self-monitoring, which are backed up by unlimited personal liability. These will be more effective than formalized managerial controls at minimizing 'free-riding and shirking' (Fama and Jensen 1983; Leibowitz and Tollison 1980).

Overall, therefore, in a professional service firm, the interests of the owners are best served when they are aligned with the interests of the professionals. The partnership form of governance is designed to achieve this outcome. Both sets of stakeholders (i.e. owners and professionals) may still represent competing claims on the firm. However, by combining the roles in each partner, the partnership structure ensures that the conflict is ultimately reconciled at an individual *and* organizational level.

Clients

Just as managers of a professional service firm need to balance the competing claims of owners and professionals, so too must they balance the competing claims of owners and clients. Given the distinctive characteristics of professional work the client must be certain that he or she can trust the professional to focus on maximizing quality of service rather than on maximizing profits.

When clients approach a professional service firm they may not fully understand the nature of their problem and cannot sample the firm's services prior to purchase. This puts the professional in a position of considerable power relative to the client. The client's trust of the professional will be based on a complex set of factors, such as personal relationship and organizational status or reputation (Alvesson 2001; Podolny 1993; Uzzi, Lancaster, and Dunlap in Chapter 5 of this book) but the partnership form of governance has traditionally represented an important source of reassurance. Unlimited personal liability, combined with the emphasis on internal ownership, ensures that partners share their clients' financial interests in maintaining quality standards and are not expected to prioritize the interests of external shareholders over those of their clients (Shafer, Lowe, and Fogarty 2002).

Partners may, of course, choose to prioritize their own interests over those of their clients, but the intensive inculcation of standards of professionalism through formal training and informal socialization supposedly militates against such a tendency (Sharma 1997; Tolbert 1988). This embodies the 'social trusteeship' model of professionalism which Royston Greenwood describes in Chapter 9 of this book. The protracted system of promotion to partner is designed to ensure that an individual's professionalism can be trusted by clients and partners alike (Anderson-Gough, Grey, and Robson 1998; Galanter and Palay 1991).

Pressures on partnership

In theory, at least, the partnership seems unambiguously to be the optimal form of governance for professional service firms. However, as discussed in detail by Greenwood and Empson (2003), a variety of forces are at work that threaten the professional partnership. These are present to varying degrees across a range of professional sectors and in part help to explain the variation in the extent to which different professions have moved away from the partnership form of governance.

Increasing size and complexity

The partnership form of governance has been a victim of its own success. As partnerships have expanded into multiple service lines and multiple countries, the traditional processes of collective decision-making and informal methods of mutual monitoring have proven impractical as large professional service firms adopt more 'corporate' methods of hierarchical and bureaucratic control. These trends of 'creeping corporatism' have been particularly marked in the largest accounting firms, which were among the first professional service firms with more than 1,000 partners.

Increasing demand for capital

Partnerships find it difficult to raise substantial loans and investment capital. In the past this was not a particular problem as the capital needed to run a professional service firm was typically not significant, at least relative to those other forms of business where incorporation and outside ownership were common. But by the mid-1980s, investment banks were finding it increasingly difficult to meet the rapidly rising capital demands of their underwriting and trading activities. In the 1990s, the requirement to invest in sophisticated IT infrastructures and knowledge management systems increased the need for capital within global management consulting firms. In the past two decades, therefore, there has been a large-scale flight from partnership within the investment banking and consulting sectors. For law firms the demand for capital has been less significant so it has been easier for them to retain the partnership structure.

Increasing commodification

The development of sophisticated firm-wide information management systems has facilitated the trend towards commodification in certain professional service firms. This trend is not associated with any specific professional *sector* but reflects strategic choices made by specific professional *firms*. As the expertise of professionals becomes commodified and knowledge is no longer proprietary to individuals, there is less need to secure their cooperation by offering them a share of ownership and a say in the management of the firm. In this context, the limitations of partnership start to outweigh its benefits.

Increasing litigation

In certain professional sectors, where fault can be unambiguously established (e.g. accounting), the dramatic increase in litigation has prompted increasing numbers of partnerships to convert to LLP status in order to avoid the crippling costs of partner indemnity insurance. Within the consulting sector in particular the changes in the legal form of governance reflect trends in litigation. For example, the clients of actuarial consultants are becoming increasingly litigious and there are no longer any partnerships among the top ten actuarial firms. By contrast, in the strategy consulting sector, where it is relatively difficult to demonstrate actionable negligence, the partnership is more common.

Changing social trends

The lure of partnership persuades junior professionals to make personal sacrifices for the prospect of future rewards in the 'heaven' of partnership (i.e. the principle of 'deferred gratification' embodied within a legal structure). However, current economic and social trends are challenging this orthodoxy. Those junior professionals who are motivated primarily by the need for money and status find that both can now be obtained more quickly by joining investment banks. Those junior professionals who seek a more balanced lifestyle turn away from the prospect of partnership as they observe the extraordinary pressures under which partners are now required to operate.

The partnership, therefore, appears to be the optimal form of governance for professional service firms but it is struggling to adapt and survive in the changing competitive environment. With this in mind, I wanted to understand better what exactly partnership was. It seemed unlikely that the lawyer quoted at the start of this chapter could feel so committed to—and get so emotional about—a legal construct. There was certainly nothing in their firm's partnership agreement which seemed likely to inspire such passionate feelings. If there was an ethos of 'partnership' that existed beyond the legal definition, how exactly was it created and sustained? In answering this question, I could begin to understand how partnership might be encouraged to survive and thrive in an increasingly hostile environment.

Recognizing the partnership ethos as distinct from partnership as the legal form opens up two possibilities. The first is that partnerships can continue to operate as a legal form long after the partnership ethos has ceased to exist in any meaningful sense. The second is that publicly quoted corporations can embody the most meaningful and valuable aspects of the partnership ethos whilst avoiding the legal trappings of partnership.

The research study

Together with my Oxford colleague, Chris Chapman, I undertook a two-year empirical study into the implications of changing forms of governance in professional service firms. We set out to explore forms of governance in three major professional sectors: law, accounting, and consulting. Over the two-year period of data collection we conducted 215 interviews and recorded 350 hours of interview material. We also conducted a detailed analysis of the archives of the relevant professional associations in order to understand changing attitudes towards governance over the previous twenty years.

We studied four firms. One was a US-based consulting company that had gone public four years previously. The remaining three were partnerships: a leading UK-based accounting firm, a major European consulting firm, and a global law firm. All the partnerships had recently converted from unlimited liability to LLP status. They provided a rich context for data collection as the partners had gone through a period of careful reflection on the nature of partnership as part of their conversion to LLP. For reasons of confidentiality we are required to anonymize the identities of all four firms.

The partnerships varied considerably in terms of size (from 50 to over 500 partners), geographic spread (from one to thirty-three countries), methods of growth (from primarily organic to merger-driven), and partner remuneration (from pure lockstep[5] to performance-related). It is perhaps surprising, therefore, that we found a remarkable degree of consistency across firms in terms of how the partnership ethos was articulated and how it was created and sustained. In each firm the partnership ethos was strong and highly prized. This may in part reflect one factor which each firm had in common. Although all the firms had grown rapidly in recent years, each contained a significant and influential group of senior professionals who had joined at the start of their careers and had worked together for two or more decades.

In the research study I asked interviewees in the law, consulting, and accounting firms, 'what does partnership mean to you?' and, based on their answers, began to build a framework which identified the dynamics of partnership. As this chapter appears in a book about managing law firms, in the following analysis I draw primarily on my interviews with lawyers to illustrate the framework I developed. However, it is important to emphasize that the framework itself was derived from the much broader-ranging analysis across all three professions.

Dynamics of partnership

As a legal form, the partnership is highly geographically and institutionally specific. Typically, however, a partnership is distinguished from alternative legal forms by two key characteristics (beyond the basic fact that the firm does not have a legal identity independent from its partners). First, ownership is confined to an elite group of professionals within the firm. Second, partners share unlimited personal liability for the actions of their colleagues. It quickly became clear to me, however, that when professionals talked about what partnership meant to them, they were not referring to the legal form of partnership but to its 'ethos' (i.e. the 'characteristics beliefs and behaviours of a community': *Oxford English Dictionary*). It was this ethos of partnership that inspired strong sentiments.

The core tension encapsulated within the partnership ethos is represented by Figure 2.3a. The dynamics of partnership through which that ethos is created and sustained are represented by Figure 2.3b. This Dynamics of Partnership framework is explained in more detail in the following sections.

Partnership ethos

The two legal features of collective ownership and unlimited personal liability represent the foundations on which the partnership ethos is

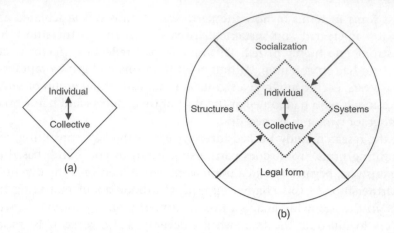

Figure 2.3 (a) Partnership ethos; (b) Dynamics of partnership

constructed. As owners of the firm, partners have a clear imperative to maximize their individual autonomy. They are, after all, effectively shareholders and what is the point of a firm if it is not to serve the interests of its shareholders? This individualistic impulse is tempered by unlimited personal liability, which serves to bind all partners together by making them individually liable for the actions of their colleagues (though the partners I interviewed were keen to stress that becoming an LLP did not constitute a licence for individualism). Partners, therefore, have a clear financial imperative to operate collectively and to monitor and support each other, both at a personal and professional level.

This tension between individualism and collectivism is fundamental to understanding the dynamics of partnership. The legal form of partnership creates the tension—the ethos of partnership resolves that tension.

In some partnerships, the balance may be tipped strongly towards individualism—partners are free to pursue their personal priorities, whether it is income-maximization or self-actualization. In such an environment, partners can make their own lifestyle choices. Rather than argue that the partnership ethos is absent in such firms, it is more accurate to recognize that the partners in such firms have chosen to strike the balance between individualism and collectivism in such a way that favours the individual.

In other partnerships, the balance may be tipped strongly towards the interests of the collective (i.e. the firm). Senior management will have a clear mandate from the partners to manage the firm on their behalf for their common financial gain. In such firms, constraints on individual partner autonomy may be quite extensive, with clearly defined rules within which a partner must operate, clear performance targets, and serious penalties for failing to achieve these targets. Rather than simply dismiss these firms as 'corporate', it is more accurate to recognize that the partners in such firms have chosen, at some point in their history, to strike the balance between individualism and collectivism in such a way that favours the collective (Tony Angel develops this argument in far more detail in the concluding chapter of this book).

In each of the firms I have studied, however, there is a strong and dynamic tension between the interests of the individual and the interests of the collective. The management of partnerships are in effect engaged in a constant struggle to identify and resolve the tension between the individual and the collective. In this context, a commonly understood partnership ethos represents a powerful unifying force which serves to counteract the potentially self-serving impulses that drive each partner individually.

In firms with a large group of long-serving partners, this sense of collectivity is associated with strong personal relationships. This may partly reflect the long hours worked together over the years and the absence of opportunities to build relationships outside work.

> One of the things my wife always says 'All your best friends are your partners, you've got hardly any friends who aren't your partners'—I always say 'Rubbish, what about X and Y?'—and she says 'But when did you last see them?' (Practice Head: Law Firm)

When personal friendship is not practical or possible, strong social norms of mutual support have much the same effect on behaviours.

> The partners really do look out for one another. I might be working flat out day and night but if one of the others comes in to my office and says—'Look, I've got a personal issue. I need to drop this hot potato and go and deal with it'—I will take it on. (Salaried Partner: Law Firm)

Rather like brothers and sisters in a family, the expectation of mutual support is not necessarily associated with harmonious relationships. But the common bond of partnership holds the partners together in an obligation to each other, even if that obligation may sometimes seem irksome.

> The sense of community can become strained at times but it is strained in a constructive way. You've got several hundred individuals, each has their own ideas and their own ego—there are difficult and sometime abrasive people in

21

any organisation such as this—but if you can harness their skills it can be fantastically effective. (Salaried Partner: Law Firm)

When I asked the partners in all of the firms I studied to explain what partnership meant to them they sometimes reverted to literary references. The ones I heard most frequently were 'One for all and all for one' (*The Three Musketeers:* Dumas) and 'Band of brothers' (*Henry V:* Shakespeare). It is worth noting that both references are military in origin and are, by definition, exclusively male. Whether it is the Three Musketeers' rallying cry or Henry V's speech to his troops on the eve of the Battle of Agincourt, both embody the sense of a collection of individuals coming together to defeat a common enemy. The Three Musketeers and the English army at Agincourt are famous for winning fabulous victories against seemingly impossible odds. If this is what partnership really means to the people I interviewed, no wonder it is something they prize so highly.

While the partnership ethos is clearly associated with partnership as a legal form, it is not explained by it. Three additional elements help to create and sustain the partnership ethos: the structures, the systems, and the socialization processes with which the legal form is typically associated.

Socialization

The dictionary definition of to 'socialize' is 'to prepare for life in society' (*Oxford English Dictionary*). Within a partnership, socialization is the process by which an individual is evaluated and prepared to join the society of partners. The process begins in the initial recruitment phase at entry level, where interviewers may be asked to consider whether they could imagine the candidate as a potential partner of the firm. Thereafter, socialization follows the traditional apprenticeship model. The professional observes the partners and learns the appropriate technical and interpersonal skills. Socialization typically culminates in a protracted and intensive process of partner selection.

> I have a friend who is a member of the SAS.[6] When I told him what I had to go through at our partner selection conference he said it sounded horribly like what he went through... the whole process is intended to strip away the natural barriers you are allowed to build up in your everyday communications with people, to get you to basically make a quick-fire judgment. (Salaried Partner: Law Firm)

During the process of socialization, a professional is developing the requisite technical skills to make partner. Whilst these are essential, they are not sufficient. It is the personal qualities of the professional, specifically the extent to which he or she is valued by clients and colleagues, which represent the deciding factors.

> You may be working with a lawyer over a ten year period. We spend a lot of time working in groups together and on the road so you see what people are really like. Do they have good client skills? How are they at mentoring the juniors? Can they hold their own over dinner? Can they have a few beers in the bar and make sense the next day? Have they got the intellectual stamina to keep going through two or three all-nighters? Can they withstand criticism? Are they able to take the knocks? (Practice Head: Law Firm)

Throughout this apprenticeship period, the potential partners are learning to subsume their own identity into that of the profession, the organization and, ultimately, the partner group. They are becoming a professional, learning to identify themselves as a member of their firm and their profession as a necessary precursor to becoming a partner. When they reach this goal the sense of pride in their achievement is phenomenal.

> How did I feel the day I made partner? I was over the moon. It was something I had worked for eight years to achieve and I had achieved it as quickly as I had dared to think possible. It was a real landmark in my career. So, yeah, I was ecstatic. I still do cherish that achievement. I know it's not like winning gold at the Olympics, but it's the closest I am ever going to get to it. (Partner: Law Firm)

This process of socialization is fundamental to the partnership ethos, which requires the interests of the individual to be reconciled with those of the collective. The individual must demonstrate that he or she has the necessary confidence and strength of character to exercise independent judgement and to behave with authority towards clients. At the same time, the prospective partner must show that he or she can be trusted to act in accordance with the wishes of the partnership as a whole.

As part of this process of socialization, professionals come to believe that partnership is superior to the corporation as a form of governance. It is necessary that they develop this somewhat rose-tinted view of partnership in order to become fully committed to the partnership ethos. As a consultant and a lawyer both explained to me:

> People here are generally doing things in the best interests of the firm as a whole. In a corporation, you hear stories emerging about how people can get ahead by doing other people down. It's that kind of internal competition, cynical behaviour that we do not experience in the partnership. (Partner: Consulting Firm)

> One of the great things about being a partnership rather than a corporation is that we're all sort of shareholders, which means we're answerable to ourselves

and to each other...directly and on a daily basis, not at an AGM once a year, but daily. (Partner: Law Firm)

Through the process of socialization, the professional, in effect, learns to become self-regulating. The lawyer who told me: 'I became a lawyer because I never wanted to have a boss' is perhaps unaware of the extent to which he will have internalized an extensive set of norms through his professional and organizational training and is, therefore, constrained in his capacity to exercise truly independent judgement. These norms do not seem oppressive to him because they have become an integral part of his own identity. This attitude, in an extreme form, is summed up by a partner in an accounting firm whom I interviewed as part of a previous study (Empson 2004):

> As a partner I have a huge amount of personal independence. No one tells me what to do...I do what I want, but the things I want are likely to help the firm because that is the way I have been trained. At one level we are completely independent, but we all march to the same tune without even thinking about it. (Partner: Accounting Firm)

Systems

Traditionally, becoming a partner has been rather like getting into heaven—you have to be very good to get in but once you are admitted you are very unlikely to be thrown out. Whilst some partners take this as an opportunity to brush up on their harp playing, the innate drive of most professionals, together with their sense of commitment to the partnership, ensures that they continue to generate and maximize profits on behalf of the firm.

> Do I feel pressure to bring in work? Yes I do. I think I have a responsibility to the firm to keep feeding the machine, and I personally take that responsibility very seriously and I do go out and get work. But I don't think the machine is forcing me to do that. No I don't. I think it comes from inside. It comes from a sort of desire to prove myself and the only way I can really prove myself, once I have become a partner, is to keep bringing in the work. (Partner: Law Firm)

In order to make partner, a professional must demonstrate his or her ability to be self-regulating. However, partnerships do not rely on this entirely. The systems for evaluating, rewarding, and sanctioning partners are fundamental to creating and sustaining the partnership ethos, and are backed up by informal processes of peer pressure.

Under a lockstep system, rewards are shared equitably amongst the partners on the basis of time served rather than individual contribution. In those law firms which have retained this method of remuneration, lockstep is seen as fundamental to the partnership ethos. The reward system is the practical embodiment of the desire to reconcile the interests of the individual with the interests of the collective.

I don't think the partners here are in it for their personal gain—well not solely for their personal gain. I think we're here to build a business and there is almost like a sort of co-operative feel to it. This stems from the lockstep. Lockstep means we are all working for the common good. (Salaried Partner: Law Firm)

It comes down to 'What is your purpose in life?' If your purpose in life is to achieve short-term personal gain then why would you spend time helping another lawyer with something? But with lockstep someone else's success is my success. (Practice Head: Law Firm)

The attachment to lockstep amongst several of the most successful UK and US law firms perhaps reflects their exposure to the extreme alternative form of remuneration, 'eat-what-you-kill'. They look at the eat-what-you-kill Wall Street firms and resolve that they would never want to be like that.

The worst thing you can have in a partnership is the cult of the individual. We don't want people who are motivated by what they personally earn or who feel it is important to earn more than other people. (Partner: Law Firm)

This extreme dichotomization of lockstep versus eat-what-you-kill is peculiar to law firms. In other professional sectors, neither extreme form of remuneration is particularly common. A study of firms of consultants and accountants found a different rhetoric, of a strong sense of partnership ethos thriving within modified lockstep and performance-based methods of remuneration (Chapman and Empson 2005). In spite of what many lawyers believe, lockstep is neither a necessary nor sufficient condition for the creation and maintenance of the partnership ethos.

Whilst lockstep may help to ensure that the interests of the individual coincide with those of the collective, when it is allowed to operate without sanction it can become a licence for individualism. Partners can free-ride on the effort of their peers. The intense socialization process prior to partnership is intended to guard against this, but cannot prevent it.

I had a partner come into my office recently saying—'I am sick to death of getting in the office at 7:30 every morning and watching X walk in at 9:10 and leave at 5:00 after doing bugger-all all day. I want him out. Get him out of here because he is pissing me off and if he doesn't go soon, I will'. (Practice Head: Law Firm)

Traditionally partnerships have dealt subtly and informally with under-performing partners. As the senior partner of a consulting firm explained:

There is a limit to what I can do because I need to respect their rights as a partner. So, I put it to them very diplomatically and subtly that people would appreciate it if they did this or stopped doing that. Or, do they realise that this is what people think about them, and what are they going to do about it? If somebody has dug their feet in, I don't think I've got the right to try and force them to do something. This is delicate stuff . . . I need to use a mixture of encouragement and suggestion without causing emotional upset. (Senior Partner: Consulting Firm)

With flagrant under-performers, partners signal their displeasure with their colleagues in much the same way that school children marginalize and ostracize their peers who do not conform to their norms of behaviour.

It's usually the judgment of the peer group which is the most lethal, not anything that the management does. I mean, management might put questions into the frame but it's when the peer group gives up on someone that he is really sunk. (Partner: Law Firm)

Occasionally partners go beyond peer pressure to employ more extreme methods of exclusion. As a partner in an accounting firm I studied put it, 'We are like a wolf pack. We hunt together but, when a partner is seriously wounded, the rest of us will turn and savage him.' When partners have 'grown up' together they will understand the subtle ways in which they are being punished and are likely to feel shame at being excluded from the group. With a less stable and more heterogeneous partner group, such informal processes are less likely to prove effective. More formalized systems of evaluation and sanction become necessary. As one law firm partner reflected somewhat nostalgically:

When we were a smaller firm you could get rid of partners by saying 'You've lost the confidence of your peers old boy. You either piss off now and we'll give you a year's money and be nice to you, or you can stay and we'll make it bloody uncomfortable for you'. . . . It isn't so simple nowadays. (Partner: Law Firm)

Structures

Whereas the partner management systems define how the partners are managed by the management, the governance structures define how the management is managed by the partners. In a publicly quoted corporation, managers must act in the interests of shareholders who delegate authority to them to build and sustain shareholder value. The priorities of governance are, therefore, relatively unambiguous. Not so in a partnership, where the shareholders or owners are working within the firm. In a global law firm there may be many hundreds of owners and each one may simultaneously embody multiple competing objectives. Senior managers must not make the mistake of reifying the organization. They must not lose sight of the fact that the interests of the collective are made up of the interests of multiple individuals and that at any moment these individuals may stop thinking as part of the collective and start acting on the basis of their self-interest. The following comment from a lawyer caricatures the differences in managerial authority between a corporate and a partnership structure.

> In a normal corporate hierarchy where, in theory at least, there is no questioning of authority—he's my boss, he can tell me what to do whether I like it or not, I've go to do it or I can get fired—I'm assuming that's the basic corporate premise, right?—but in a partnership it's, 'I don't like what you're telling me and I'm not going to do it so you can just bugger off'. (Practice Head: Law Firm)

A key task for management, therefore, is to arrive at a clear understanding of the collective interests of the partners and to communicate these coherently and consistently so that they become the established 'truth' within the firm. Leadership in this context may need to be subtle and indirect, guiding partners towards an understanding of how their individual interests can be reconciled with those of the collective.

> The partners want leadership, but a leadership that reflects rather than directs the general tenor of the partnership. It's a very difficult thing to get right. (Practice Head: Law Firm)

> The key is to understand the currents that flow around this place—the surface may be fairly wave free—four foot waves, five foot waves—but it's the currents going backwards and forwards underneath that you really need to be aware of. Every now and then a big wave will break and cause the place to change. That's something that is primarily in the hands of the leadership team. They need to create enough waves going in the right direction for people to say okay, if that's what we've got to do then let's just get on with it. (Partner: Law Firm)

The ability of senior management to exercise effective leadership in a partnership is severely hampered by the ambiguous nature of their authority and the highly contingent governance structures within which they must typically operate. They have been elected by a majority of their peers and can be deposed by them at any time. The following comments by two practice heads express this dilemma:

> It's like I'm the eldest brother. I'm not the Dad; there is no Mum and Dad. It's like I've got to the top because I'm the oldest or the tallest or whatever, but I'm still their brother. (Practice Head: Law Firm)

> I am responsible for a large group of partners, all of whom are very bright, at least as bright as I am, all of whom have big egos, all of whom are owners of the business with as much right to vote and draw profits as I have. The process of being in charge or leading is about building consensus—it's not easy because most people are attracted to this business because they are independent, they like doing their own thing. Essentially they want to be left alone until it's something that kind of connects them and then it's—'why wasn't I consulted?' (Practice Head: Law Firm)

My studies identified three components of the formal governance structures which are particularly important in determining the nature and extent of managerial authority in a partnership. The first is formally delegated authority—specifically, what issues require a full partnership vote and what size majority is required for key decisions? What decisions can be decided by the managing partner and his or her team? The second is the process by which the management team is selected. Is the managing partner able to nominate or select practice heads? Is he or she required to work with whoever the partners in that practice choose to elect? The third key component of the governance structure is the delineation of roles of managing and senior partner. Specifically, to what extent is the senior partner, or anybody else, formally tasked with monitoring the actions of the managing partner and the management team on behalf of the partnership group?

  But the formal governance structures only represent one aspect of managerial authority. My analysis identified various personal factors which distinguished effective managers in partnerships from their less effective peers. When partners praised their senior managers to me in interviews they spoke in the following terms. First, the individual was an exceptionally gifted professional, either with clients or in technical terms. Being perceived as 'cleverer' than your peers, or at least harder working, is an important source of your authority as a manager in a professional service firm. Second, it is equally important not to be seen to seek or enjoy power. Many successful senior managers in my study had led their colleagues to believe that they were more interested in the advancement of the firm than in their personal advancement. Whether this was true or not is irrelevant—the point is that their fellow partners believed it to be true. Third, the most effective senior managers were able to combine a clear sense of direction with a tolerance for ambiguity. They were able to step back from the day-to-day complexities presented to them by their fellow partners and retain a clear sense of purpose, both for themselves and the firm as a whole.

Earlier in this chapter I referred to the phrases 'One for all and all for one' and 'Band of Brothers' as expressions of the partnership ethos. It is worth remembering that, while the English knights at Agincourt submitted to the authority of their brilliant and inspirational leader, the Three Musketeers were an extremely heterogeneous and ill-disciplined collection of individuals who won through because of their remarkable skills with the sword. Some law firms resemble the Three Musketeers—others have more in common with Henry V and his knights. A partnership ethos may operate very powerfully and effectively in either case.

There were only Three Musketeers (plus D'Artagnan), whereas the English knights at Agincourt numbered 900. If a large partnership must inevitably adopt more 'corporate' practices, should large partnerships simply bow to the inevitable and incorporate? If partnership is the optimal method of balancing the competing claims of its professionals, owners, and clients, then it is logical to conclude that professional service firms should make every effort to remain partnerships. Contemporary management writing on corporations would support such an argument.

Imitating partnership

There is anecdotal evidence to suggest that the flotation of professional service firms has had damaging consequences for clients, professional staff, owners, and even society as a whole (Augur 2000; Shafer, Lowe, and Fogarty 2002; von Nordenflycht 2003).

In recent years, as Gerson (2005) has shown, management writers have exhorted corporations outside the professional services sector to emulate professional partnerships. They see such firms as embodying many characteristics essential for operating within the knowledge-based economy. Some corporations have deliberately set out to imitate aspects of partnership, to try to create the ethos of partnership within a corporate form.

McKinsey & Company, for example, incorporated in the 1950s but, to the outside world and to the consultants within it, still embodies many of the qualities of a partnership. As Marvin Bower (Managing Director, 1950–67 and described on McKinsey's website as 'the soul of McKinsey') says 'we find it takes intensive and continuous effort to preserve the real and useful partnership spirit.' (Bower 1997: 59). McKinsey does not rely simply on the 'spiritual' approach but seeks also to mimic the structure of a partnership. For example, the Managing Director is elected by 270 of the most senior 'partners'. The term partner is still used informally within McKinsey because 'even though it may not be legally accurate it can bring out some of the best qualities in people' (Bower 1997: 60). Whether McKinsey is genuinely like a partnership is not the issue—what matters is that it has sought to create the impression of partnership amongst its clients and professional staff because it can be 'useful' in business terms. McKinsey has succeeded in effect in 'imitating' partnership.

McKinsey was once a partnership, albeit fifty years ago, and has remained privately owned. Is it possible to create and sustain a partnership ethos within a publicly quoted firm with no history of partnership? My research suggests that the answer is *yes*, up to a point, but it is not easy.

As part of a study of governance in professional partnerships I studied a consulting firm (the 'Company') which had floated on the New York Stock Exchange in 2000 (for full details of this study see Empson and Chapman 2006). Although the Company had never been a partnership, its shareholding structure closely resembled one at the time of the flotation (i.e. initial public offering, or IPO). Shares were held internally by a broad cross-section of employees, with no individual owning more than 1.5 per cent. Post IPO, 50 per cent of the Company transferred to external investors.

Reflecting attitudes associated with traditional professional partnerships, the CEO recalls a time prior to the IPO:

> I remember eight years ago having conversations with people who would say things like, 'Do we really need to be in business to make a profit? Aren't we here to serve our clients?' (CEO: Consulting Company)

Preparation for the IPO prompted a more overt emphasis on commerciality and a drive for growth and revenue enhancement, which has become stronger post IPO. These changes are subtle, however, with the emphasis on encouraging professionals to develop a more explicit focus on cost control and revenue growth, within the Company's broad strategic agenda—sound management practice in any context, partnership or corporate. A practice head explains how management has sought to contain the impact of the IPO:

> There's been less change than one would imagine. We've been maintaining a balance between long- and short-term benefiting employees and benefiting shareholders and so far that's turned out very well.... I thought the recession would test it, but the CEO told the analysts that we were reserving a fair amount (of profits) for the bonus pool—the reaction from the analysts was, 'Good, your product is your employees and if you try to pay out too much in dividends you blow the whole thing'. (Practice Head: Consulting Company)

Just as in a partnership, the CEO has recognized the inherent tension between the needs of the individual and the needs of the collective. However, in the Company the 'collective' has been expanded to embrace external shareholders. The CEO recognizes his responsibility to act in the interests of the shareholders but he also knows that for his 'decisions' to be effective, he must first build consensus among his colleagues.

> We don't have a classic management structure that says 'you shall'. The CEO creates opportunities and platforms for new ideas, but he very rarely says 'you shall'—he says 'you should listen to what John has to say about XYZ', but he will rarely ever say, 'we're going to do this programme'—it doesn't work like that. So it becomes a very time-consuming process of selling your ideas to people. (Functional Head: Consulting Company)

The painstaking process of consensus-building is embedded within the organization structure. The Company is structured as a matrix, with each member responsible to dual reporting lines of practice and geography. All key decisions require approval from both sides of the matrix. Where agreement on management issues cannot be reached between peers, the decision is moved up to the next level of the matrix. Consultants argue that better quality decisions get made after careful consultation and consensus-building. However, as often happens in a partnership, there is frustration about the time taken to reach decisions. By substituting the word 'partnership' for 'matrix' in the following quotations, it is possible to see how the matrix structure in the Company has been used to imitate some of the best and worst aspects of a partnership.

> The nice thing about the matrix is that you can bounce decisions back and forth, very freely and openly. It is not like you have to hide anything.... In the matrix we know we are all in this together. (Practice Head: Consulting Company)

I have laid off senior people and it has been ferociously difficult. The quantitative information on them was categorical. In other words there was no ambiguity about whether they were terrible or not or whether we were losing money on them, but it still took months, and in one case years, to get rid of a person because of the inherent conservatism of the matrix. (Practice Head: Consulting Company)

Whilst the matrix prevents professionals from acting unilaterally with regard to internal management issues, professionals have considerable autonomy with regard to client issues (e.g. which clients to serve and how to deliver the service).

There is a certain amount of flea market mentality here. Each senior consultant has their own booth at the flea market, renting space from the flea market operator. (Practice Head: Consulting Company)

This place gives me room. It is very trusting. It relies on my entrepreneurial spirit to move forward ... this place lets you use your brain cells and lets you try; it gives you the opportunity to sell, to persuade. (Functional Head: Consulting Company)

For these consultants, the autonomy they prize is not about resisting managerial control but about acting entrepreneurially—in other words, the freedom to make money any way they like. The management of the Company have recognized that, as long as their professionals are left alone to do what they most care about—to serve their clients—they will accept many of the internal management constraints associated with being part of a large corporation.

Will the incorporation and flotation of a partnership inevitably have damaging consequences for its shareholders, the professionals that work within it, and the clients they serve? This study says no. The pressures to change may be strong but they are not inexorable. Within alternative legal forms of governance, it is possible for professionals to imitate the most valuable aspects of a partnership without necessarily being restricted by its legal form. However, for this process to be effective, professionals and their managers must be strongly committed to the partnership ethos and work actively to create and sustain it. While it is possible to reconcile the competing claims of owners, professionals, and clients within a corporate structure, this is not a stable equilibrium. Incorporation and flotation may not automatically destroy the partnership ethos, but they certainly do not encourage its survival.

Conclusion: evolution of partnership

The partnership ethos can survive within the challenging contemporary context in which professional service firms must compete, but only under certain conditions. Managers of professional service firms must develop a sophisticated and subtle understanding of what exactly the partnership ethos means within their firm and how to use their systems, structures, and socialization processes to ensure that this ethos adapts and survives. In other words, it is up to the managers of professional service firms to ensure that the partnership *evolves* rather than simply becoming *extinct*.

Partnership ethos

Whilst the partnership ethos reconciles the tension between individualism and collectivism within a professional service firm, the precise manner in which it is manifested and enacted will be highly context-specific. It is important for managers to understand what it means within their own particular firm and just where the balance should be drawn between the needs of the individual and the needs of the collective.

Perceptions of the partnership ethos may vary considerably within the firm, between junior and senior professionals, among junior and senior support staff, as well as externally with clients and with potential recruits. Whilst the partnership ethos can meld a disparate group of senior professionals into a collective entity, the very exclusivity which makes it attractive to those within the partnership serves to exclude, and potentially alienate, all those outside the partnership. Do salaried partners, for example, feel included or excluded from the partnership? Do junior professionals understand the partnership ethos and do they aspire to be partners? Does the partnership ethos relegate high quality senior professional managers to the status of second-class citizens? Are juniors and support staff expected to tolerate extreme and inappropriate behaviours from partners who view themselves as owners of the firm? Are clients and potential recruits aware of the partnership ethos and do they understand its significance?

By addressing these questions carefully, managers can develop a clearer understanding of what partnership means to the key stakeholders. What has it meant traditionally? What is challenging traditional attitudes? What aspects of partnership are vital to preserve? How can the partnership ethos adapt to the changing competitive marketplace? With this foundation of understanding in place, the next step is to understand how the systems, structures, and socialization processes can be managed to ensure that the most valued aspects of the partnership ethos evolve—to survive and thrive in a changing world.

Socialization

As socialization processes cannot easily be observed, they are also very difficult to change. Formal processes can be redesigned but individuals may struggle to articulate the plethora of informal ways in which they signal to their colleagues what is and what is not legitimate within the firm.

As well as being difficult to change, these socialization processes represent a potentially serious block to change more generally. By socializing and selecting individuals to join the elite company of partners, a partnership risks becoming a self-perpetuating collection of 'clones'. Evolutionary psychology (Nicholson 1998) argues that we humans are 'hard-wired' to be drawn to people who are like us and to distrust people who are different. In contemporary partnerships this is no longer an adequate or appropriate basis for partner selection. In the next chapter of this book David Wilkins describes the compelling economic and ethical rationale for introducing greater racial and gender-based diversity into partnerships. Geographically dispersed and diversified partnerships need the ability to recognize high quality professionals working in different countries and in different kinds of businesses.

In this context, it is vital to make the processes for socializing and selecting potential partners explicit. The partnership ethos can be strengthened not just by promoting those professionals who embody it, but by dealing with those partners who do not—and making this obvious to their fellow partners and to aspirant partners. Partners may grumble that more explicit procedures for selecting and sanctioning partners smack of bureaucracy and will inevitably lead to partners becoming corporate 'clones'. It is ironic that these developments may instead encourage heterogeneity, by making it easier to recognize and accommodate the strengths of idiosyncratic individuals who nevertheless embody the partnership ethos. In seeking to promote professionals from diverse backgrounds, partnerships can still remain exclusive and homogenous, but the homogeneity and exclusivity will no longer be based on class, gender, racial, or religious grounds. Instead it will derive from the extent to which individuals embody the partnership ethos.

Structures

As partnerships grow large it is inevitable that governance structures will evolve, requiring partners to delegate authority to a select group to manage the firm on their behalf. This is a necessary precondition for growth. This delegation of authority need not lead to the destruction of the partnership ethos, however. As already discussed, the worst elements of 'corporate' style management structures can be held in check by retaining and developing socialization processes and partner management systems which support and sustain the partnership ethos (a point developed by Tony Angel in the concluding chapter of this book). If the systems and socialization processes are strongly aligned with the needs of the partnership, then greater authority can be safely delegated to management through the governance structures. Management will not act against the interests of the partnership as a whole because they have been socialized appropriately and know that they will be rejected by their fellow partners if they overstep their mandate.

Managers of publicly quoted companies are subject to increasingly stringent oversight of their activities. By contrast, in some growing partnerships, management are formally delegated authority or assume greater authority without a concomitant increase in the oversight of their activities. The roles and responsibilities of non-executive directors of corporate boards are clearly defined and are becoming increasingly onerous. The roles and responsibilities of senior partners and partnership boards in relation to managing partners and management committees are resolved on an ad hoc basis through each firm's partnership agreement. As partnerships evolve, one of the key responsibilities of the senior partner should be to exercise this oversight of management and to act as a custodian of the partnership ethos.

There is much, therefore, that managers of professional partnerships can do to preserve the partnership ethos within their firm, whether they choose to retain the partnership in its legal form or to move towards incorporation or flotation. The key is to recognize what exactly the partnership ethos means in the context of their own firm, what is threatening it, and specifically how it can remain valuable in a changing competitive context. As a law firm grows, and its structures, systems, and socialization processes evolve, senior managers are responsible to their professional colleagues, owners, and clients to ensure that such changes serve to support, rather than undermine, the partnership ethos. Ultimately it is up to the law firm's management to ensure that the ethos of partnership survives and thrives in a changing world.

Notes

1. Empson, L. and Chapman, C. 'Consequences of changing forms of governance for the management of professional service firms', Economic and Social Research Council of Great Britain (RES-000-22-0204).
2. Sections 9 and 10 of The Administration of Justice Act 1985 amended The Solicitors' Act 1974, enabling solicitors' practices in England and Wales to incorporate. These provisions ultimately came into force in 1992.
3. *Equal Employment Opportunities Commission* v. *Sidley Austin Brown & Wood*, 315 F.3d 696 (7th *c*. 2002).
4. For the sake of simplicity the term 'owner' rather than 'shareholder' is used generically in this chapter to describe the owners/shareholders of all professional service firms, whether corporate or partnership.
5. Under a lockstep system each partners' compensation is based on chronological seniority (i.e. how long they have been a partner).
6. The Special Air Service is an elite British special forces army unit noted for its exceptionally tough selection and training programmes.

3

Your people

Valuing diversity: some cautionary lessons from the American experience

David B. Wilkins
Harvard Law School

Introduction

Discussions about diversity have become a staple of modern law firm life. This is easiest to see in the USA where there is a thriving industry consisting of organizations, consultants, marketers, and legal recruiters whose primary purpose is to advise law firms about how to achieve diversity and maximize its value (Wilkins 2004a). But diversity has become a prime topic of discussion for lawyers in other parts of the world as well. In Britain, for example, both the Bar Council and the Law Society recently published lengthy reports containing specific directives and policies designed to ensure equality and to promote diversity among their respective members (Bar Council 2004; Law Society 2004). At the same time, managing partners of law firms in the UK with global aspirations declare, in the words of Clifford Chance's former senior partner, that 'the question of culture is critical' and affirm their intention 'to create a genuinely multi-cultural firm' (Clark 2000).

Although diversity is unquestionably now an important topic, there is far less agreement about *why* diversity matters, *what kinds* of diversity should count towards these goals, and *how best* to bring about the diversity that firms claim to seek. Traditionally, those advocating greater attention to diversity in law firms have grounded their arguments on the legal profession's moral obligation to rectify the effects of its exclusionary past and to live up to its bedrock commitment to equal opportunity. As the Scottish professor Donald Nicolson argues, 'discrimination in the allocation of the benefits which accompany professional membership is particularly odious given that the adherence to high ethical standards is a central justification for professional status' (2005: 201). Given this justification, advocates have concentrated their efforts on convincing firms to recognize that achieving diversity is 'the right thing to do' by eliminating discrimination against groups such as women and members of racial and religious minorities who in the past were expressly denied the opportunity to become lawyers, and who, even after the fall of *de jure* barriers, continue to be underrepresented in the profession as a whole, and in large law firms in particular (Abel 1989, 2003; Gellhorn 1968; Nicolson 2005).

In recent years, however, this social justice paradigm has been joined, and in many respects supplanted, by a new justification for paying attention to diversity. According to this new account, diversity is not simply 'the right thing to do'. It is also 'good for business'.

The emergence of a 'business paradigm' for addressing diversity issues can be seen most clearly in the USA. Consider, for example, the following advice by the Minority Corporate Counsel Association about how to launch a successful law firm diversity initiative:

> To ensure senior partner commitment and firm-wide buy in, it is important that a law firm develop a written plan that elucidates the business case for diversity, including an analysis of the costs of not taking the issue of diversity seriously and of the interest of clients in having diverse legal counsel represent them. Hence, law firms commit to becoming diverse because their future, market share, retention of talent, continuation of existing relationships with corporate clients, and performance depend on understanding and anticipating the needs of an increasingly diverse workforce and marketplace. (Mitchell 2001)

Recent events appear to confirm this advice. In 2003, Sara Lee Corporation's general counsel, Richard Palmore, issued a 'Call to Action' to his fellow corporate counsel urging them to commit themselves to putting pressure on law firms to increase diversity, and to stop doing business with firms that fail to show progress on this issue (Jones 2005). In the last three years, hundreds of general counsel have signed up to Palmore's initiative. Wal-Mart has now gone even further. In June 2005, the giant retailer declared that it intended to review the company's relationships with its 100 top-billing law firms in order to determine whether Wal-Mart should designate a woman or minority lawyer as the 'relationship partner' in charge of overseeing all of the company's legal work. As of October 2005, Wal-Mart has switched forty of these relationships, in the inelegant but revealing phrase employed by an assistant general counsel, 'from a non-diverse to a diverse attorney' (Hobbs 2005). Not surprisingly, the fact that this change is occurring in a company that spends over $200 million on outside legal services a year strikes many observers as conclusive proof of the merits of the business case for diversity. As one prominent academic observed:

> Law firms are going to have to get serious about hiring and maintaining women and minorities, so that when a Wal-Mart comes calling, they'll be ready. (Hallman 2005, quoting University of Pennsylvania Law Professor Georgette Poindexter)

In this chapter, I want to explore the implicit assumptions underlying this optimistic assessment of the business case for diversity in large law firms. Specifically, I will examine how market-based arguments that were first developed to persuade corporations of the value of diversity are likely to affect why law firms value diversity, the kinds of diversity that firms are likely to value, and how these institutions might go about achieving this goal. I do so on the basis of almost two decades of research on the efforts of black American lawyers to become integrated into the large law firms and corporate legal departments that comprise what Heinz and Laumann refer to as the corporate 'hemisphere' of the bar (Heinz and Laumann 1982; Heinz et al. 2005). To chronicle these efforts, I have interviewed over 200 lawyers, conducted a survey of over 650 black Harvard Law School graduates, and helped to coordinate an ongoing ten year longitudinal study of lawyers' attitudes and careers that tracks over 4,000 lawyers who entered the bar in 2000 (American Bar Foundation 2004; Wilkins 2000).

Although my research is therefore primarily limited to the American context, the turn to market-based diversity arguments in the USA is likely to have important implications for law firms in other parts of the world. As Nicolson observes, one can already begin to see this influence in the UK in the manner in which both the Bar Council and the Law Society justify their efforts to promote greater diversity. Both organizations give a passing nod in their respective reports to the duty of a profession dedicated, in the Bar Council's words, to 'uphold a person's rights without fear and favour' to exemplify these noble values in its own conduct (Nicolson 2005: 216, quoting Bar Council 2004). These statements, however, are, in Nicolson's words, 'swamped by references to the commercial benefits of equality and diversity' (2005: 216). Given the size and importance of the American legal market and the fact that US firms pioneered the model of the large law firm that has now spread to virtually every important commercial centre around the world, one can reasonably expect that as law firms in Europe and elsewhere focus more attention on diversity issues, they will continue, as Clifford Chance's former senior partner remarked in discussing the value of cultural integration, to be 'driven by what happens in the US' (Clark 2000).

For the reasons below, however, law firms and advocates interested in diversity in countries around the world should be both cautious and critical when seeking to draw lessons from the American experience. There are good reasons to believe that breaking down the homogeneity, cultural rigidity, and intolerance that have unfortunately characterized elite law firms in the USA (and most other places around the world) is crucial to the ability of these institutions to continue to thrive in today's increasingly multicultural and cut-throat global marketplace. That said, however, to establish whether linking progress on diversity to the demands of the marketplace will in fact produce either greater diversity or increased productivity for large law firms requires a closer examination of the connection between 'diversity' and 'business' in this context than most advocates of the business case for diversity in the USA have undertaken or even acknowledged. Diversity advocates in the legal profession tend to assume uncritically that the same arguments that have persuaded large corporations to embrace the diversity agenda will be persuasive for law firm leaders as well. But for all the talk about the legal profession becoming more like a business, there are many important differences between the business of large law firms and the business clients that these firms typically represent. These differences, as I argue, are likely to magnify some of the limitations of the business case for diversity that have already begun to emerge in the business context for which these arguments were originally developed.

The rest of this chapter elaborates these concerns. The first part briefly recounts the changes that have encouraged diversity advocates in the USA to embrace market-based justifications for promoting diversity in law firms. The second part then explores the most common arguments raised in support of the business case for diversity in the corporate context and examines the implications of these arguments for large law firms. I conclude by arguing that law firms in today's globally competitive market for legal service can profit by paying attention to diversity, but only if they are willing to examine how their *failure* to achieve diversity calls into question the continuing validity of key cultural and structural realities of law firm life.

From morals to the marketplace

It is not hard to see why diversity advocates in the USA are increasingly embracing the business paradigm. Specifically, three aspects of the US legal services market make market-based arguments particularly appealing. First, since the mid-1970s there has been a dramatic explosion in the number and size of law firms and other legal employers seeking to hire talented law students and lawyers (Galanter and Palay 1991; Heinz, Nelson, and Laumann 2001). At the same time, the percentage of white men graduating from law school has been steadily shrinking. Women now comprise almost 50 per cent of all law school graduates in the USA. Racial minorities now constitute an additional 20 per cent (Chambliss 2004). Given these demographics, law firms that seek to grow by 'hiring the best lawyers' can ill afford to ignore such a substantial percentage of the available talent pool.

Second, as indicated above, corporate clients have become much more focused on diversity. Responding to the changing demographics of their own workforce and customer base both in the USA and globally, many companies have made achieving diversity in every phase of the organization, including 'supplier diversity', a core goal (DiversityInc 2003). As important suppliers of professional services, law firms are increasingly covered under such policies. Moreover, the lawyers in charge of making corporate purchasing decisions are themselves an increasingly diverse group. Ironically, many of the women and minorities who left large US law firms in the last thirty years have found their way into the expanding in-house legal departments of top companies. Today, some of these big firm dropouts have risen to senior positions. Women now comprise more than 15 per cent of all general counsel at Fortune 500 companies, and by some estimates, almost a third of all lawyers employed in corporate legal departments (*Corporate Legal Times* 2003). The percentages for minorities—6 per cent and 12.5 per cent, respectively—although smaller, are still impressive. Not surprisingly, many of these new corporate legal purchasing agents, like Palmore at Sara Lee, have made diversity a central concern. As the Wal-Mart example discussed above makes clear, law firms ignore these concerns at their peril.

Finally, in a world of growing global competitiveness, market-based diversity arguments appeal directly to what US law firms appear to value most: the bottom line. In so doing, such arguments also sidestep some of the controversies that have increasingly surrounded affirmative action and other similar policies designed to make progress on diversity (Thernstrom and Thernstrom 1997). If corporations want more minority lawyers working on their matters, the argument goes, then hiring and promoting such lawyers is a matter of economic necessity—not, as some critics of affirmative action have asserted, an unjustified 'preference' for minorities that harms innocent whites. It is small wonder, therefore, that a growing number of diversity advocates have abandoned the contested domain of moral theory for the seemingly neutral imperatives of the competitive marketplace.

Collectively, these three features of the American market—changing student demographics, corporate diversity initiatives, and the rise of market values—do indeed make a persuasive case for exploring the value of the business case for diversity. Indeed, it is increasingly clear that all three of these changes are now at the front and centre in many parts of the globe. In most industrialized nations, women are entering the legal profession in ever-expanding numbers (Schultz and Shaw 2003). Issues of race and religion are also receiving more attention in professional circles, as lawyers in various countries begin to confront the complex legacies of colonialism, immigration, and internal ethnic division (Baxter 1998; Nicolson 2005; Thomas 2000). At the same time, companies in the UK such as Barclays have begun to demand, in the words of a recent article, 'US-style trends for corporate responsibility' by demanding 'staff diversity statistics from every firm it uses for external counsel' (Middleton 2006). Finally, global competitiveness is concentrating the minds of lawyers everywhere on finding ways to increase profitability and efficiency. Given these trends, it is clear that diversity is no longer just an American concern. While few law firms have gone as far as Freshfields Brukhaus Deringer, which hired a French professor of organizational behaviour to help the firm avoid 'stereotyping', and the tendency to be 'blind to our own culture' after the merger between UK and German firms that created this global powerhouse (Freshfields Annual Report 2001), managing partners in many jurisdictions are likely to begin looking for a business connection between the rapidly globalizing market for corporate legal services and the growing diversity of the lawyers who practise in these institutions.

Unfortunately, this is where the analysis tends to stop. Saying that law firms now have good economic reasons for paying attention to diversity is not the same as demonstrating that these economic drivers will produce the diversity that advocates in the USA and in other countries around the globe claim to seek. To see why, it is necessary to look closely at the arguments typically deployed in support of the business case for diversity and to examine critically the implications of accepting these arguments in the context of large law firms.

Limitations of the business case

Until very recently most law firm leaders (like the corporations they served) assumed without question that homogeneity, not diversity, was what was good for the business of large law firms. As Erwin Smigel documents in his classic study of Wall Street law firms in the 1950s and 1960s, these institutions confined their recruiting almost exclusively to 'Nordic [men who have] pleasing personalities and "clean-cut" appearances, are graduates of the "right" schools, have the "right" social background and experience in the affairs of the world, and are endowed with tremendous stamina' (Smigel 1969: 3). The English bar maintained similarly exclusionary practices. Needless to say, these practices excluded virtually all Jews, women, and racial minorities. As Smigel's respondents made clear, however, the primary purpose of these recruiting practices was not to discriminate against lawyers from groups considered to be unworthy of becoming members of the bar—although discrimination against all of these groups was open and notorious during this period. Instead, Smigel's Wall Street lawyers deeply believed that recruiting lawyers who shared a common background and outlook was essential to a firm's ability to produce high-quality legal work and to relate to clients who came from similar stock.

Indeed, even after a lawyer was hired through the use of these highly exclusionary criteria, Smigel's respondents emphasized that when deciding whether to elevate the new recruit to partnership eight to ten years later, partners considered the candidate's ability to fit into the firm's tightly knit social structure to be almost as important as the number of hours he worked or his potential for bringing in business. As a typical partner told Smigel:

There are intangibles. We see a man for long hours over the years, see his wife, know his family background, what outside charity activities he participates in. You get to know about these people over a ten year period. You see them in your home or when you're away on a trip with them—the word comes down about them from judges and clients. We encourage extracurricular activities. On a personal level, if we never see a man at functions we wonder if he has the qualities we want—if he measures up. He must be able to play team ball—if he can't we will not take him, for we are also looking for personal qualities, including his ability to get along with you. (Smigel 1969: 106)

Notwithstanding the many important changes in the years since Smigel's study, there are good reasons to suspect that many partners continue to cling to these beliefs. Paul Barrett discovered in his revealing book about race in large law firms, for example, that there are still many partners who believe that the real reason why firms have so few black partners is that there are too many incompetent black lawyers who have been 'polished up' by affirmative action to look like Harvard Law School graduates (Barrett 1999). Sommerlad and Sanderson uncovered similar attitudes in their study of women solicitors in England and Wales (Sommerlad and Sanderson 1998). More fundamentally, as Empson demonstrates in Chapter 2, lawyers continue to think of the 'partnership ethos' as akin to joining a very exclusive club in which 'fitting in' to the existing norms and practices of the group is paramount. It is against this background that proponents of the business case for diversity must state their claim.

Those pressing this new framework seek to meet this challenge by pointing to the unique benefits that diverse lawyers bring to their work. An influential brief filed by General Motors Corporation in support of the continuation of law school admissions policies that take race into consideration summarizes the benefits from creating a workforce with 'cross-cultural competence':

Such ... competence affects a business' performance of virtually all of its major tasks: (a) identifying and satisfying the needs of diverse customers; (b) recruiting and retaining a diverse work force and inspiring that work force to work together to develop and implement innovative ideas: and (c) forming and fostering productive working relationships with business partners and subsidiaries around the globe. (General Motors Corporation 2003: 12–13)

Nicolson finds a similar set of justifications in the recent diversity reports by the Bar Council and Law Society. In explaining why achieving diversity is now a pressing need, he summarizes both reports as emphasizing the market value of:

... providing better services to an increasingly diverse client base, thus opening up access to new markets; better chances of obtaining work from organisations which impose equal opportunity and diversity requirements; access to a wider pool of talent in recruitment... [and] increased innovation and creativity through fresh thinking and new ideas.[1] (Nicolson 2005)

Each of these arguments, which I have reframed slightly under the general headings of serving new markets, managerialism, and problem-solving, highlights important advantages that can flow from promoting an open and diverse workforce. My research on black lawyers, however, under-scores that in the context of corporate law firms, each has significant—and largely unexplored—complexities.

Serving new markets

As indicated in the previous section, many American businesses, in the words of the General Motors Brief 'are truly international companies' (General Motors Corporation 2003: 7). Given this reality, managers fre-quently see the need, as Thomas and Ely put it, for 'a demographically more diverse workforce' to 'gain access to these differentiated segments' and to 'understand and serve [their] customers better and to gain legit-imacy with them' (Thomas and Ely 1996). It is therefore not surprising that in the corporate world, blacks have made substantial inroads in heavily regulated industries such as communications and insurance, that Asian Americans are well represented in technology companies that do substantial business with Asia, and that Proctor & Gamble has one of the best records for hiring and promoting women (Thomas and Ely 1996: 83).

Black lawyers in the USA have experienced similar career benefits from changes in the market for corporate legal services. Consider, for example, the rise of black political power in many major American cities. When black politicians were elected mayor in cities such as Los Angeles, Detroit, Chicago, and New York City, they often demanded that black profes-sionals receive their fair share of city business (Thomas and Ely 1996; Wilkins 1999b). As a result, law firms that competed for city business—or represented the many corporate clients who depend on the good graces of city officials to conduct their own business profitably—began to see a strong 'business reason' for caring about diversity. The consequences of this increased concern were dramatic. Of the more than seventy black lawyers at major Chicago law firms I interviewed in the late 1990s, most claimed that the election of that city's first black mayor in 1983 had a direct and substantial impact on their ability to build stable and successful practices (Wilkins 1999b).

A similar story can be told about the implications likely to flow from the rise in women and minority general counsel over the last decade. There is ample evidence that minority general counsel make an effort, in the words of one prominent black in-house lawyer, to ensure 'that matters go to minority lawyers' (Deger 2003). Most black lawyers in large law firms have benefited significantly from these efforts. As one black partner succinctly stated, 'virtually every important client relationship I have has come through a minority or woman in-house counsel' (Confidential Interview 71). Statements in support of diversity by leading general counsel, such as those by lawyers at Sara Lee, Wal-Mart, and Barclays discussed above, will only strengthen the ability of women and minority in-house counsel to channel work to women and minority lawyers inside firms.

Although these trends in the legal services industry are therefore likely to benefit the cause of law firm diversity, it is doubtful that changes in the demographic composition of in-house legal departments will have as powerful an effect on the careers of women and minority lawyers in law firms as the corresponding growth in minority purchasing power has had on the careers of minority managers in the corporate world. Once again, the prior experience of black American lawyers attempting to capitalize on an increase in the demand for their services by certain clients is instructive. As indicated above, the rise of black political power in many major US cities did spur the demand for black lawyers who could connect with these new elected officials. But building a career based on political connections is by its very nature an unstable route to success in a large law firm. While many black lawyers saw their fortunes rise rapidly with the election of black mayors, several saw their positions just as quickly erode when the political winds changed. As one prominent black lawyer— promoted to equity partner in large part because his Chicago law firm saw him as valuable after the city elected a black mayor—described the impact of that mayor's untimely death four years later: it was as if 'the ground . . . caved in and everything fell apart'(Confidential Interview 16). With the black mayor gone, and a white mayor in his place, this lawyer's contacts in city government became far less valuable, thereby making him less valuable in the eyes of his partners and clients, who no longer saw a strong business reason for employing his services. Within a few short years, this lawyer was eased out of his prestigious partnership.

Black lawyers who have sought to build practices on the changing demographics of corporate legal departments and the growing corporate commitment to diversity have experienced a different set of obstacles— but ones that have proven just as damaging to the 'business case' for diversity as the shifting political fortunes discussed above. Although minority—and indeed many white female general counsel—often want to give business to black lawyers, they often find themselves constrained by the fact that most companies already have strong relationships with outside counsel. Moreover, when corporate counsel do select new lawyers, they face tremendous pressure to hire counsel whose 'merit' is beyond question, in part to protect themselves in case something goes wrong. This pressure is particularly strong for minority in-house lawyers who, like black politicians, face charges of favouritism if they select less prominent minority lawyers over better-known whites (Wilkins 1999a).

In the past, these combined pressures have severely limited the effectiveness of programmes designed to encourage corporate clients to give law firms a business reason for hiring and promoting minority lawyers. Prior to Palmore's Call to Action, there were two other initiatives by corporate counsel designed to press law firms to hire and promote more minority lawyers: a letter from the general counsel of General Motors in 1987 that was endorsed by dozens of major corporations and the American Bar Association, and a letter in 1996 from the general counsel of Bell South that was eventually signed by over 350 companies (Pearce 1988; Fritz 2002). Yet notwithstanding the fact that both initiatives received substantial attention and support, neither produced lasting change. In each case, after an initial flurry of activity, most corporations did little more than send their outside firms the same letter every year 'requesting information' about their progress on diversity and doled out a few small projects that were often below the pricing structure of most large law firms (Wilkins 2004a). In the end, as one black partner in a major California law firm bemoaned in comments that were typical of the people I interviewed, these well-intentioned efforts proved:

> ... totally useless as far as black partners or black associates in major firms [were concerned]. The only thing it's done is to encourage the corporations and other major institutions to spin off and siphon off some pissy-ass collection effort or something else to a minority lawyer. (Confidential Interview 109)

Of course, one can hope that the current Call to Action and related initiatives will prove more potent than their predecessors. The fact that many of the general counsel who are leading these new efforts are themselves women and minorities, for example, seems likely to give this new round of corporate pressure some added push. Nevertheless, there are still reasons to be concerned about the long-term efficacy of this current crop of what I have elsewhere referred to as 'demand-side diversity initiatives' (Wilkins and Gulati 1996).

To begin, arguments that have proven effective in convincing corporations in the consumer products area to focus on diversity may not translate well to the work of corporate lawyers. To the extent that these arguments are grounded on the value of having a workforce that reflects and understands the culture of the company's customers, making a similar appeal to law firms may end up undermining, rather than promoting, opportunities for minority lawyers. When a multinational corporation is considering a new joint venture agreement, for example, it wants lawyers who know how to operate in the complex world of strategic planning and corporate finance. Notwithstanding the demographic changes discussed above, that world remains overwhelmingly white and male.

Indeed, to the extent that arguments about 'new markets' promote diversity, it is likely to be of a different kind than the diversity sought by American advocates currently pressing the business case for diversity. Most of the new markets that large law firms are interested in cultivating are in Europe and the emerging economies in Asia. It is far from clear whether the resulting national and cultural diversity of the client firms will produce the opportunities for US-born minority lawyers that diversity advocates in this country sometimes assume. For example, in 2003 the Minority Scorecard, an annual headcount of the number of minorities employed by large law firms conducted by the *Minority Law Journal*, reported a significant drop in the number of minorities at several prominent firms (*Minority Law Journal* 2003). When the editors inquired about the reasons for the decline, they were informed that the firms in question had stopped including the *foreign nationals* in Europe and Asia working in their *foreign* offices in their overall diversity statistics. Firms, in other words, were beefing up their diversity statistics for a publication whose express goal is to increase opportunities for US minority lawyers by treating, for example, a Spanish lawyer working in Spain as a 'minority'. As I argue below, this practice reveals a great deal about the lengths that firms will go to cultivate an image of diversity. For present purposes, however, the fact that removing foreign nationals working abroad from the minority pool significantly reduced not only the total number but the percentage of minorities working in many firms demonstrates the fact that few US-born minorities work in the overseas offices of US firms. Put somewhat differently, although US law firms are increasingly 'going global', their US minority lawyers apparently are not.

Nor are US minorities in large law firms benefiting significantly from the changing demographics of the US population or the growing economic clout of minority businesses and consumers. As indicated above, advocates for the business case for diversity frequently point to the fact that the USA is rapidly becoming a 'majority minority' country in order to bolster their contention that diversity is now a business imperative (General Motors Corporation 2003: 3). But most of these new minority consumers—whether individuals or small minority businesses—simply cannot afford the high-priced legal services offered by corporate lawyers. As a black lawyer reported when leaving a partnership in a major law firm to take up one in a small minority firm: 'most of my clients are small businesses [and] many are minority business' who simply could not afford the $250 an hour that his old firm charged for his services (Gill 1992). The net effect is that in spite of the impressive growth in minority purchasing power *in the aggregate,* the growing purchasing power of minority consumers, like globalization, is having less impact on the careers of minority lawyers in large law firms than this trend is having on the careers of minorities in other areas of corporate life. This reality, in turn, affects the strength of the managerial arguments offered in support of the business case for diversity.

Managerialism

In addition to producing new consumers for American business, both globalization and the changing demographics of the American population are also dramatically reshaping the American workforce. Developing a managerial elite capable of overseeing this increasingly diverse workforce is one of the major business imperatives cited by diversity advocates.

Those asserting this position frequently point to the experience of the USA military during the Vietnam War. Although the number of black soldiers in the enlisted ranks had increased significantly following the Second World War, the percentage of black officers remained extremely low. As a result, the military experienced 'increased racial polarization, pervasive disciplinary problems, and racially motivated incidents in Vietnam and on posts around the world' (General's Brief 2003). To remedy this problem, the military launched an aggressive affirmative action programme expressly designed to increase the number of black officers. The success of this programme—and the military's vigorous defence of it in the same Supreme Court case in which General Motors invoked the business paradigm to defend its own affirmative efforts to hire and promote minority managers and executives—is frequently cited by diversity advocates in law firms as strong support for the business case for diversity in these institutions.

The argument from managerialism, however, is far less compelling in the context of large law firms. As the Generals' Brief underscores, 'almost 40 per cent of servicemen and women are minorities . . . including 21.7 per cent African-Americans' (2003: 6). As indicated above, however, minorities comprise just over 14 per cent of all law firm associates, and just under 4 per cent of all of the partners in these institutions (Chambliss 2004). These percentages present a far less urgent need for managerial diversity than the comparable percentages and trends in the armed services or even in much of corporate America. Although women constitute a far bigger percentage of the typical law firm's legal professionals (over 40 per cent) this has been true for more than two decades, yet women still constitute just over 16 per cent of law firm partners (Catalyst 2001). Clearly, the changing demographics of law firm associates has not been sufficient to produce a corresponding change in the percentage of women partners.

Indeed, it is not clear that law firms give significant weight to management considerations in making partnership decisions at all. Associates are promoted to partnership primarily on the basis of their legal skills and projections about their ability to bring in business (Wilkins and Gulati 1998). There is little indication that whether a given lawyer will also be a good manager plays much of a role in this process. Given this underlying reality, it is not surprising that the final set of economic arguments about diversity—that diverse teams make better problem-solvers—has recently garnered so much attention.

Problem-solving

It is a testament to how far the US business community has come in the years since Smigel's study of Wall Street law firms discussed above that many corporations have now officially endorsed the proposition that diversity, as opposed to the homogeneity that corporate America once craved, is what really produces innovation and creativity. This same history, however, should make us cautious about accepting this new commitment at face value.

Three issues relating to the relationship between diversity and 'problem-solving' have made moving from rhetoric to action on the basis of this aspect of the business case for diversity troublesome in corporate America. First, as the arguments about new markets underscore, there is considerable disagreement over exactly what constitutes diversity for these purposes. Since many kinds of attributes and talents play a role in problem-solving, the tendency has been to expand the definition of diversity to include everything from geography to organizational position to personal habits and taste in food or sports (Edelman, Fuller, and Mara-Drita 2001). Given this expansion, the extent to which companies value the link between *demographic* diversity and problem-solving remains an open question.

Second, as even the proponents of the problem-solving diversity argument concede, 'empirical research on whether and how diversity is actually related to work group function is limited...and the evidence is mixed' (Ely and Thomas 2001). Moreover, the most promising research in this area suggests that whether work group diversity improves productivity depends on the attitude and orientation that group members bring to their work. To the extent that group members do not value 'diversity as a resource for learning how to do their core work', these groups are less likely to benefit from their diversity and may even perform less well than homogeneous groups that do not have to negotiate the kinds of conflict and communication issues that often beset diverse groups (Ely and Thomas 2003).

Finally, not every kind of 'diversity of viewpoint' is valued by corporate America. Specifically, views or attitudes that too strongly challenge existing understandings or practices are often not well received by managers—despite the fact that fostering dissent is one of the primary ways that diversity improves decision-making (Ellemers, Spears, and Doosje 1997; Sunstein 2003). Given their history of marginalization, minorities are likely to be especially fearful of being perceived as being too 'diverse' in this way (Carbado and Gulati 2000; Morgan 2002). Paradoxically, this fear may lead minorities not to present divergent views (or worse yet, not to speak at all) thereby reinforcing the view that their diversity makes no positive contribution to group problem-solving (Herring 1992).

None of this should be taken to mean that diversity in general, and demographic diversity in particular, does not contribute to better decision-making or that diversity advocates ought to stop trying to convince law firms and their corporate clients that it does. Studies in a variety of areas demonstrate that under proper conditions, diverse groups can produce innovation and greater productivity (Ely and Thomas 2003). My own work on black lawyers highlights the unique value that those traditionally deemed to be outsiders often bring to their work (Wilkins 2004b).

Nevertheless, sweeping statements that seem to draw easy causal connections between general trends in the economy like 'globalization' and increased profits and the need for diversity, or which draw conclusions on the basis of management speak about the value of incorporating 'multiple perspectives', seem likely to reinforce, rather than dissipate, background scepticism about the value of diversity that undoubtedly lingers in the minds of many lawyers brought up under the old unspoken credo that it is really homogeneity that is good for business. And the more sceptical law firm managers are of the business case for diversity, the more likely they are to manipulate this construct—to 'play the game' without believing in the goal.

Dangers of cosmetic diversity: the numbers game and race matching

If diversity is valued primarily for its business advantages, but achieving these advantages is 'costly' (e.g. because it requires firms to deviate from normal routines and long-standing assumptions), then we should not be surprised to find firms looking for ways to appear to be complying with diversity directives without actually changing existing practices. If this does not work, firms may also seek to economize on what they perceive as the costs of compliance by looking for places where the economic benefits of diversity are most likely to be found. In either case, the end result is likely to be diversity that is, as Krawiec has observed in a similar context, more 'cosmetic' than real (Krawiec 2003).

Recall the creative accounting used by law firms who claimed foreign nationals working in their native countries as minorities for purposes of reporting their diversity statistics to the Minority Corporate Counsel Association. This manipulation underscores the risk that firms will respond to business pressures for increased diversity by taking steps to appear to be making progress on this issue when little or no progress is actually being made. I have elsewhere called this manipulation 'the numbers game' (Wilkins 1999a).

There is ample evidence that some law firms are manipulating their diversity statistics in order to avoid just the kind of pressure from corporate clients upon which much of the hope for the business case for diversity rests. My interviews are replete with examples of black lawyers who have been trotted out to impress a black politician or corporate counsel and then trotted back into the oblivion from whence they came never to see the work that their diversity helped to produce. The following comment from a black associate who worked at a large Washington, DC firm in the early 1990s is typical:

> [I was] rolled out to every presentation for a black mayor or black CFO or a black city treasurer or what have you.... Now, I'm the junior most person in the whole department. So clearly it wasn't because my presence was of any substantive relevance to their presentation. It was purely facial, purely for cosmetic purposes. (Confidential Interview 101)

Even when black lawyers are formally assigned to work on matters for clients who have expressed an interest in law firm diversity, they often have difficulty translating this experience into commensurate work for other clients. Having satisfied the literal terms of the first client's request (placing diverse associates on their matters), firms often proceed to ignore black lawyers whose value they see as strictly tied to their status as peons to the few meddlesome clients who demand diversity. This, in turn, reinforces the tendency towards race-matching that has unfortunately become a significant by-product of the rise of market-based diversity arguments.

When corporations look for a business reason to hire minorities, they frequently find it in areas where race already plays a prominent role. In consumer marketing, minorities often market exclusively to minority communities, just as 'in investment banks ... municipal finance departments have long led corporate finance departments in pursuing demographic diversity because of the typical makeup of the administration of city halls and county boards' (Thomas and Ely 1996: 83). Not surprisingly, law firms have tended to pursue a similar strategy. The plurality of the black corporate lawyers I interviewed specialize in 'labour and employment' law, which, in many large law firms, often means defending discrimination cases. When the large number of black corporate lawyers who specialize in litigation (where the heavy concentration of minorities in urban jury pools is increasingly significant), and municipal bond practice (where black city officials are often the ones who dispense the work) are added to this number, it is evident that a very large percentage of black lawyers (probably over 50 per cent) are engaged in practice areas where their race might be thought to be an important credential.

The danger is that these are the only places where firms will see minorities as adding value. As one respondent bluntly put it, black lawyers who market to other blacks or otherwise work in areas where their race is a significant credential frequently find themselves trapped inside a 'black box' that severely limits their ability to broaden their horizons or, in many cases, to advance in the firm (Confidential Interview 175). For example, a well-regarded black litigator from a large law firm complained bitterly to me that, notwithstanding his many successes in trying cases all over the country, both potential clients and the press continue to highlight his appeal to 'minority jurors' in 'criminal cases'—thus making it harder for him to attract the kind of lucrative corporate litigation upon which his success as a major rainmaker in his firm ultimately depends (Confidential Interview 166).

To make matters worse, minority lawyers sometimes find themselves being 'matched' in areas in which they have no interest and to which they have no business being involved—a danger that has ironically been accentuated for Latinos and Asians by globalization. A Puerto Rican associate working in a large New York law firm, for example, reported that she was often pulled off general corporate deals where she was the senior associate to work on transactions involving Latin American clients where her responsibilities were little more than translation (Confidential Interview 226). Similarly, a Japanese-American litigator reported being summoned by corporate partners to come to a meeting at which the firm was soliciting transactional work from a Korean company (Confidential Interview 227). Minorities who feel that they are being pressed into service solely because of their race frequently come away from such encounters feeling devalued and exploited. As the black lawyer who found himself 'rolled out' for every meeting with a black politician said with disgust:

> That was I think probably the biggest slap in the face. To spend your life getting properly validated only to get pimped once you get in the law firm and have no control over it unless you leave.... I worked in that area for three years until it got to the point where.... I just couldn't take it. (Confidential Interview 101)

If law firms are going to move beyond cosmetic diversity—let alone begin to achieve the positive benefits that can and should be associated with building a more open and inclusive workforce for today's global marketplace—then these institutions must begin seriously to explore how achieving diversity affects their core mission. As Donald Nicolson argues with respect to the UK, to achieve this result 'it is essential...that attention is clearly focused on the ethical case for eradicating discrimination and promoting diversity' (2005: 216). Without this attention, diversity efforts will be hostage to the changing winds of self-interest of both law firm leaders and their corporate clients. To be sure, these winds are currently blowing in the direction of promoting diversity. But as Lauren Edelman has demonstrated in the corporate context, when organizations 'managerialize' diversity by moving from a 'civil rights' paradigm where fairness to previously excluded groups is the legitimating force, to a diversity paradigm where such efforts are justified solely by their effect on corporate profits, there is a danger that the unique problems and potential contributions of women and minorities will be lost in the general effort to maximize the general value of everyone's unique diversity (Edelman, Fuller, and Mara-Drita 2001).

In previous work, I have attempted to lay out a normative case for ensuring opportunity and inclusion for black lawyers in large law firms that ought to appeal to partners, corporate clients, and—a constituency too often forgotten or taken for granted in this context—black lawyers themselves (Wilkins 1993, 1998a, 1998b, 2004a). I will not repeat these arguments here. Instead, in the remainder of this chapter I want to emphasize that, notwithstanding Edelman's important caution, paying attention to these normative arguments can actually facilitate a law firm's ability to compete in today's increasingly multicultural global marketplace.

To achieve this objective, however, firms will need to spend less time obsessing about how they can *profit* from diversity and devote more attention to what they can learn from their *failure* successfully to integrate women and minority lawyers during the last thirty years. Law firms, as Leblebici demonstrates in this volume, are 'connected systems'. As a result, it is very difficult to alter any given practice (in Leblebici's example, billable hours) without also changing practices in other areas (in Leblebici's case, associate evaluation and partner compensation) that undergird and support the practice one is trying to change. Leblebici's analysis is equally applicable to the diversity issues under consideration here. Law firms will never achieve significant diversity—let alone learn how to profit from the diversity that they do achieve—until they are willing critically to examine those aspects of their culture and structure that continue to reproduce homogeneity. Ironically, those firms that are willing to engage in this kind of critical introspection are not only more likely to achieve the narrower objective of demographic diversity, but will also learn valuable lessons that will help them to meet the broader challenges associated with global competition.

Conclusions: learning from diversity

Of all the factors that have contributed to the failure of most US law firms to hire and promote a significant number of women and minority lawyers, two have emerged in my own research, and the research of other scholars, as being of particular importance: (*a*) the exclusion and alienation that many women and minorities feel from traditional law firm culture, and (*b*) the built-in biases of the 'tournament of lawyers'. Understanding both of these themes, I submit, will be crucial for lawyers in Europe and the USA who wish to build stable and successful global law firms for the twenty-first century.

Managing the culture wars

As the statements from Clifford Chance and Freshfields referenced earlier in this chapter underscore, achieving cultural diversity has become a major topic for large law firms, especially for those with global ambitions. Global mergers require melding national as well as professional cultures. Often, linguistic differences will be present as well. And because law and lawyers are intimately connected with national sovereignty and identity, the attorneys who make up these global firms will come from different normative and substantive legal traditions embedded with differing, and potentially conflicting, notions about law, lawyering, and professionalism. Given these realities, the barriers to integrating these diverse ideas, styles, and practices into a functioning global firm are considerable indeed.

The US experience of trying to integrate minority and women lawyers highlights both the importance and the difficulty of cultural integration. Minorities and women consistently report feeling excluded and alienated from the prevailing culture of many law firms. Thus, women lawyers often feel trapped between an 'old boys" culture that views women as unfit for demanding work assignments and an implicit expectation that women must play a demanding but unappreciated role as 'nurturers' inside the institution. Minority lawyers frequently complain that they are left out of the informal social networks in their firms, thereby isolating them from the information, opportunities, and relationships that invariably flow through these channels (Wilkins and Gulati 1996). Research on women and minority solicitors in the UK has reached similar conclusions about the exclusionary effects of traditional law firm culture (Shiner 2000; Sommerlad and Sanderson 1998). The net result is that lawyers from both groups in the USA and the UK often fail to reach their full potential because of what they correctly perceive as the firm's oppressive and exclusionary culture. If firms are going to make real progress on improving their retention of women and minority lawyers they must find ways to change these prevailing cultural norms.

The problem is likely to be even more acute with respect to the issue of 'cultural integration' faced by firms like Clifford Chance and Freshfields. For all the talk about a separate 'female' or 'black' culture in the USA, the women and minority lawyers who are joining large law firms are similar in most important respects to the lawyers who have worked in these firms for generations. Virtually all are American, most are graduates of the same elite schools as their white peers, and many come from similar class and social backgrounds (Wilkins 2005).[2] The fact that US firms are having difficulty integrating US women and minorities into the institution's cultural fabric does not bode well for their ability to form global partnerships with lawyers who come from substantially different national, linguistic, and professional backgrounds.

If global firms are to avoid having foreign lawyers feeling as excluded and marginalized as US minorities have traditionally felt, they must begin, as Garth (2006) has argued, 'to start thinking like anthropologists', and question some of their fundamental assumptions about what it means to be a 'professional' in a multicultural society. Lawyer professionalism, to paraphrase the sociologist Lewis Coser (1974), has traditionally been a 'greedy' ideology. Through legal education and professional socialization, lawyers are expected to adopt a 'professional self' that subsumes all other aspects of their personal and moral identity (Nelson and Trubek 1992). According to this standard account 'such apparent aspects of the self as one's race, gender, religion, or ethnic background... [are] irrelevant to defining one's capacities as a lawyer' (Levinson 1993: 1578).

'Bleached out professionalism', as Sanford Levinson has aptly labelled this traditional ideology, is a problematic normative ideal for global lawyers. Once again, the American experience with diversity underscores this conclusion. As a preliminary matter, women and minorities stand as a constant reminder of the falsity of the implicit claim of bleached out professionalism that the current norms of professional conduct exist independent of any particular pre-professional identity. Consider the claim that the traditional career path (under which associates must work sixty to eighty hours a week for eight to ten years in order to be considered for partnership) is the only appropriate way to train young lawyers to be competent and ethical practitioners. Although these claims are often expressed in the neutral language of professionalism, it is clear that this system, like every social system, is a product of the historical times in which it was produced (Epstein et al. 1995). With respect to traditional career patterns, this historical period was one in which there were overt discriminatory policies against hiring women. Concepts of professionalism developed in this era were therefore framed to fit the identity of those who were eligible for such positions—young men with wives who did not work. Given this historical pedigree, it is simply not true that women who ask that their identities be recognized when judging what constitutes a professionally acceptable career path are engaged in an unprofessional act of special pleading.

Moreover, by stigmatizing as unprofessional those whose identity-related commitments fail to conform to traditional understandings, bleached out professionalism stifles innovation. Many of the most important critiques of long-standing professional practices have been launched by lawyers challenging the manner in which existing standards fail to recognize particular aspects of their non-professional identities. Consider, for example, the alternative dispute resolution movement in the USA. Feminist scholars in the USA have long claimed that the American adversary system, with its emphasis on aggressive winner-take-all combat, reflects a distinctly 'male' form of identity (Menkel-Meadow 1985). Although such claims have always been controversial—even among women academics (Rhode 1993)—many of the scholars and practitioners who levelled these charges have also been instrumental in pressing legislators, courts, and litigants to seek more consensus-oriented means of resolving disputes (Menkel-Meadow 1995). The resulting shift towards negotiation and mediation has been one of the most important innovations in American law in the last quarter century.

Similarly, black lawyers in the large law firms have often used identity-based organizing strategies to cope with the isolation and subtle obstacles that still haunt their careers. For example, black lawyers working in large law firms appear to be more likely than their white peers to engage in *pro bono* work, to have spent time in government or other public service, and to be active in bar organizations (Wilkins 2004b). My interviews reveal that for most black lawyers, this heightened commitment to public service is the result of two factors. The first is a strong belief that as black professionals they have an obligation to use their legal skills to improve the situation of the black community generally. The second and equally strong belief is that the experience, visibility, and contacts that flow from public service will be especially useful in helping them to overcome the obstacles that they face as minorities in the corporate world.

In the process, however, many black attorneys have found that their engagement with public service also has helped them to develop an integrated sense of their own identity that rejects the stark dichotomy of bleached out professionalism between personal identity and professional role. The following comment from a black partner in a mid-size law firm is typical of those I heard from black lawyers about public service. Against the advice of friends who believed that it would hurt his career, this partner agreed to become the president of the local black bar association, primarily as a means of fulfilling an obligation that he felt to assist other black lawyers and the black community generally. After doing so, however, he discovered that the visibility and access associated with being a bar president—even of a small minority association—increased his stature both inside and outside his firm. Although these career benefits were certainly important to him, in the end they are not the primary reason he now urges other black lawyers to get involved in public service. As he emphasized during our interview, public service 'helps you develop your business, but it also helps you keep your sense of yourself. A lot of people live internally at the firm—totally. [But] you've got to balance the two' (Confidential Interview 6). Those black attorneys who have managed to achieve this integration have been able to rise within the profession while at the same time continuing to hold the bar and the country as a whole accountable for continuing inequality between blacks and whites (Wilkins 2004a).

Each of these lessons from the experiences of minorities and women that bleached out professionalism stigmatizes lawyers who are different from those who created existing professional norms, discourages identity-related innovations in professional practices, and deligitimates the kind of integrated self-consciousness that promotes individual growth, collective organization, and service to others—has important implications for the success of global law firms. Lawyers from around the world who are increasingly being brought together in US and UK law firms with global ambitions are unlikely to work efficiently together if some believe, as the cultural anthropologist hired by Freshfields warned in the quote cited earlier in this chapter, that they are stigmatized for beliefs and practices that they consider to be intimately connected to important aspects of their national or legal culture. Similarly, firms with global ambitions will be less likely to respond to the rapid changes that increasingly characterize the global marketplace if they discourage innovation by lawyers from other cultures who disagree with the firm's often taken-for-granted policies and practices. Finally, the fact that firms too often fail to allow associates and partners to develop an integrated sense of their own identities plays an important role in the growing problem these institutions have with lawyer attrition. To see why, one must first understand how diversity highlights important limitations in traditional law firm hiring and promotion practices.

Real rules of the tournament of lawyers

The basic structure of the modern large law firm has remained the same for more than a century. Associates are hired directly out of law school for a probationary period, typically lasting from six to ten years, during which they are expected to demonstrate their ability and commitment to the firm. At the end of this period, the firm selects the 'best' of these young lawyers to become partners. Those who are not selected are let go or, in rare circumstances, allowed to stay with the firm as permanent associates or 'of counsel'. The structure is often analogized to a 'tournament' in which associates compete on an equal playing field to demonstrate their abilities with the top performers selected for partnership (Galanter and Palay 1991). It is this image of the large law firm—as an efficient, professional, and meritocratic institution that best serves the needs of lawyers, clients, and the public at large—that US lawyers like to show to the world.

This image, however, masks important structural biases in the manner in which the competition for partnership takes place. Given the pyramidal structure of most elite firms—a small number of partners at the top supported by many associates at the bottom, particularly in the junior tiers—good work and mentoring will inevitably be in short supply. Contrary to the 'survival of the fittest' rhetoric of tournament theory, therefore, success in large law firms is less a matter of innate ability and hard work (most of those who get hired by elite firms possess these qualities) and more a function of gaining access to valuable, but limited, opportunities—opportunities that are invariably mediated through relationships. And relationships of all kinds are invariably mediated by issues of identity (Wilkins and Gulati 1998).

There is now a substantial body of evidence in fields ranging from cognitive psychology to organizational behaviour that people tend to favour people who are like themselves when reaching subjective evaluations about merit (Kang and Banaji, 2006). Given that most lawyers in large law firms continue to be both white and male, particularly at the partnership level, this unsurprising but nevertheless powerful tendency means that minorities and women are less likely to gain the kind of important opportunities and encouragement that give them an incentive to invest in building a long-term career in the firm. And, of course, the less women and minority associates invest in their own development, the less likely it is that partners will be willing to invest their own scarce time in developing these outsiders. The result of this vicious cycle is that women and minorities are much more likely to leave their law firms after only a few years than their white male peers (National Association of Law Placement Foundation (NALP) 1998).

In the last several years, however, it has become abundantly clear that early attrition has become a critical problem for large law firms with respect to *all* of their associates. Over 40 per cent of the associates who join large law firms in the USA leave before the end of their third year (NALP 1998). Moreover, research suggests that many departing white associates are now leaving for the same reasons that women and minorities have been departing corporate practice for decades—they do not see a viable long-term future with these institutions. For example, in a nationwide survey of over 4,000 lawyers who entered the bar in 2000 (that I am helping to coordinate), lawyers working in large law firms are the most likely to say that they intended to leave their jobs within the next two years—and the most common reasons given for seeking a new position were dissatisfaction with mentoring and opportunity for advancement (American Bar Foundation 2004). Given the realities of the modern tournament of lawyers these results are hardly surprising. The same pyramidal structure that makes it difficult for minorities and women to get access to good work and meaningful developmental relationships ensures that these opportunities will be scarce for all lawyers. In a world where young professionals have a growing number of opportunities—including for many women the option of leaving the workforce altogether—it should not be surprising that many are becoming increasingly dissatisfied with jobs that, while high paying, do not offer the rewards and opportunity for advancement that they had promised.

Facing history—and ourselves

If US law firms' painfully deliberate experience with integration in the last fifty years provides an important cautionary tale for the global ambitions of large law firms, then the careers of the women and minorities who have managed to overcome these obstacles underscore just how deliberate law firms must be if they hope to make progress on achieving both cultural integration and institutional change in the coming decades. Law firms cannot simply expect that the passage of time will produce the integration and innovation upon which their futures depend. Instead, they must work to ensure that lawyers from all backgrounds feel that they have a fair chance to succeed within the context of organizations whose traditional boundaries are being remade by changing career patterns.

At the core of this effort must be a willingness to redefine both cultural norms and established organizational structures. Law firms must move beyond the implicit belief that there is only one way to be a 'true' professional. Just as women and minorities have chafed under a law firm culture from which they have felt excluded, lawyers from around the world are unlikely to work efficiently together if some feel that they are stigmatized for beliefs and practices that they consider to be intimately connected to important aspects of their national or legal culture.

At the same time, the 'retention' crisis discussed above emphasizes that we can no longer expect lawyers to spend all or even the majority of their careers with a single employer. Firms that want to compete for talent in such an environment could learn a great deal by examining the careers of successful women and minorities who have had to look outside the organization for the career support that they have so often been denied in their own workplaces (Wilkins 2004b). Firms that encourage their associates to explore relationships and build opportunities outside the firm will expand the firm's network of potential relationships when these lawyers leave to pursue other opportunities. Indeed, firms that actively discuss career options with their associates may actually reduce the pressure that young lawyers currently feel to leave a law firm after only a few years for fear that staying longer may decrease their lateral mobility if either they or the firm decides that they are not likely to become partners.

In the last analysis, however, none of this will matter unless firms are willing to move beyond traditional patterns of work assignment and promotion that increasingly limit opportunity to an ever smaller percentage of new associates. Needless to say, breaking free of these established structures will be difficult. But innovation in times of crisis is the key to survival. Once again, attention to diversity is critical to this process. Large law firms are less likely to respond effectively to the rapid changes that increasingly characterize the global marketplace if they discourage innovation by those who believe that existing structures and practices do not allow them to express their own individuality or creativity. Firms that fail to acknowledge this truth will continue to find that their lawyers are alienated from their work, isolated from crucial sources of development and support, and prone to seek more meaningful careers at the first available opportunity.

Notes

1. Nicolson also points to the benefits of avoiding discrimination suits. Although the corporate and military briefs in *Grutter* do not mention this motivation, my guess is that those who drafted these legal documents were concerned about these costs as well.
2. As Nicolson demonstrates, this may be less true in the UK, where elite law schools like Oxford and Cambridge are less integrated than similar institutions in the USA and where class divisions are arguably more important and lasting (2005: 208–11).

4

Your expertise

Developing new practices: recipes for success

Heidi Gardner
London Business School

Timothy Morris
Saïd Business School, University of Oxford

Narasimhan Anand
Tanaka Business School, Imperial College London

Introduction

How do professional service firms create a new practice area? How should a fledgling practice be nurtured? What can derail the creation of a new practice? Our research shows that nearly half of all new practice attempts fail, often despite considerable investment of time and resources from both individuals and firms. This chapter seeks to explain why certain initiatives grow into fully fledged new practices, while others stall and fade away or fail soon after they become stand-alone practices.

Successful firms often build their reputation on one or two core practices and work to ensure that these stay cutting-edge. Critically, these firms also innovate to meet, and indeed lead, market demand by creating new specialist groups that serve emerging client needs in new areas. Our research examines what it takes to make these new practices succeed. In our intensive multi-year study, we examined forty examples of new practice development in professional service firms in the legal and consulting sectors. Overall, we found that almost half of all new practice efforts failed, and ongoing discussions with professionals suggest that failure rates may be even higher if we count early stage dropouts as failures. As we discuss in this chapter, each failed example was missing one or more of the essential 'ingredients' for success.

It is vital to understand why so many new practice initiatives fail. Such knowledge can help firms realize value from the considerable attention and resources they devote to their new practice efforts. It can also enable firms successfully to align their portfolio of practices with changing client demands.

In this chapter, we begin by discussing why new practice creation is an important strategic activity for professional firms. We then present some commonly encountered myths surrounding new practice development in law and consulting firms. With careful digging and rigorous analysis across firms and initiatives, we have uncovered the surprising truths that lie behind these myths. Based on our interviews, observations, and study of internal documents, we find that three ingredients are necessary to ensure success. We have also identified three robust 'recipes' that guide the success of new practice initiatives. We call them recipes because each has certain required ingredients along with a set of instructions for how to combine them into a successful outcome. Our objective in this chapter is to describe these recipes for developing successful new practices.

Imperative for new practice development

One point was abundantly clear from both the existing literature on professional firms and from our prior work in this area: developing successful new practices is essential for firms' long-term prosperity and survival. New practices allow professional firms to grow organically and diversify in order to meet ever-changing client needs.

By way of a definition, we consider a 'practice' to be an organizational subunit comprising professionals with related expertise, typically focused on a particular set of clients (e.g. utilities sector) or client issues (e.g. mergers and acquisitions). In addition to organizing existing expertise and providing a stable income, a practice serves as the vehicle for exploring new markets and adapting to changing competitive circumstances.

Growth and diversification

Professional firms have an inherent imperative for both organic growth and diversification. The 'up-or-out' tournament system by which juniors are promoted to partner creates an endogenous bias for organic growth

(Galanter and Palay 1991). For the firm to be viable, newly promoted partners must develop reputations in the client marketplace through which they can attract work and then deploy junior professionals to execute this work (Gilson and Mnookin 1989; Morris and Pinnington 1998). The continued profitability of a professional firm rests on partners' ability to leverage their reputation by deploying increasing numbers of junior staff (Maister 1993).

Beyond this, professional firms have an imperative to diversify in order to hedge against possible shrinkage in their client markets and to exploit underutilized firm resources (Hitt et al. 2001). The diversified structure also allows the firm to spread the collective risk of its partners efficiently (Gilson and Mnookin 1985). Consequently, a firm seeks to develop multiple groups of professionals who work within different areas of expertise or practices as they are conventionally termed.

The joint imperative for internal growth and diversification of its service offering compels professional service firms to adapt and reconfigure their portfolio of practices. This is done, most importantly, by developing thriving new practices.

Challenges surrounding practice portfolio reconfiguration

We know from existing research that professional firms face a number of challenges in renewing their configuration of practices. Professionals' desire for autonomy in the conduct of their professional tasks and their control of client relationships produce a dispersed distribution of power within the professional firm (Hall 1968). This dispersion limits the ability of the top management to exercise absolute control over strategic initiatives concerning diversification and organic growth. Such strategic decisions are likely to be undertaken at a relatively decentralized level by individual partners since they are most aware of opportunities in their client markets (Hinings, Brown, and Greenwood 1991). However, the lack of a legitimate central planning authority or the absence of an appropriate strategic planning process often leads to internal disputes over the boundaries between practices.

We thus began our study with two clear, interrelated ideas. First, developing successful new practices is essential for professional service firms. Second, the process of new practice development is fraught with difficulties. What are the key ingredients of the new practice development process? How do these ingredients fit together? What are the keys to success? With these questions in mind, we used in-depth case studies to delve into the process of new practice development. Before explaining in detail how we went about collecting and analysing data and what exactly we discovered, we briefly identify the myths that we encountered in the course of our research.

Myths about how new practices are built

When we started talking to senior partners and others about how new practices had developed in their firms, we heard three types of stories. As with myths in the classical sense, professionals use these stories to articulate ambiguous situations and explain events which are otherwise difficult to understand. They also embellish these tales through the use of narrative devices such as heroes, hazardous journeys, a happy ending, or a tragic crash. Each myth consists of a kernel of truth that is useful to our understanding of the process of new practice creation.

Myth of the hero

The first of these myths about how new practices arise is 'all it takes is a hero'. Here the practice's heroic founding partner is held up as the quintessential entrepreneur, whose own vision and intelligence define the practice, whose charisma garners valuable clients and dedicated associates, and whose personal sacrifice and dedication see the practice through to success. According to this myth, any failed practice initiatives are the result of having a weak or ineffectual founding partner—the equivalent of a tragic hero who simply does not have the mettle.

Myth of the market

The second myth about new practice development in professional service firms is 'The market dictates the course'. Here the client is often held up as the omniscient being, wisely leading the thirsty lawyer or consultant to a hidden oasis made possible by a change in law or an expanded scope of business. Another version of this myth holds up the grey-haired professional sage as the seer of market niches to come, strategically steering the firm past hazards towards new and prosperous possibilities. The myth of the market suggests that failures to develop new practices result from firms' inability or unwillingness to spot and capture opportunities that their clients and visionary leaders put forward.

Myth of serendipity

The third myth surrounding new practice creation is 'serendipity rules'. The mythical princes of Serendip were travellers who constantly made unexpected and wonderful discoveries through sheer luck and happenstance as they progressed on their journey. Likewise, these tales in professional firms suggest that there is something almost magical about the confluence of events, professionals, timing, clients, and market conditions that allows a new practice to surface and thrive. Proponents of the myth of serendipity are usually unable—and indeed unwilling—to explain why certain practices have failed, except to put forward vague notions about 'bad karma' and things 'not coming together' in the necessary way.

Time and again we heard these stories, across partners, across firms, and across different professions. Yet when we started digging deeper and combining these tales with thorough analysis of how practices are actually built and developed, we discovered that, underlying these myths, there are three robust recipes for creating a successful new practice. Our findings show that relying on a single champion is not enough to ensure success, that the market alone is not a sufficient guide, and that placing faith in the magic of serendipity is not always required. In creating successful new practices, there are clear paths that can be followed.

Research study

We conducted a two-phase, multiple case study research programme to investigate how new practices arise and develop in professional service firms. We studied forty separate examples of new practice development in eight firms.

We focused this first phase on management consulting firms because they operate in a particularly fast-changing market and therefore need to innovate almost continuously by developing relevant new practices. Each of the four consulting firms we studied had started with a core practice and later diversified its portfolio through the creation of one or more successful new practices. The four firms range in size from one of the largest consulting firms in the world to a more 'boutique' consultancy that has offices in only a handful of locations. They also vary significantly in terms of their core practice areas, including information technology–enabled organizational transformation, corporate strategy, wage determination and executive recruitment.

The four law firms in our sample are all based in London; three have overseas offices and the fourth has two other offices in the UK. They vary substantially in size: one has twenty partners, one has fifty, and the other two have more than one hundred partners. The two largest firms provide a range of services to the corporate sector, while the smallest specializes in intellectual property and patenting. The medium-sized firm in our sample offers both corporate legal services and a thriving private client practice.

Our primary source of data was semi-structured interviews conducted over more than fifty hours with a carefully selected set of informants of varying levels of seniority within the law and consulting firms. To analyse nearly 600 pages of resulting transcripts, we used case study analysis to uncover the fundamental building blocks of successful new practices and see how they fit together in particular patterns. In order to verify the robustness of the patterns that we uncovered, we revisited the firms to seek further cases of successful as well as unsuccessful new practice attempts. In total, we investigated forty examples of new practice development across the eight firms.

Whilst the firms were drawn from two very distinct professional sectors, and differed dramatically on a number of key dimensions, we found a remarkable degree of consistency in our findings across all firms.

Recipe ingredients required for a new practice

While analysing our research, we realized we could describe a practice development effort in terms of a recipe for building an organization. In the conventional sense, a recipe consists of two parts: ingredients and instructions for combining the ingredients. We therefore begin our discussion with an overview of the necessary ingredients before expanding on how to mix them together. Our analysis revealed that the three critical ingredients for a successful new practice are 'turf', 'expertise', and 'support'.

As we elaborate below, we consistently found that all three ingredients are necessary in order to make a complete (and successful) recipe. Depending on the type of new practice effort, however, the 'flavour' or variety of each ingredient may differ. One dimension on which the type of new practice can vary is its novelty. Is it based on a brand new concept that the market has never seen before? Or does it already exist within

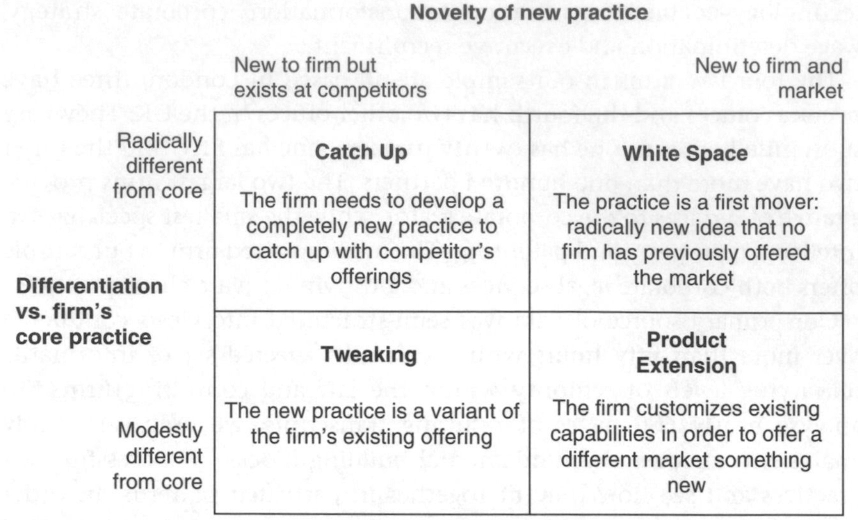

Novelty of new practice

	New to firm but exists at competitors	New to firm and market
Radically different from core	**Catch Up** The firm needs to develop a completely new practice to catch up with competitor's offerings	**White Space** The practice is a first mover: radically new idea that no firm has previously offered the market
Modestly different from core	**Tweaking** The new practice is a variant of the firm's existing offering	**Product Extension** The firm customizes existing capabilities in order to offer a different market something new

Differentiation vs. firm's core practice

Figure 4.1 Four different types of new practices, based on novelty and differentiation from core

competitor firms, and is it simply being developed as a new offering in the focal firm? A second dimension along which new practices vary is their differentiation from the firm's core offering. Some new practices are radically different, while others are seen as incremental adjustments to existing offerings. Figure 4.1 shows how these dimensions fit into a two-by-two matrix, creating four different types of new practice, which we have called Catch Up, White Space, Tweaking, and Product Extension.

Turf

Our research clearly shows that a new practice must delineate and defend its turf within the firm. Our findings suggest that successful turf creation comprises three aspects: (*a*) removing barriers to acceptance of the new practice especially by key stakeholders within the firm, (*b*) using external sources, such as powerful clients, to legitimize the new activity, and (*c*) using internal sources of persuasion in order to carve out an autonomous territory. Because professional firms are characterized by a limited hierarchy and a lack of centralized strategic decision-making, attempts at internal change rely on mobilizing power through coalitions of like-minded partners and supportive clients (Greenwood and Hinings 1996). While a number of consultants told us that they needed to demonstrate 'proof through revenues', it is clear that the promise of potential fees is not enough on its own to create turf that is safe from encroachment by others within the firm: founders of new practices also have to convince others that they have proprietary knowledge, and that they have already made significant in-roads using this new approach.

Considering turf issues by type of practice, we see that a new practice in the Catch Up space (radically different from the firm's existing offering, but existing elsewhere) faces challenges in gaining credibility with clients because other firms have already staked their claim in the domain and the firm has no related expertise or reputation. Practices that are not very different (Tweaking) may be able to convince clients that the firm has a viable offering, but founders must focus on the internal politics of defending their turf from colleagues who do similar work. In contrast, practices that are very new both to the firm and to the market (White Space) must rely on both proof of concept and the reputation of the practice's founding partner(s) to convince clients and internal stakeholders that the idea is viable. Finally, we see the fewest turf considerations when firms simply expand modified versions of their existing offerings into new markets; not only do they have a related reputation on which to rely, but there also are few, if any, competitors (Product Extension). The first row in Table 4.1 shows these relationships.

Expertise

In our study we found that professional firms constantly develop new expertise through client assignments. The debatable question then becomes: when is a body of newly developed knowledge different enough to constitute the basis for a new practice? Clearly this issue is intertwined with claims that aspiring practice founders can make about the relative uniqueness of their expertise. The body of knowledge should be distinctive, yet share an approach to structuring client work that is commonly understood within the firm. For example, one law firm we researched built a new practice in legal aspects of private equity capital that was linked to its core expertise in finance and capital markets, but recognized internally as being distinctive and reflective of growing demand in a new domain of activity. In part, the new expertise was technical and required an understanding of private equity financing law; it also involved an understanding of the mechanics of private equity markets, including the nature of the markets' dynamics, the major players, and the jargon conventionally used by market actors.

71

Table 4.1 Turf considerations, sources of expertise, and organizational support needed for different types of new practice

New practice type ingredient	Tweaking (differentiation: low; novelty: low)	Catch Up (differentiation: high; novelty: low)	Product extension (differentiation: low; novelty: high)	White space (differentiation: high; novelty: high)
Turf considerations	Internal legitimacy hard to gain without clear differentiation Difficult to defend turf against encroachment from colleagues	External credibility harder to build because other firms and professionals have staked their claim	Fewest turf considerations: leverage existing reputation without having to fight off competition	First mover advantage: credibility depends on the strength of the offering and firm's or individual's reputation in other areas
Sources of expertise	Strong possibility to build on existing expertise and adapt or copy other firms' approach	New knowledge most readily available from lateral hires	Export knowledge from existing offices or practices to new locations	Technical expertise is paramount for first movers—need to build from scratch
Organizational support needed	Cross-selling of the new practice to existing clients	Firm resources for hiring and developing lateral hires or for investing in knowledge-building initiatives by existing partners	Budget and resources for setting up new locations, including investments in local market knowledge	Political backing to 'sell' the idea internally and protect the founder from revenue pressures while starting the new venture

The second row in Table 4.1 illustrates how different types and sources of expertise come into play for the four types of new practices. Practices that seek to Catch Up with competitors are likely to find the best source of talent by hiring experts from other firms that already offer that service. Practices that occupy the Tweaking space should be able to source their expertise internally, since current members of the firm work in related areas, and they only have to imitate approaches laid out by competitors. First movers, those practices in the White Space, rely primarily on technical expertise that they need to build from scratch. Finally, practices that are part of a firm's Product Extension can import their expertise from existing areas to new locations.

Support

Support relates to the supply of both tangible and intangible resources from the firm for the budding practice. For example, the supply of trained associates is an important form of organizational support for an emerging practice, as is cross-selling of the new practice by partners with long-standing client relationships. Political sponsorship is widely seen as a crucial form of organizational support, with examples ranging from the managing partner bolstering the practice founder's reputation at a partner conference, to providing 'breathing space' from normal client pressures while the founder initially devotes time to building the new practice.

The nature of the support required varies according to the type of new practice, as shown in the third row of Table 4.1. Support for Catch Up practices that source their expertise through lateral hiring requires resources and processes for attracting, hiring, and socializing new members. Practices in the Tweaking quadrant generally require colleagues to cross-sell the modified offering to their clients. Founders of White Space practices need political support: it is crucial for powerful partners (or the managing committee, firm leadership, etc.) to help bolster the founders' internal capital in order to protect them from revenue pressures while they are focusing on starting the new venture. Finally, practices in the Product Extension domain require support in the form of a budget and resources, such as local staff with requisite knowledge, for establishing themselves in a new market or new location.

Combining the ingredients

Of course, just like in a cookbook recipe, the three new practice ingredients do not come together to form a finished product of their own

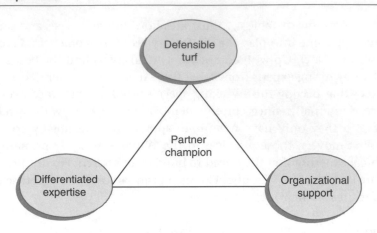

Figure 4.2 Essential ingredients for new practice creation

accord: in a professional service firm, a practice founder needs to play the role of chef—or 'champion' if you will—gathering the ingredients of turf, expertise, and support, and adding them in the right amounts and proper order. It is essential to have an effective practice leader with the skill and motivation to champion the efforts of others. There is an element of the myth of the hero in describing the work of a champion, but the crucial difference that we found is that a sole partner acting on his or her own as the lone ranger—no matter how entrepreneurial or skilled— cannot build a new practice in the absence of those three necessary ingredients. Figure 4.2 shows how we conceptualize these ingredients as interconnected, with the partner champion as a central player who pulls together all three components.

Our research shows that there are three different ways of combining these ingredients—three distinct recipes—based on whether the practice founder begins the initiative by focusing on turf, expertise, or support. In all recipes, the most essential instruction is to ensure that all three ingredients are present in a practice development effort. As we describe in more detail below, too many firms believe that they can make up for the absence of one ingredient by adding more of the others. For example, one law firm we researched developed a new patent law practice in Germany on the back of support from a major government client, indicating the presence of turf as an ingredient. The firm also had internal expertise to start the client work. However, the practice suffered from internal squabbles about who should resource the new practice—lack of support caused the practice to fail at the start-up stage.

New practice development recipes

While the three ingredients—turf, expertise, and support—must be present in each successful recipe, the three distinct ways of combining them make a difference to how the process unfolds. We describe each of the three recipes below, using real (albeit disguised) examples from the consulting and law firms to illustrate lessons of success and failure.

We start with the Turf-driven recipe because in many respects it is the riskiest: as it requires partners to leverage their relationships with trusting clients, failure in the new practice attempt can damage existing business. We then move on to the Expertise-led recipe, which we tend to see as the toughest one to complete successfully—often because this is the only option for more junior partners who have neither strong enough client relationships to create turf, nor enough internal clout to muster resources from scratch. Finally, we describe the Support-centred recipe. We have generally found this to be the most controversial approach. When it works, founders often try to bolster their own reputation as rainmakers by minimizing the role of the firm in advancing their success; when a Support-centred approach fails, the founder needs to answer to peers who feel their resources have been squandered.

Both the Turf-driven and Expertise-led recipes are examples of emergent processes of new practice development, meaning that they are essentially 'bottom-up' processes and may already conform, to varying degrees, to the firm's existing strategy. In contrast, the Support-centred recipe can be characterized as more strategically driven than the other two recipes, meaning that this route is more closely directed from the top down and thus is expected to have greater alignment with the planned direction of the firm. Despite these differences, the principle that there are three necessary components applies to all of the processes.

Turf-driven recipe

Firm A specializes in intellectual property law and patenting work. It has recently expanded in South East Asia in response to the growth in manufacturing and outsourcing in that region. Its clients include both major multinationals and local firms. One of its largest clients, a multinational consumer products firm which was increasingly sourcing products from China, had been using a range of law firms in each country in the region but proposed to rationalize its arrangements. The client approached a partner in Law Firm A offering the chance to take over all of its intellectual property work in the region if Firm A would open offices in each of the countries in which the client was located. In considering this proposal, the regional managing partner of Firm A could see that while it was consistent with the firm's core expertise; some new knowledge of local trading conditions and laws would have to be developed, primarily through lateral hiring. Because there was likely to be growing demand from other firms for this sort of service and the client was able to guarantee a certain volume of work for the start up period, Firm A's management team approved the proposal. It appointed a local partner as champion of the project and allocated resources to open offices in countries where there was no representation.

This example shows the typical pattern for a Turf-driven recipe: a professional leverages an existing client relationship for developing and testing new ideas in order to carve out a new territory that she or he can develop into a stand-alone new practice. In our consulting interviews, we heard that partners often strike a deal with clients to 'co-invest' in knowledge building (i.e. add a gratis associate onto the team in exchange for freedom to experiment, or add an extra week's consulting free of charge to test a new methodology). For example, the drive to obtain what he called 'bragging rights within the firm' led the founder of one firm's post-merger support practice to persuade a 'friendly client' to let him experiment with a new consulting proposition. This partner said:

> It was a big enough client relationship . . . a client that we'd worked with before so there was a degree of confidence that something would come out. . . . We didn't really know very much about mergers and acquisitions, but we had a great relationship with the client and we went in and offered a 'diagnostic' that could be helpful.

When the new expertise or method proves viable in the initial client tests, the founder can then use this experience as a launching pad to refine and test the ideas with other clients. This requires either that the partner has additional clients of his own who will let him experiment, or that he begins to convince the 'gatekeepers' of other clients to let him in. During this time, the founder needs his team to codify the knowledge so that it can be easily replicated in a broader setting and so that he can use it for 'internal marketing' in order to garner firm support. Ultimately, a Turf-driven practice succeeds when experiments with the client lead to significantly differentiated knowledge that attracts the support of the organization and can be deployed on assignments with other clients.

One corporate finance lawyer described the Turf-driven recipe as a 'high-beta approach' to building new practices—meaning that it carries higher-than-average penalties for failure but equally high rewards for success.[1] These disproportionate results stem from the fact that generally only partners who are already fairly powerful have access to clients for the purposes of experimentation. If the idea for the new practice works with their client, then they can draw on their personal reputation and track record to make claims on their territory. On the other hand, by leaning on trusting clients to try out novel ideas or methods, they risk losing a stable income stream if the experiment fails badly. Another risk is that the time that partners spend building the new practice distracts them from maintaining the client relationship. In either of these two examples, the formerly powerful partner will be worse off than before he or she attempted to start the new practice.

What are the main reasons for failure in the Turf-driven recipe? Overall, we saw three kinds of problems that ultimately derailed new practice attempts. Figure 4.3 summarizes these problems and displays them graphically.

One difficulty that some would-be practice founders faced was an inability to back up their proposition with a clearly delineated knowledge base. In one law firm, Robert used his existing client base in the retailing and consumer sector as a platform to develop a niche to serve clients as they set up new business ventures in the online arena. His intention was to demonstrate specialized expertise in the emerging internet domain, and use this as a way to expand across sectors into media, financial services, and others. As word of his success grew within the firm, however, other partners doubted that it took unique legal knowledge to work in this arena, and they simply offered a similar service to their own clients. 'They thought they could just replicate my work—clearly I had failed to convince them that e-commerce was its own niche, with its own unique set of issues and answers.'

Another problem was the founder's failure to secure strong organizational support for the nascent practice. We interviewed Andrea, a consulting partner who had used a set of engagements in the utilities sector to develop an innovative methodology for optimizing the costs of resource scheduling. Although other partners recognized the potential for selling additional work based on this idea, the firm's top management perceived the effort as not having enough scale to be a fully fledged practice and denied her request for dedicated associates to staff these projects. In the end, Andrea's idea was folded into the existing utilities practice.

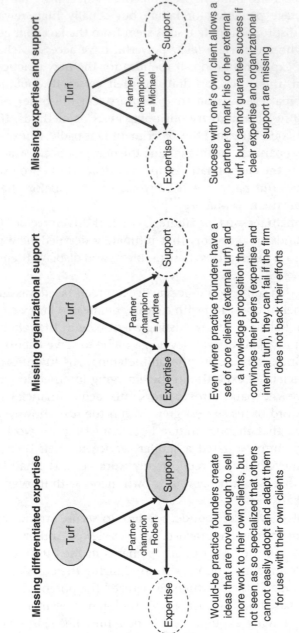

Figure 4.3 Failures of the Turf-driven recipe

Returning to the recipe metaphor, Robert and Andrea failed in their efforts because they did not add expertise or support, respectively, to the Turf-driven recipe. The third failure of new practices that are based on turf happens when the founder builds neither distinct expertise nor organizational support for the practice. In one consultancy, a junior partner called Michael was keen to 'build his personal brand' by developing a new customer management practice based on work he had done at some packaged goods multinationals. Although he developed some new analytical frameworks and innovative organizational designs for his clients, other partners' teams could easily replicate this work with different clients. Michael admitted to us, 'Consultants who worked on these projects didn't really need a lot of specialised expertise.... Aside from me, there was nobody pounding the table in support of the idea, and I just couldn't go it alone.' In this example even the initial knowledge-building attempt was feeble and clearly there was no support from the wider organization; the effort was therefore unsuccessful.

What lessons can law firms draw from these examples of the Turf-driven recipe? As already stated, one overarching theme is that all three ingredients—turf, expertise, and support—are necessary for a practice to succeed. Adding more of one cannot compensate for the lack of another. A more nuanced point is what it takes to create and defend one's turf in order to get the recipe started. First, professionals need external credibility with their clients. The partner in Law Firm A would never have been approached by the consumer goods company if that client did not already believe that Firm A either possessed or could quickly develop the capabilities to handle the increased scope of work. The second component of turf is gaining internal legitimacy with peers. Often professionals can leverage their external credibility with clients in order to convince their peers—gatekeepers to other clients and holders of firm resources—that their new ideas are novel but trustworthy. If the partner in Firm A had not been able to convince her regional managing partner of the potential for sustained revenues, she would never have been given the green light to begin building up local resources.

Expertise-led recipe

Law Firm B has a strong reputation in the area of finance and capital markets. It had hired a partner from a competitor firm who brought expertise in the growing area of financial services regulation and proposed to develop a fully fledged practice in this area. While it was clear that this was a growing area of work, there were still questions about whether it would best be positioned as a separate practice or as part of a larger existing practice group. Some partners were sceptical about the extent to which the expertise was really distinctive from other practice groups, and thought that a new practice might confuse the market rather than generate more work. The partner who championed this initiative had a strong reputation in his area and could point to successful examples elsewhere but, as a relatively recent hire, his network among the other partners was somewhat limited. He therefore had to build internal support for the idea by drawing largely on the experience of other firms to convince the other partners that the proposition was viable. For a time the practice was located within a larger one and therefore could share resources and costs; when the flow of work began to increase and look more predictable the practice was given its own budget and formally recognized as separate. In addition, the champion had to build a team of associates who were interested in this work and prepared to work for him exclusively, and to ensure that any work in this area was directed to the practice rather than taken by others. Securing control over the flow of work proved to be a considerable challenge requiring persuasion and emphasis on the new practice's growing credentials because there was no strong central control over work allocation.

In a similar example from one consulting firm's retail banking practice, a consultant who was 'hungry to make partner' consciously sought to enhance his personal reputation by founding a new practice area. His first step was to develop new consulting know-how in the area of retail banking, and then conduct an early engagement for a prominent client to show that the knowledge he had developed was commercially viable. This led to sufficient consensus within the firm that retail banking held unique knowledge and insight distinctive from the firm's canonical strategy practice. With broader support in the form of political backing from powerful partners, the practice was able to negotiate turf within the firm to access clients and grow its business.

As we see in these examples, the trigger to initiate this recipe is typically an ambitious professional who seeks to carve out a personal niche by building up distinct expertise in an area that is new to the firm. Junior professionals often follow this recipe out of necessity: they lack strong client relationships that would otherwise help them to generate legitimate turf, and they are not powerful or connected enough inside the firm to rally support for an untested idea. Instead, the professional identifies a market opportunity that could be targeted with a distinctive knowledge base. After refining and testing this knowledge, the professional—often acting in concert with colleagues—successfully leads the initiative to acquire clients and draw support from the wider organization. In one of the firms in our sample, a partner had joined from a larger law firm in order to have the freedom to develop his own practice. As he puts it:

> The key was to build up the idea of permanence in the minds of 'management' and the rest of the staff (by bringing in clients over a decent time period). In that way I could attract and retain good people. Without an established client base it took me two to three years of marketing myself and my fledgling practice, plus a lot of support from the centre as there are always opportunities to sell employment law to existing clients.

In both law and consulting firms, we observed three clear-cut ways in which the Expertise-led recipe failed. Figure 4.4 explains each of these reasons for failure. In short, even after creating distinctive knowledge or expertise, the founders were unable either to create sufficient turf or to obtain organizational support, or both.

In one consultancy, Joanne attempted to start an operations efficiency practice at the firm's London office with a proposal to assemble a small team that had built up specialized knowledge in the area. The consultant even managed to get a major client interested and hence was able to legitimize her patch of turf in the London office. However, the practice stalled because the global top management of the firm was equivocal about supporting the initiative. Ultimately it lost out to an internal rival practice that had started in the US at about the same time. Joanne said, 'We got swallowed up by the US group after [the managing partner] made it clear that he favoured their approach.'

One law firm example illustrates how the lack of defensible turf leads to failure. David, a partner in one of our sample firms, had returned to London after a number of years working in South East Asia. He had no client base in London but saw an opportunity in project finance. At that time, project finance was a growing market as new forms of financing were developing to fund large-scale construction and energy projects. However, his expertise was in corporate law and he found that his initiative was quickly taken over by a group of construction and finance lawyers. As he said, 'The practice was clearly viable as a business proposition but I didn't have a ready-made client base which I could work with or the expertise on my own to make it work. They had the contacts to make it work.

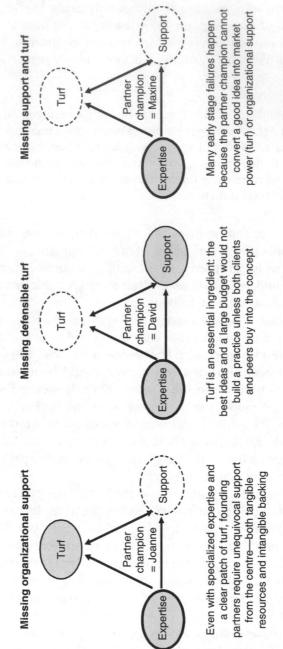

Missing organizational support

Turf

Partner
champion
= Joanne

Expertise

Support

Even with specialized expertise and
a clear patch of turf, founding
partners require unequivocal support
from the centre—both tangible
resources and intangible backing

Missing defensible turf

Turf

Partner
champion
= David

Expertise

Support

Turf is an essential ingredient: the
best ideas and a large budget would not
build a practice unless both clients
and peers buy into the concept

Missing support and turf

Turf

Partner
champion
= Maxine

Expertise

Support

Many early stage failures happen
because the partner champion cannot
convert a good idea into market
power (turf) or organizational support

Figure 4.4 Failures of the Expertise-led recipe

I thought about re-training but it was clear we had enough expertise among the partners to make my role superfluous.'

Another pitfall within this recipe is failure to add both support and turf to the mix; no matter how outstanding the knowledge base, a practice cannot survive without both appropriate levels of support and a territory that the founder can defend against 'internal encroachment'. In an example from consulting, the corporate social responsibility practice initiative at one firm got underway when Maxine drew together the firm's thinking on the topic and began to activate a network of internal and external individuals interested in conducting original research. However, when she raised a formal proposal to obtain resources to start up a practice, the partnership committee expressed doubts about potential profitability and legal liability, and refused to support her. As one managing partner whom we interviewed explained: 'We only require relatively flimsy business plans in the first year—a proposition and agreement from me that the champion can get on with (building the practice). But we do agree a budget which is an important two-way commitment and "the centre" will provide marketing and cross-selling support to kick-start the practice.' But because there is limited central control over resource allocation in professional firms, the centre cannot necessarily provide all the resources: one partner we interviewed echoed the view of several others when she said that the most difficult part of the process was to persuade other practices to 'lend' associates to grow the practice when there was little direct pay-off for them.

We believe that it is unlikely that a lawyer would be able to move into a completely unrelated area in the same way as a consultant. Compared with a consultant, it is harder for a lawyer to develop credibility in a completely unrelated practice. However, the reputation of the firm offers some room for manoeuvre—and therefore clients may well be prepared to try out or co-develop a new practice. In one example, a partner moved into a specialist area of insurance litigation which was related but not very close; the combination of her own and the firm's reputation in litigation was enough for her to convince the clients the area was viable, pick up the law quickly, and then learn the market know-how. Also, we found that the novelty of the domain in the market makes a difference to the expertise required: technical knowledge is more of an issue in areas where the firm wants to be first mover (i.e. the first into a new area like private equity or derivatives), but for a late mover, the issue is not so much technical know-how as market know-how.

Support-centred recipe

A core practice in Law Firm C is litigation and the partners in that area had recognized for some time that changes in the demand for their work focused around the growth of arbitration. The central management team therefore supported a proposal that came from the litigation practice to start an arbitration practice. The know-how for this was partly sourced from within the firm as several partners had done work in this area, but the management team also went out and hired new partners to enhance the expertise of the group. The team decided to ring-fence the new practice in terms of its expected contribution for up to two years while work was generated. Three partners agreed to head up the initiative from within the litigation practice, acquired resources in the form of staff and marketing budgets, and developed a plan to start up the practice. In making this initiative work, the firm faced two problems: turf issues and concerns from some of the partners about the costs involved. The latter concern mainly related to the added costs to the firm of the lateral hires, who had all been senior partners in other firms but, because this was a relatively new domain of work, did not yet have large client followings. The concern with turf arose because other parts of the firm were also involved in some arbitration work: for example, some of the banking practice partners were undertaking arbitration for insurance clients and did not want to give up control of this work. While the centre agreed that the arbitration practice should be located within the litigation area and should have sole rights to undertake this work, it was unwilling to force a confrontation over internal jurisdictional rights. It therefore took some months before an internal agreement was worked out that the new practice should take on this work with certain 'concessions' to the other affected partners.

The Support-centred recipe typically kicks off with a professional who leads a new practice effort in an area that the firm's top management or partnership committee has clearly identified as a market opportunity. Often, the firm selects a leader who either has a track record of starting and successfully finishing new projects, has expertise in a related area, or whose current client base could provide a launching ground for the new initiative. Our research suggests that consulting firms prefer to seek this new practice leader from existing partners within the firm, and in most cases will turn to the external labour market only where no suitable internal candidates are available (or, perhaps, willing to take on the challenge). Law firms appear to be somewhat more amenable to lateral hiring, although managing partners also generally tend first to look in house for practice founders. After designating a practice leader, the firm provides him or her organizational support in the form of political backing and tangible resources to create the practice's turf and to develop differentiated knowledge to tackle the market opportunity.

One consulting firm's managing partners seized the opportunity to capitalize on changes in UK legislation surrounding executive pay by creating an executive compensation practice in the London office. They brought in a partner, Paula, with experience in the US market, which was more advanced in this area, to lead the new practice. Paula described how the firm's management board played a critical role in 'mediating potential conflict-of-interest issues' that arose from providing the new service along with the firm's core services, and in granting support in the form of personnel to staff the new venture. Paula instituted a formal workshop-based course that consultants needed to complete before they could take on executive compensation assignments. Ostensibly, this move helped to maintain high quality standards for professionals in her practice, but it also clearly marked the knowledge base as proprietary and helped to delineate the new practice's turf in the London office.

This sort of top-down direction setting can be problematic in professional service firms, which tend to be characterized by dispersed decision-making and relatively autonomous professionals. Again, we found three reasons for failure, depicted in Figure 4.5. First, we found examples where partners had managed to secure initial resources from the firm to build up expertise for a new practice, but ultimately failed to convince their colleagues of the effort's merit. In one telling example, a strategy consulting firm granted a partner, Justin, the better part of a year and several dedicated associates to create an elaborate set of 'how-to' documents for conducting client engagements in a new organizational learning practice. Other partners doubted the initiative's revenue potential—'It was never going to spin fees on its own,' they said—and blocked his access to their clients. Justin's interpretation is that they resented the firm's sizeable investment in his practice start-up costs, given that other partners needed to fund their 'pet projects' from their own operating budgets. In any case, the new practice failed to establish its own turf, and soon thereafter Justin resigned from the firm.

A number of cases from the legal field followed similar patterns. Law Firm D tried several times to start up a New York office. Having seen the need for a US presence, the firm designated a partner, Chris, for the project. They gave him plenty of resources, but the initiative failed

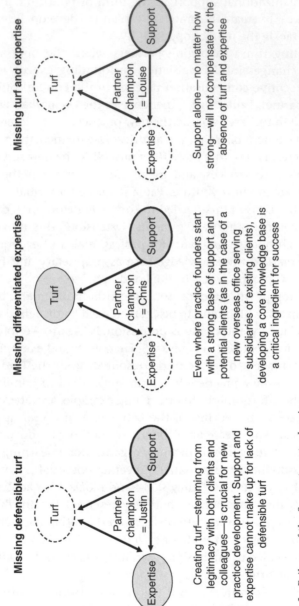

Figure 4.5 Failures of the Support-centred recipe

because neither he nor they had access to local referral networks that would deliver the quality of work they wanted. Similarly, the managing partner of the UK-based Law Firm A strongly backed Louise to start an office in Washington DC. The effort soon folded, however, when Louise realized that she could not offer the incentives to attract the top talent from competitors. Without local expertise and connections, it was impossible for Louise to bring the new practice to fruition.

These examples make it clear that intangible support like the 'official blessing' of a management committee, or even concrete resources like a project budget are not enough to guarantee success in a law firm, or indeed, any professional service firm. Partners who are tasked with building a new practice often need to divert attention from their client work during the start-up phase. Not only do they relinquish a potential source of external legitimacy but they also see their power diminished within the firm at a time when they are occupied with creating and defending new turf. Firms can help these partners establish turf by gaining the commitment of other partners to cross-sell the new practice's work into their existing clients. In addition, in the absence of compelling and differentiated expertise, resources and turf are not enough to sustain a new practice initiative. Firms need either to invest in internal knowledge-building efforts or to hire expertise from outside.

Even where the Support-centred recipe provides new practice leaders with the resources to develop distinctive expertise and the internal legitimacy to mark their territory within the firm, the issue remains: how can a professional develop credibility with clients to provide a new service? Our analysis of turf considerations (Figure 4.2) offers some clues. Partners need to assess what sort of new practice they are creating: for example if they are in the White Space quadrant, they need to develop *and demonstrate* their own reputation for technical expertise as soon as possible; if they are in the Catch Up quadrant they need to remember that there is a premium on demonstrating market familiarity and expertise, for example by having good networks with other actors in the marketplace and understanding how the market works. Where product expansion is planned by moving into a new jurisdiction, professionals can use their firm's reputation to build a practice, but they will need to call on resources and the appropriate backing from other senior partners to deliver on their offer. Where the practice is in the Tweaking quadrant, defending against encroachment internally is more likely to be the pressing concern while, ironically, the client market will already have recognized the need for the practice by going to competitor firms.

Conclusions

We started this chapter by suggesting that practitioners often explain new practice development in terms of what we called the three 'myths': the entrepreneurial hero, the market, and serendipity. While we believe there is some truth to each of these, it is possible to understand the process of new practice development in more systematic terms. We used the idea of a recipe, with ingredients and a process by which these are mixed together, to explain how new practice development occurs.

From our study of consulting and law firms, we propose that there are three key ingredients—turf, expertise, and support—and that they have to be mixed together by a 'champion' who has the skill and motivation to make the recipe work. In short, our findings stress the active role of individuals, rather like the hero myth, but demonstrate that success also requires that the other ingredients are present and that the champion(s) can interact effectively with colleagues and clients to make the process work: this is not a solo effort. Further, our research shows that each ingredient is necessary but not sufficient on its own: all three have to be brought into play by the champion in order to succeed. Failure often results from professionals assuming that one can compensate for the absence of an ingredient by adding more of another.

We also showed that there is more than one way in which the ingredients can be combined: our research has revealed three different recipes depending on whether the founder or champion focuses first on developing turf, expertise, or support. Each has its challenges. A Turf-driven recipe has the advantage of clients who will often offer some form of co-investment, but failure risks damaging individual and firm reputations. The Expertise-led approach is the most difficult in our view because there is no ready-made client work offering a springboard to start the process. A Support-centred recipe differs from the other two in that it is a more top-down process, while the others are bottom-up initiatives, but it, too, can be controversial in terms of the allocation of honours if it succeeds, or blame if it fails.

Looking across the three recipes, we note a number of important patterns. First, regardless of which ingredient kick-starts the process (i.e. turf, expertise, or support) we find that any successful new practice initiative always combines all three ingredients. Even highly skilled partner champions with vast organizational resources (support) and a new idea (expertise) cannot succeed unless they convince their clients that the idea is credible, and their colleagues that it is financially viable and intellectually defensible.

Second, we emphasize that the role of the centre can take various forms and degrees of intervention. In some firms, the managing partner (sometimes along with his or her committee or board) plays a key role in shaping firm direction and long-term strategy; here, the centre's part in new practice development is likely to be a stronger, more active role along the lines of portfolio management. Elsewhere, the centre plays a much less active role, preferring to leave decisions up to the 'knowledge market'. This approach defers to a combination of both the internal and external selection environments (i.e. colleagues and clients) for deciding which new practices are viable and important. Here, the firm strategy tends to reflect, rather than direct, new practice development. Across firms, however, we found that even in emergent processes (those where practices start with turf or expertise), the centre still exercises control over the portfolio by granting or withholding organizational support at some stage in the process.

Third, we note the implications from our research having focused primarily on the establishment of new practices that build up and develop over time. The new practices tend not to threaten significantly the firm's existing core practice area. As these types of new practice build up, the firm has time to adjust to them. We recognize and advise caution, however, that the same case does not hold for firms that buy a whole existing practice. Early evidence suggests that successful integration of a whole group of professionals into an existing firm is highly dependent on the degree to which that new practice can create and defend its own turf by bringing along existing clients—assuming that it has both enough organizational support and a knowledge base that is clearly differentiated from the incumbent practices.

Finally, it is important to recognize the impact of context for the recipes we have described. In particular, we suggest that the questions of how novel and how different the practice is must be taken into account. Practices in what we call the White Space quadrant (novel to the firm and industry, and radically different from the core) have a first-mover advantage, but face very different types of challenges with respect to turf, support, and expertise from those in the Tweaking quadrant, for example.

In practical terms, other important contextual issues may also affect the recipes we have described. For instance, turf considerations may be more acute when the market is contracting and practices are fighting harder for work, than when it is expanding. Compensation systems also undoubtedly affect the extent to which partners are prepared to cooperate with each other in sharing resources, information, or clients: lockstep systems appear to be more amenable to the sort of collaboration necessary for new practice development than highly individualistic reward systems, although this may be offset by the more limited motivational aspects of the lockstep model. Some firms are clearly more directive than others even if they are all formally organized as partnerships: the more directive firms seem better able to sort out disputes over internal legitimacy and arbitrate more actively over encroachment issues, but they may also stifle bottom-up initiatives more than their less directive competitors. Our research continues to explore these issues.

While our research findings suggest that our model of new practice development, involving ingredients and combining processes, is generalizable to different types of professional service firms, we recognize that subtle differences between sectors may have to be taken into account. As already suggested, one difference relates to expertise. In consulting, expertise is often based on a more fluid model of knowledge that is not constrained in the way that legal knowledge is. Consultants have a greater degree of freedom than lawyers: the former can decide what is new and effective knowledge by asking 'does it work for clients?' while lawyers must work within a wider legal framework, asking not only 'does the client buy my solution?' but also 'is it technically sustainable?' This may well have implications for the ability of lawyers (or other types of professionals who work with externally determined knowledge bases) to create new practices. Nonetheless, we believe that this is a difference of degree rather than type, and that our recipes for success in new practice development are applicable not only to law and consulting, but across the professional services sector as a whole.

Note

1. 'Beta' is a mathematical measure of the sensitivity of rates of return on a given stock compared with rates of return on the market as a whole. For example, a beta of 1.5 forecasts a 1.5% change in the return on an asset for every 1% change in the return on the market—disproportionate rewards for success or penalties for failure.

5

Your client relationships and reputation

Weighing the worth of social ties: embeddedness and the price of legal services in the large law firm market

Brian Uzzi
Kellogg School of Management, Northwestern University

Ryon Lancaster
Department of Sociology, University of Chicago

Shannon Dunlap
New York University

Introduction

The winds of change have been blowing through the law firm market during the past decade, and for many in the industry, the breeze is carrying a far-from-pleasant odour. Gone are the days of unfailingly loyal clients. Gone is the gentlemanly restraint from cherry-picking competitors' talent. Gone are the scads of new law school graduates prepared to spend every waking moment vying for a partnership.

A driving force in this increasingly competitive market is a series of major changes among firms' clients. Mergers and acquisitions have shrunk the client base. Old relationships with a single law service provider are starting to fray. Legal exposure is growing for big business, while legal budgets are holding steady. This means that corporations are not only courting offers from multiple firms for outside legal work, but also expanding their in-house legal departments in hopes of increasing efficiency and cutting costs (Figure 5.1).

Adding to the pressures from clients are the internal pressures within the law firm industry. Talented young lawyers are turning to positions

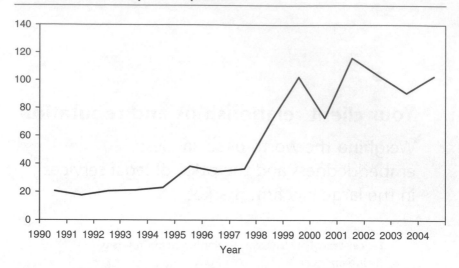

Figure 5.1 Number of US *Fortune 250* corporations with in-house counsel departments of more than 60 attorneys

within corporations rather than battling for partnerships. Firms have become unabashed about raiding their competitors' talent. Mergers and acquisitions between law firms have led to major restructuring and ambiguity about the best ways to optimize profits.

This harsh evolution is not affecting all firms equally. In fact, there are clear winners and losers within this changing market. The gap between average revenues and the revenues of top law firms has been steadily increasing since 1994 (Figure 5.2).

The rapid increase of competition within the legal industry has heaped greater importance on managerial decisions, such as how to price legal services. The winners in Figure 5.2 understand how markets set prices and use that knowledge to their advantage. Most people are accustomed to thinking of pricing as an economic process, influenced by factors such as bargaining power, production costs, and product specialization. What often goes unnoticed, however, is that pricing is also a social process tied to relationships.

The impact of social relationships on prices may be intuited by lawyers and other members of the professional services sector. During the course of our research, we spoke to lawyers who had observed that certain social factors, such as the relationships they formed with clients, could impact the way they priced their services. Because this area is only beginning to

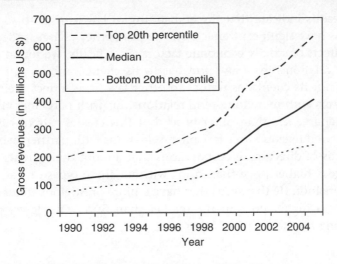

Figure 5.2   100 largest US law firms' gross revenues, 1990–2004

be explored by researchers, lawyers have lacked a reliable way of understanding these social effects.

In response to this issue, we designed a study of mega law firms of the USA to clarify how social factors such as firm–client relationships, board memberships, and status (or reputation) influence pricing. In an article in *The American Sociological Review*, we discussed information we had collected on this issue, both through a study of large statistical effects and through interviews we conducted with lawyers (Uzzi and Lancaster 2004). Our findings are not only pertinent in the context of sociological theory, but show signs of having practical implications for lawyers in all types of firms. Because the research suggests that small differences in social factors can have a multimillion dollar impact on a firm's bottom line, we were eager to translate our earlier article into this chapter for practising lawyers. This chapter focuses on the broad lessons of interest to practising lawyers. For a detailed explanation of the theoretical context and statistical analysis conducted, please refer to our *American Sociological Review* paper.

Our goal was to give managers of professional service firms a broader social and economic perspective on what they should consider when setting prices by examining how relationships influence the rates that law firms can charge their corporate clients. As a backdrop for our findings, we will first take a look at *embeddedness*, the theory that informed the way we constructed our study.

Our results indicate that the embedding of law firms into social relationships have significant effects on the prices they charge, independent of the effects of strictly economic factors. Specifically, we found that the network relationships a law firm has to its clients, and to corporations that are not its clients, as well as to other law firms, affect their market price. Firms with more long-term relationships with particular clients on average charge *less* than other firms, but this creates a trade-off with a more assured revenue stream. Conversely, firms with partners who sit on the boards of directors of corporations that are not their clients are able to charge a higher price than firms without these types of ties. Finally, our results indicate that firms that have a more prestigious status are able to charge a higher price in the market than firms with lower prestige, controlling for the effects of other factors.

Embeddedness

The social framework that our research was built upon is embeddedness theory (Baker 1990; Coleman 1988; Granovetter 1985; Podolny 1993; Powell 1990; Uzzi 1996, 1997, 1999; Uzzi and Gillespie 2002; Uzzi and Lancaster 2003, 2004). In contrast to conventional economic approaches to firm behaviour, which argue for efficient markets and faceless one-shot relationships, embeddedness refers to the fact that the players in an economic transaction do not exist in a vacuum, but rather in a system of social relationships. These affiliations can affect the types of information they receive as well as their motives for profit and profit-sharing, generating new potential to shape the value created during a transaction. This allows for a different outcome from a market model (a system of impersonal relations) or hierarchical model (a system of formal contractual relations). A pure economic relations model, for example, is represented in Figure 5.3, with an ask price from a client company and varying bid prices from law firms determining the winning law firm and the final sale price. In this model, the price is determined by the quality of the firm, the bid price, and the ask price.

In contrast, the embeddedness model accounts for the social relationships that can make pricing more complex. In Figure 5.4, we have offered one potential scenario of how social ties might change the model. Factors like status, board ties, and repeated relationships with clients make the model far more complicated and variable and influence the final sale price of a transaction. The embeddedness model adds considerations of the

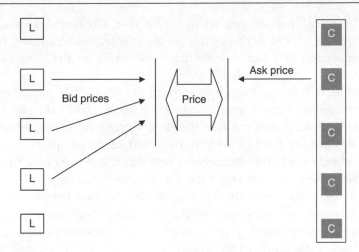

Figure 5.3 Standard economic model of price setting

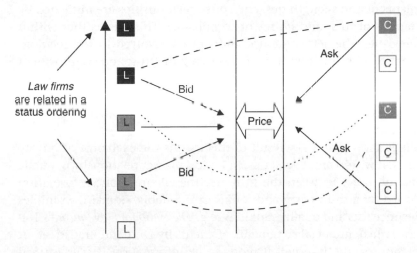

Figure 5.4 Embedded model of price setting

Note: In Figure 5.3 and 5.4 'L' stands for law firms in competition with one another and 'C' stands for corporations that the law firms are competing for. Dashed lines represent repeated relations, and dotted lines represent board ties.

ways in which law firms and corporations have pre-existing relationships that also affect the prices set in the marketplace. Instead of simply examining the bid and ask price and the quality of services provided, the embeddedness model also looks at how other types of relationships, such as board ties with non-client corporations or long-term relationships with clients, affect what price gets set in the market. Furthermore, law firms are related to one another not through direct economic relations, but by being embedded in a status order that ranks firms on the basis of their prestige.

Embeddedness theory takes into account the *relationship quality* and the *network positions* of those involved. In examining relationship quality at the most basic level, ties can be either arm's-length or embedded. Arm's-length ties are the kind of socially detached relationships that require no prolonged or repeated interaction between the two parties. In arm's-length ties, one does not know the other party well, so people rely on formal agreements rather than norms to dictate their behaviour. These simple relationships work well for the exchange of public information, like financial statements, government filings, performance rankings, or other kinds of standardized reports.

In contrast, embedded ties tend to be much more complex because they involve social attachments and affiliations. Rather than using the formal agreements of arm's-length ties, embedded relationships are mitigated by expectations of trust and norms of compliance. This means that within embedded ties, the actors (i.e. the individuals involved in the relationship) behave with the intention of preserving the trust and reciprocity of the relationship, rather than just thinking about short-term incentives of their actions. While there may be formal agreements involved, actors are willing to go beyond the specific contractual terms in order to preserve their relationships.

Findings show that a key result of this trust is the exchange of private information within embedded ties. In typical market relationships, public information flows between the firm and the client. Public information is collected by a third party and found in the public domain. Examples include price lists and quality rankings (e.g. *The National Law Journal*'s Top 250 Law Firms), financial statements of clients by Dun and Bradstreet, or information on the internet. It tends to be information that is verified by third parties and fairly accessible to everyone in the market. As a consequence, while its objectivity gives it power, its availability lowers its value. In contrast, private information is more subjective and not verifiable by a third party. Private information gives buyers and sellers knowledge about each other's distinctive capabilities even though it lacks a prepared, standard, and public presentation, such as a profit and loss statement. Private information includes data on a market actor's idiosyncratic capabilities, intangible assets, client loyalties, disruptive board politics, dispute resolution strategies, or a person's word. The lack of a standardized format and third party verification mean that private information is typically undocumented, unprepared, and interpretive. Because of this, we tend only to share it with those we trust. Private information can be extremely valuable and can give individuals an edge during high-stakes decisions. This trustful exchange of information lowers the governance cost of transactions within embedded ties and leads the actors to expect a sharing of costs and profits that will mutually benefit them both.

Network structure is a second factor that can affect the flow of information. All organizations have a network, a system of interlocking relationships. A person's placement within this network can affect what information he or she can access. Some network positions serve an intermediary function between two other parties in the network. For example, a stock analyst mediates between companies and traders. These positions are enviable because they allow the person holding them to witness the exchange of private information between others. As with embedded ties, the behaviour of the people in these roles is regulated by social norms that increase trust.

In this study, we examine two particular types of network structure. The first is that of lawyers from a firm sitting on the boards of directors of corporations. This practice is common in the USA, and becoming more common in Europe. In the USA, lawyers are very rarely directors of corporations which are clients of the law firm, due to potential conflicts of interest, such that they typically serve on boards of corporations that are not their clients. However, these relationships are important, as we discuss below, not because they increase the relationship between the law firm and a particular client, but because they provide unique information about how boards of directors make decisions about hiring outside counsel, giving law firms an advantage in the marketplace with corporations who are their clients.

A second type of network structure that we examined was status. When discussing status, we mean the intangible or symbolic characteristics of law firms that distinguish them from one another, otherwise known as reputation. Factors such as name recognition, the prominence of selected clients, or the street address of a firm, all create small differences that are used to distinguish firms when quality is roughly equivalent or hard to measure. Dividing the market into 'A+ firms' or 'silk-stocking firms' implies different status characteristics.

It is worthwhile to note that embeddedness is not intrinsically positive. Increased trust can sometimes lead to the collusion of the two parties to engage in unethical behaviour. Also, embedded ties do not necessarily lead to the most efficient outcome when factors like prejudice enter the relationship. Typically, however, because of the discipline of the market, the relationship quality and network structure of embedded ties promote private information exchange and lowered transaction costs (the costs associated with conducting any particular exchange in the market), a distinction not unlike the one made in the relational contracting literature familiar to lawyers (Macaulay 1963; Macneil 1980).

Based on this, we believed that embeddedness was very likely to influence pricing. We also felt that different types of embedded ties would lead to significantly different outcomes. Therefore, we designed a study to gain qualitative and quantitative knowledge about these effects.

Who we studied

A new kind of law firm began to materialize in the 1990s. These 'mega firms' were a new breed amongst the standard law firms of the past, employing hundreds of lawyers so as to cater better to large corporations with diverse legal needs. Table 5.1 furnishes some general statistics on the mega firms that emerged in the USA during the years 1989 to 1995. While somewhat dated, this table shows the tremendous differences among law firms providing corporate legal services, which is as true today as it was ten years ago.

Serving big businesses means being able to handle a wide variety of legal issues, many of them complex and multidimensional, such as mergers and acquisitions or securities management. Mega firms are well suited to this challenge, not only because of the sheer number of lawyers they employ but also the diversity of their expertise (tax, litigation, real estate, labour law, etc.). This wide array of talent comes together in project teams. These teams are typically comprised of associates led by a partner in charge.

The type of legal work that mega firms do varies widely in complexity. This fact will be essential to our discussion of pricing because complex work and routine work are usually priced at different hourly rates. Complex work is usually handled by a partner. It often requires original research and the synergy of multiple areas of expertise. Because of this, it gives firms ample opportunity to differentiate their work from the competition. Routine work is usually handled by associates within the project teams. Because routine work is less challenging, it offers fewer opportunities for product differentiation.

Table 5.1 Descriptive statistics of the mega law firms, 1989–95

	Characteristics of law firms					Client legal staff			Billing rates, range ($)	
Size quintile	Age (yr)	Offices (n)	Attorneys (n)	Partners (n)	Associates (n)	Costs-starting salary ($)	Main office in major city (%)	In-house attorneys at clients (mean)	Partner	Associate
1	98	10.6	510	178	312	75,307	76.8	53.3	190–350	94–218
2	100	6.9	291	115	162	70,456	64.8	43.9	187–338	97–201
3	86	5.9	217	95	113	65,290	56.0	49.3	177–314	94–188
4	79	4.7	174	77	90	62,301	57.9	43.5	167–299	93–180
5	88	4.6	142	64	72	60,668	36.8	34.4	163–286	90–174
Mean	91	6.5	267	106	150	66,812	58.3	45.7	173–309	93–187
F-statistic	1.09	141.82				170.48	38.00	5.32	8.45, 16.01	3.34, 8.45

Note: Data are from The National Law Journal and the Of Counsel 500. Firms are organized into quintiles based on the total number of attorneys at the firm, with the first quintile being the largest 20% of firms. The number of cases range from 1,052 to 2,000 due to missing data for some of the variables. Major cities include New York, Boston, Philadelphia, Chicago, Houston, Dallas, San Francisco, and Los Angeles. The F-statistic tests the equality of the means in each column except for size, which is used to separate firms into categories. The F-statistics for billing rates were calculated for the high and low price and are reported separately above.

To ascertain whether the work of mega firms is priced fairly, corporate clients usually rely upon their in-house legal divisions. The in-house lawyers carefully track which lawyers staff a case, the hours they work per day, and the rates being charged. They are also well-versed in the public information available about mega firms. Materials like the *Corporate Scorecard* and the *Best Lawyers in America* survey allow them to judge the law firm's quality and the credentials of its partners. Furthermore, as practising lawyers themselves, they have an extensive network through which they can access information about law firms.

Though competition does keep the industry very market-oriented, we felt that social relations were also playing a dynamic role in the operation of law firms. To examine this possibility, we designed a quantitative study of US mega firms. From this study, we hoped to gain a better understanding of the effect and the magnitude of the effect that embedded ties, board memberships and status have on the pricing of legal services. We also gathered qualitative data during interviews at three law firms and two corporations in a large Midwestern city. We spoke with nine lawyers (seven of whom were partners) about issues such as partnership models, production efficiency, training, cultures, profitability, client development strategies, inter-firm ties, and pricing tactics. We also interviewed a commercial banker and an insurance company executive in order to gain a better sense of the client's perspective on these issues.

Research study

The study required the accumulation of many different types of data about law firms. A main source for this data was an annual survey done by *The National Law Journal* (*NLJ*) on the 'Top 250 Largest US Law Firms'. For this survey, a partner provides information about the firm's number of partners, associates, offices, practice areas, and branch locations, as well as information about the firm's hourly rates. The nature of the survey, however, leads to a different set of firms being surveyed each year, so that some firms are surveyed more frequently than others. For the purposes of our study, which compares a law firm's ties to clients in one year to the ties in another year to ascertain how changes in firm–client relationships affect pricing, we needed to use firms that were surveyed at least twice, so our data set included information on 133 law firms during the period from 1989 to 1995.

We focused on law firms in the USA to reduce the complexity of looking at the global marketplace for legal services. By studying the dynamics of price setting within one important national market, we gained a fine-grained understanding of how prices get set for corporate legal services. Because of data limitations, we only collected data through 1995, which may appear somewhat dated, but we expect the patterns which we observed to hold in the present marketplace.

We also used two other surveys by the *NLJ*—'Who Represents Corporate America', which surveys the Fortune 500 and 'Who Represents Financial America,' which surveys the 200 largest US banks. These surveys provided information about which firms the surveyed corporations and banks used most (in other words, repeated firm–client ties) as well as the names and firms of the lawyers that sit on their boards. For data on law firm quality, we turned to the *Best Lawyers in America* survey and the *Martindale-Hubbell Directory*.

We used multiple regression analysis to study how different factors affect price. Multiple regression is a powerful statistical tool that enables researchers to isolate the effects of multiple factors on the variable of interest, in this case, price. This allows us to test how different variables affect the average price, while netting out the effects of other variables. For example, we expected embedded ties to have an effect on the price a law firm charges in the marketplace. However, we also expected that the costs a firm faces have an impact on that firm's price as well. Multiple regression allows us to isolate the effect of embedded ties on price, 'net-net' of the effects of all other factors on price.

In addition to our quantitative study, we also interviewed a number of partners of top US law firms to look at the impact of relationships on price. We used these to develop concrete measures for our variables, as well as giving us a more detailed understanding of how relationships affect price. Quotations from these interviews are used below in our analysis to show how our quantitative results play out in terms of the challenges managers of top firms face in setting prices in an increasingly competitive market for corporate legal services. A full list of these variables, where we obtained them from, and what theoretical concept they are measuring, is presented in Table 5.2.

Price was, of course, the main outcome variable to be explained throughout the three different parts of the study. The pricing of partner and associate work differs because of the complexity of the work. There are also high- and low-end rates for both partners and associates supplied in the *NLJ* survey. In our study, we examined both partner and associate

Table 5.2 Variables used in statistical analysis and their measurement

Variable name	Data source	Measurement	Underlying concept
Embeddedness Measures			
Embedded ties	NLJ	A relationship between a firm and a client that lasts two years or more—client firms gave the names of the top 5–7 laws firms they have worked with over the last year.	Repetitiveness indicates when a firm–client relationship is based on trust and private information exchange rather than arm's-length price information only
Board memberships	NLJ	The presence of a partner from the law firm sitting on the board of a corporation that is not a client of the law firm	Indicates a law firm's ability to get private information from the market not available to firms that lack board ties
Law firm relational status	NLJ	A law firm's network of ties with all its client firms ranked by the profitability of the client firm—higher-profit clients have higher status.	Indicates the wealth and power of a law firm's client base; firms with similar clients are viewed as being in the same status bracket
Firm Characteristics			
Human capital quality	NLJ	The percentage of partners with degrees from the eight most selective US law schools	Indicates the rigour of academic training that the lawyers in a firm have experienced
Best lawyer quality index	Best Lawyers in America survey	The number of lawyers in the directory of best lawyers that each firm employs multiplied by the average number of associates assigned to each partner at that firm	Indicates a law firm's quality as measured by success multiplied by the impact he or she has on the firm
Costs of goods sold	NLJ	The average yearly starting salary of a firm's associates	Measures the production costs of a firm's services
Size	NLJ	The log of the number of lawyers in the firm	Measures size of firm
Number of offices	NLJ	The number of offices	A second indication of a firm's size
Age	NLJ	The log of the number of years since a firm was founded	Indicates a firm's strength of reputation, inertia, and operating knowledge

Client Characteristics			
Number of in-house counsel	NL_j	The average number of in-house counsel a firm's clients employ	Indicates the client's capability to assess the pricing and quality of law firms
Number of clients	NL_j	The total number of clients a law firm service	Indicates a law firm's dependence on their clients
Average bank assets	NL_j	The average assets of a firm's bank clients	Indicates the power of a firm's bank clients to bargain down prices
Average corporate revenues	NL_j	The average assets of a firm's corporate clients	Indicates the power of a firm's corporate clients to bargain down prices
Market Controls			
Indicator variables for key practice areas	NL_j	Whether at least 20% of a firm's work was done in each of these areas: banking law, commercial/securities law, litigation, labour law, and tax law	Indicates differences in composition of the firm's practice areas
Law firm client demand	NL_j	The yearly change in a law firm's employment growth or contraction	Indicates how much demand for a firm's services exceeded its manpower or vice versa
Indicator variables for location	NL_j	The categorization of a firm as being located in the northeast, midwest, west coast, south or in one of nine major US cities	Indicates differences in demand and competition due to location
Dependent Variable			
Average firm partner price per hour	NL_j	Self-reported firm average price charged for one hour of a partner's time	Indicates the price per hour fee structure of the firm
Average firm associate price per hour	NL_j	Self-reported firm average price charged for one hour of an associate's time	Indicates the price per hour fee structure of the firm

103

prices, where price is understood as the hourly rate charged by firms. Our principle results were based on the estimated average hourly rates for partners, along with a second model on the estimated average hourly rates for associates. In addition, we also looked at the range of billing rates for both partners and associates to confirm our results. In order to operationalize these variables, we averaged the high- and low-partner rate and the high- and low-associate rate for each firm. We lagged these figures one year so that the rates would coincide with the causal factors that set the prices. That is, we wanted to ensure that we had causation correct, so we used explanatory variables from the year prior to the year we measured price, which ensures that we can statistically assess that these factors cause price, as opposed to price affecting the nature of relationships. We also checked to make sure that the distribution of work over different specialties (which can differ in price) was not skewing our calculated average rate.

We also needed to control for certain variables throughout the study. For example, we needed to control for the difference in the cost of a law firms' production, and we did this by using the starting salary of the firm's associates. We accounted for factors like differences in firm size (the number of lawyers and the number of branches) and differences in inertia and operating knowledge (the firm's age).

Because firm quality was a crucial and multidimensional factor to account for, we operationalized quality in two different ways. One measure of law firm quality is the rigour of the academic legal training of its lawyers. We accounted for this through a variable that we called the *firm's human capital quality*, in which we measured what percentage of the firm's partners received their JD from one of the country's top eight US law schools (Columbia, Duke, Harvard, Stanford, UC Berkeley, University of Chicago, University of Michigan and Yale). While it would have been preferable to use data from both partners and associates on this measure, not all firms publicize information on their associates' degrees. However, when we looked at the firms that did provide data about associates' degrees, we found a very high correlation between the percentage of partners and the percentage of associates with elite degrees. This is because partners tend to hire associates with JDs from the schools from which the partners themselves graduated.

Academic training, however, is not the only measure of quality; we also wanted to account for actual experience. To do this, we created a variable called the *firm's best lawyer quality index*. We created this using information from the *Best Lawyers in America* survey, in which lawyers are asked to identify the best lawyer outside their firm in their specialty area. Because this is a perceptual measure, we wanted to test it against a behavioural measure. We did a confirmatory check of our findings with data from the *American Lawyer Corporate Scorecard*, which provides data on the volume and size of a firm's deals.

We also controlled for certain variables associated with the firms' clients. For instance, the number of in-house counsels affects how carefully and comprehensively a company can assess the quality and price of the law firm it hires. We also tried to account for power differences by using the bank assets or corporate revenues of the clients. Finally, we controlled for some market variables, such as region, differing practice areas, and law firm client demand.

Embedded ties in firm–client relationships

From the *NLJ* surveys, we can see which law firm ties are embedded (i.e. which firm-to-client ties repeatedly occurred during the years we studied). However, we cannot determine the intensity of the ties, because we do not necessarily know the start date. Therefore, we considered a tie to be embedded if it lasted at least two years, and we lagged the first year of the sample back two years to obtain consistency. We then calculated the percentage of a firm's total ties that were embedded.

When we used this information in our regression model, we found that the more embedded ties a firm had, the lower their prices were. Specifically, a firm's percentage of embedded ties had a significant and negative impact on partner rates. The effect was in the same direction for associate rates, but the impact was only marginally significant. By using regression analysis, we are able to quantify these effects. Firms in which two-thirds of their large corporate clients are in long-term relations on average charge $4.07 less per hour for partners and $1.60 less per hour for associates than firms in which only one-third of their large corporate clients are in long-term relations.

Paradoxically the lower rates may translate into higher profits in the following way. Consistent with our understanding of the social embeddedness of markets, we argue that embedded ties may lower the transaction costs of firm–client transactions below the transaction costs of firm–client relationships that lack embeddedness. These lower costs can permit higher profits for the firm; even though the absolute price they charge the client is lower, the price-cost mark-up is larger in embedded relationships (the amounts shown are small on an hourly basis but can translate into sizeable amounts over the course of a long-term relationship). The lower price charged to the client indicates that these benefits are mutually shared by both parties. Thus, embedded ties with clients are beneficial social relationships that allow a firm to maintain or increase its profit margin while at the same time providing an incentive for client retention—two key factors that are consistent with the observation that long-term ties are advantageous to law practices.

To rule out other explanations for this effect, we ran several other analyses. First, we ruled out the possibility that these results were not due to the firms' relative bargaining power (e.g. smaller firms might lower their rates to retain clients). We also wanted to make sure that the lower prices were a consequence of the embedded ties, not a cause of them (e.g. price-sensitive companies sticking to lower-priced firms). Third, we looked at the possible effects of 'price stickiness' (which could make firms hesitant to raise prices for old customers). However, after further analyses of the data, our original findings were further supported.

We also found anecdotal evidence in support of this interpretation during our interviews with lawyers. During the interviews, evidence began to emerge that the trust and reciprocity that distinguishes embedded ties from arm's-length ties was a benefit that both lawyers and clients recognized and valued. In accordance with our statistical findings, our interviewees indicated that the increased trust and information-sharing of embedded ties result in lowered transaction costs (the costs associated with making and maintaining the transaction), the benefits of which can be shared between the lawyer and client. For example, an in-house counsel had this to say about the development of trust over time:

> We begin to build a special relationship based on trust within the first year and sometimes sooner depending on if the managing partner is a relationship person and the turnover on the [in-house legal] committee. So, if we work with a law firm for two years, it is a pretty sure bet we have a trust relationship because it means we've renewed with them, we're not negotiating a new contract, and have a pattern of comfort in interaction. It also means we have worked out a fee structure. There are increases, but not like the first time you deal with them. We work with them on an annual basis and usually won't stop unless we fire them.

Lawyers at mega firms also noticed the advantages of trust in a client relationship. Below, a partner talks about how embedded ties increase trust and the flow of information:

> It's no question that trust enters into it [pricing]. I mean, it's very rare that you're gonna get the big five hundred million dollar transactions—I don't see 'em with a stranger. Chances are there's a little bit of a dance, and so forth,

that goes on before you can form a relationship. It's relationship-building, it's communication, and it is trust. For example, we have a client where the general counsel, while he's familiar with working with law firms, had not dealt with my area of law before. He was initially very sceptical about the work that it would take. And the first phone call was very uncomfortable, because he said, point blank, 'I don't believe that this is gonna take this much work. Tell me more about your experiences with other clients'. And after a while, he warmed up . . . but he was initially very sceptical. It's a process. It's a trust, a transparency.

Another partner discussed what his firm called the 'trusted advisor role.' This indicated a relationship that operated under mutual trust rather than written agreements—in other words, an embedded tie. He told us how private information-sharing could lower transaction costs:

> Knowing how a client likes to receive your legal services is important. Some don't want long memos. 'Just confirm the phone call or give me a one pager.' I know that through a relationship. Others I have to scream 'For Christ's sake' before they start to take me seriously. [So], having this working relationship, I know exactly how clients expect to receive things from me and it helps me make budget. We will limit the number of drafts. It's the benefits of the trusted advisor role. . . . A relationship allows her [the client] to be more nimble with our firm; rather than having a formal engagement in a project she may call a partner she knows directly . . . so it's very efficient for her.

A specific practice that helped law firms share the lowered transaction costs of embedded relationships (by charging clients a fee that is less than their usual rate but one that will maintain the firm's profit margins) included charging less for work because a portion of it had previously been completed for a different client. Lawyers will recognize, however, that this treads dangerously close to the forbidden practice of double billing. However, because there are financial benefits of this practice to be shared by both the firm and the client, law firms disclosed the situation to the client and received permission to charge a rate which is less than their usual rate for new work but more than the nominal charge for taking knowledge 'off the shelf'. One lawyer talked about this practice during the interview:

> If we happen to know of an answer, or be smart on an issue, everybody benefits, other than the fact that we can't charge as much as maybe the last time. If you come up with a solution that benefits more than one client, it's very tricky within our firm rules as to whether you can do multiple billings because you came up with the same answer once . . . I'm going to have to divide up that fifteen minutes by five unless we get the client's permission to bill on a different rate, which would be a premium price.

Though this creates a mutually beneficial outcome, these kinds of arrangements are difficult to create if there is not a measure of trust between the lawyer and the client. A client has no means of validating whether the lawyer is discounting the service a fair amount for work that was previously done. Therefore, embedded ties are vital in allowing these agreements to be reached. One lawyer had this to say about how embedded ties and pricing are related:

> I recognise that if I'm giving somebody the million-dollar answer in an hour, I'm thinking to myself, I'm losing on this one, because I know it and I'm delivering in an hour, and I'm not getting paid for it. All I'm getting is an hour. And so there is the sense of frustration . . . or just recognition that we sometimes have the golden answer that's going to save the client a lot of money and a lot of time. So, [with the client's permission] the . . . hourly rate is a blended rate of the great super-duper value we had, as well as times when we knew more routine advice.

The opposite kind of situation arises when there is a lack of embeddedness in the relationship. When there is an absence of trust and reciprocity between lawyer and client, the lawyer may opt to charge a contingency price to protect the firm from bearing the brunt of hidden costs should unexpected problems arise. This practice indicates that in the case of an arm's-length tie, prices will be higher to cover the cost of the unknown.

Board membership

The second part of our study involved the number of lawyers in each firm who sat on the boards of directors of large corporations. Board connections are another form of embedded tie (Mizruchi 1996). These are embedded ties because of the close relationships that develop between and among the directors that sit on the same boards. Our thinking was that lawyers who sat on boards would be able to position themselves in lucrative deal streams for the top corporations. While the law firm cannot contract directly with the corporation for which their partner is a board member, the partner can gain insight into the inner workings, bidding practices, and competitive needs of similar firms in the same industry through the exchange of private information among board members. This unique view of the corporation's needs should help lawyers identify the highest return projects and anticipate the needs of other firms in the industry, making them highly sought after for forward-looking legal advice and acumen. To obtain data on board seats, we looked at the *NLJ* surveys of the Fortune 250 and the 200 largest US banks to determine which lawyers from which firms were sitting on their boards.

From our regression model, we found that the more board seats a firm has, the higher the firm's pricing is for both partner and associate rates. The magnitude of the effect was similar for associate rates and partner rates once the range of partner and associate work was standardized. This seemingly small difference has a relatively large impact on the prices set by the firm. Firms with just one partner sitting on the board of directors of a large corporation charge $3.36 more per hour for partners and $1.77 more per hour for associates than firms with no lawyer sitting on a board of directors. In the previous section, we saw that when the complexity of the work and the uncertainty of the transaction decreased, the effect of embedded ties decreased as well. However, this was not the case with board memberships. This finding suggests that this kind of embeddedness does not rely upon the uncertainty of the market.

We interpret these findings to mean that board members have access to private information that allows them better to position and differentiate their firm's product. Previous research has focused on how board member- ships can provide power and negotiation benefits, but our study indicates that board seats provide a significant and potentially lucrative marketing advantage as well.

Our interviews reinforced these findings. Board seats provide law firms access to a wide array of private information, including what kind of offers other law firms are making and how the company evaluates these bids. The law industry has a confidential bid system, so this type of information could be highly valuable to partners and allow them better to differentiate their own firm's product. Here is how one of the interviewees described board membership:

> I think it's very important for law firms to be able to place their people on major boards, I think so, because of two things. You're gonna have the benefit of seeing what other law firms are charging if the company that you sit on is using other firms.... And you're gonna get the benefit of the commentary that your fellow board people have on legal services, and what they consider to be important. This enables you to make the last bid and reposition your firm relative to your competitors so that you can add something of low cost but high value to the client.

Board members may also enjoy a first look at business prospects or trends. This allows them to adjust their own offerings or to invest in areas of legal work that they anticipate being lucrative in the future. One lawyer noted:

109

The law firm is clearly looking for business opportunities on boards. If there's a deal, if there's a change of control, if there's some hot issue, the person's in the know or can hear it first and have an opportunity to say, 'Oh, we've got some people who can help out' and so forth.

Status affiliations

A third form of embeddedness is status or reputation. Status attempts to capture the intangible value of the firm to the client—what they get in hiring a law firm in addition to the functional quality of the firm. These intangible benefits to the client include name recognition, prestige, cachet, or other factors that are attached to the firm's name and that affect its ability to impress clients. Specifically, a firm's status adds value to the client by enhancing the client's own image and lending credibility to the client's decision-making process of selecting one firm over another. In markets where the quality of law firms may be relatively similar, these added benefits differentiate and brand a firm in a way that allows it to increase prices.

Whereas embedded ties and board ties are dyadic relationships between a single firm and a single client, a law firm's status derives from its collective web of affiliations with its corporate clients. Thus, a law firm's status can be seen as a function of the power and wealth of its clients. Taking this into account, we measured status by the type of corporate or banking client that a firm serviced. This methodology enabled us to do two things. First, we found a way to quantify a firm's status, and second, to connect a firm's status to its embeddedness. For example, it is well accepted in law that status differences exist. Typical phrases such as 'silk-stocking firm', 'Madison Avenue A-Firm', or 'Wall Street B-Firm' exemplify the sensitivity of lawyers to the importance of status. Nevertheless, such categories as 'white shoe firm', etc., while having intuitive appeal, lack quantifiable precision and fail to link a status to clear and reproducible market determinants. Our status measure enabled us to solve both these problems. Using a listing of all the mega firm clients, we identified each law firm's network of affiliated corporate firms and then ranked a law firm's position in the status hierarchy based on the profitability of a law firm's clients. These quantitative rankings closely reflected the classifications that are well known within the market—for example, firms like Cravath or Skadden have the top status bracket in our operationalization, while Baker & McKenzie, the largest law firm in the world, is in the next bracket down.

From our regression model, we found that status was positively related to pricing for both partner and associate rates (Figures 5.5 and 5.6). While status did increase price in both cases, the effect had greater impact on the prices of partner rates. Because we used a proxy measure for status, we

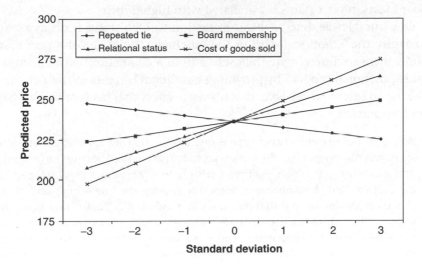

Figure 5.5 Embeddedness and partner billing price

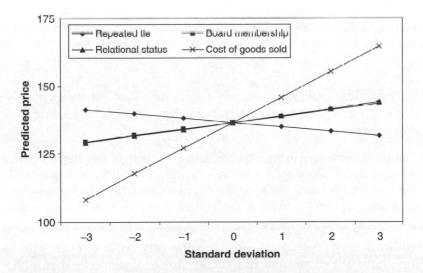

Figure 5.6 Embeddedness and associate billing price

used the statistical properties of the variable to assess the changes in price. We found that a firm that is one standard deviation higher than the mean for this variable, equivalent to a firm at the top third of the status range as opposed to the average firm, charged $9.41 more per hour for partners and $2.25 more per hour for associates than the average firm. Just as with board seats, higher status is associated with higher prices.

One interviewee described this attraction to high-status firms as a way to satisfy the 'emotional part' of the purchase. The image of a firm may allow them to differentiate themselves from a competitor with a comparable functional product by providing emotional benefits to their clients. During an interview, a lawyer described the effect that his firm's status has on consumers:

> Pricing is multi-faceted. Experience is one facet ... that we are efficient and the client gets the top gun [i.e. the top lawyer in that area]. [But] because we certainly find that when our clients get into a crisis, when there's an emotional part of the project—and there always is, somewhere along the line—they want us to give them the impression that *they're* really number one. That comes from our status. ... So, I think what clients are looking for and what they're entitled to is the benefit of our experience. And if we have the status and we're entitled to claim it, I think we have every right to expect [that] as part of the pricing they give us a premium. I think both those things have to go into the equation. I don't think there's anything exclusionary about that analysis even for inside corporate counsels. Each of those things is going to play a role in pricing.

From this, we see that hiring a high-status law firm can have several advantages. It may enhance a client's image. When a client has to spend large sums of money hiring a law firm, hiring a high-status firm is an easy choice to defend—in the event of a crisis, the hirer can more easily justify his or her choice if the firm has high status. In other words, hiring a high-status firm reduces the costs of choice validation for the client. One interviewee described why a high-status firm would be appealing to an inside counsel:

> The tax director says to herself, 'You know, I could get this [legal expertise] somewhere else. I can use a medium-size firm in Kentucky, and they're fine. But I think I'd like to be able to tell my directors I got Baker & McKenzie—a high status firm.' There's less to justify before the deal and after the fact if something goes wrong.

Standard hiring procedures in the law industry tend to accentuate the firms' status. When multiple firms are courting the same client, it is often described as a 'beauty contest'. Use of the term seems to suggest that status is an important factor in hiring decisions. An interviewee had this to say about beauty contests:

> You know there aren't that many pure beauty contests that are out there, but they're all beauty contests to some degree.... It was so the [hiring] person at the company could say whatever happens, no one's going to question my choice. In commodity work or the areas where there's more competition, we may be thrown into a beauty contest too. [But] it's not about quality. It's about is the firm better at spitting out materials and ready to answer questions?

As with board seats, status allows a firm to differentiate its product. However, in this case, the differentiation arises not from functional differences in the legal offerings, but rather from image enhancing and protocol-appropriate benefits that status provides.

Weighing the worth of social ties

How much difference in actual dollars and cents do embedded relationships make? From our regression models we can estimate actual dollar values which can help us understand the comparative importance of these variables relative to others, particularly production costs. Regression analysis fits the best linear relationship between two variables which allows us to calculate the actual amounts. For example, our variable measuring board ties was simply the count of the number of lawyers sitting on boards of directors in large corporations. In regression analysis, a line is fitted that best describes the relationship between the number of board ties and the price charged by the firm, netting out the effects of the other variables. This line has a slope and an intercept, and the slope describes the best linear relationship between the number of board ties and price. For board ties, we obtained a slope of +3.36 for our regression on partner price, which indicates that for every board tie a firm has to a corporation, the partner price on average increases by $3.36 per hour.

Furthermore, we standardized the values of our variables so that we can compare the relative magnitude of their effects across variables—that is we can say how a change in the standard deviation in a variable, say embedded ties, compares to a change in the standard deviation of another variable, say status, in affecting the financial returns of the law firm. Standardizing variables does nothing to affect our results, but it does allow us to compare the size of the effects for variables measured in different units. For instance, we measured board ties as the count of the number of lawyers sitting on boards of directors, while the measurement for embedded ties was the percentage of a law firm's clients that had long-term relationships with the firm. Since these variables have different units, we cannot directly compare the sizes of the effects. However, by standardizing the variables we are able to compare directly the size of the effects. For example, a one standard deviation increase in embedded ties leads to a $3.82 decrease in partner rate per hour (remembering that this may translate into larger profit margins overall). One standard deviation in board memberships (i.e. the equivalent of one board seat) led to an increase of $4.25 and $1.77 in partner and associate rates, respectively. Status had the largest impact on pricing, with one standard deviation raising partner rates by $9.41 and associate rates by $2.25.

While our embeddedness effects may seem like relatively small dollar amounts compared to the hundreds of dollars that lawyers charge hourly, they can still have enormous impact on a firm's revenues once aggregated across the firm and over time. For example, consider the combined effects of board seats and status on associate rates. If both of these variables are increased by just one standard deviation by the firm, the associate's hourly rate increases by approximately $5.00. If we multiply that figure by sixty hours of billing per week and fifty weeks per year, this $5.00 difference could increase revenues by $15,000. If we multiply that figure by 500 associates, we see that the small but significant effects of embeddedness could result in about $7,500,000 in additional revenues from associate pricing alone.

Conclusions

Our research demonstrates that the way in which law firms build relationships has a significant effect on price. A firm with more long-term relationships tends to have a lower price relative to other factors as the costs of the transaction lowers, allowing benefit to both firm and client. This also allows for a more stable client portfolio, as firms trade off higher billing rates for repeat business, assuring a line of revenue and a wide (but possibly not the widest) profit margin.

We also found that firms with lawyers sitting on the boards of non-client corporations also increased the average prices firms charged in the marketplace, compared to those firms without any lawyers sitting on boards of directors. While these relationships are not with clients, they do allow lawyers to see what boards of directors look for in the hiring of outside counsel and provide general market intelligence that is unavailable to law firms lacking these ties. This enables law firms to find ways of creating, and most attractively packaging, high-value services to prospective clients.

Finally, we found that the relative status of a firm had a positive impact on price. This effect held after we had controlled for quality, costs, location, and a host of other variables. This indicates that there are direct benefits of the status of a firm on the prices it is able to obtain. Much of this effect is driven by the in-house counsel in corporations, who use status to justify a hiring decision to their superiors or to cover themselves in case something goes wrong with the deal even though a lower cost firm of equal quality is available.

Our study focused on mega law firms, so further research is necessary to discover how far these findings extend. For instance, while the effects may be present in smaller firms, the magnitude of their effect may differ. Overall, we found that the types of social relationships a firm has with clients, other corporations, and their position in the social structure of the market, all significantly affected the prices these firms are able to charge. However, prices are not the same as profits or revenues. In some instances, firms can garner more long-term revenue by charging less per hour if there is also a drop in costs or an increase in the length or stability of the income stream. With long-term relationships, firms are better able to hire the number of associates needed, and better able to predict revenue streams, and the number of billable hours, allowing for greater efficiencies. In this way, lower prices in relationships can actually *increase* the bottom line for firms.

However, by relying too much on long-term clients, firms risk the possibility of losing their clients to more market-savvy firms. In related work we have done on the banking industry, we found that banks that relied too heavily on long-term relationships with their clients and those that had no long-term relationships did worse on average than banks that had a healthy mix of both long-term and transactional clients (Uzzi 1999; Uzzi and Gillespie 2002). This allowed banks to gain the transaction cost benefits of long-term embedded relations, while at the same time having access to current market conditions and market information. However, banks that relied too heavily on long-term clients were not as able as other firms to identify trends in the market or to identify new and valuable products to sell. Other banks that had greater access to this information were better able to innovate in developing new products for their clients (Uzzi and Lancaster 2003). The idea is that embedded ties are beneficial but must be part of a portfolio of diverse ties to clients in order for their liabilities to be offset.

Our results also indicate that firms benefit from having lawyers sit on boards of directors of corporations, even when these corporations are not clients of the firm. By providing access to unique sources of private information, lawyers are able to see the decision-making processes of boards, and what they consider to be important characteristics of firms that they are willing to pay for. By having access to this information, firms are able to identify low-cost, high-value services to bid for *other* clients, creating a source of profit, and higher prices, than they would otherwise be able to charge. While this practice is currently only common in the USA, this is a potential strategy for firms in other countries to pursue.

Overall, our study raises a number of important and urgent questions for those in management roles in modern law firms. Unfortunately, our work can only raise these questions without providing easy solutions. Nevertheless, these are important issues that law firms are going to be facing for years to come, and by beginning to subject these questions to sustained empirical analysis we hope to have provided some tools for navigating the new market terrain.

While we expect much further research in this area, the information in this study may be of great importance to managers of large law firms. Lucrative benefits await a firm that is able to harness the power of social relations on price and use embedded ties, board seats, and status to its advantage.

6

Your income

Determining the value of legal knowledge: billing and compensation practices in law firms

Huseyin Leblebici
University of Illinois, Urbana-Champaign

The amount of the matter in dispute, the labour of the serjeant, his value as a pleader in respect of his learning, eloquence, and repute, and lastly the usage of the court.

Factors considered to be important in determining legal fees as they were listed circa 1290 in *The Mirror of Justices*, Book II, c.5. Selden Society Edition, 1895.

Introduction

The success of every professional service firm, especially those operating in the field of law, critically depends on establishing a delicate balance between the demands of the client marketplace and the demands of its professional staff. Management issues ranging from leverage ratios and firm governance structures to the management of professional careers are direct manifestations of this balancing act (Maister 1997; Trotter 1997). The objective of this chapter is to look at one specific aspect of this balancing act—the fee structures for client services within the context of law firms. Traditionally, both in research as well as in practice, the billing practices within professional service firms in general, and in law firms in particular, have been explained by the types of clients served, or services rendered, by the firm. The compensation practices, or the partnership structures of professional service firms, on the other hand, are

117

usually explained by the types of professionals employed and the existing precedence within a particular profession (Cotterman 2001; Empson, this volume). In this chapter, I argue that these practices cannot be understood independently from each other but must be considered together in research as well as in managerial practice. Any attempt to change the existing conventions that shape client–law firm relations cannot be successful unless there are related changes within the internal operations of the firms themselves.

In this chapter, I first explore some of problems that billing poses for practising lawyers, by studying the historical evolution of the 'billable hour' and how its practice shapes the lives of individual lawyers, the success of law firms, and the reputation of the legal profession. Although billing is a central practice for lawyers, the subject receives very little attention in àcademic research. I then provide a conceptual map of the institutionalized practices in corporate law firms in order to demonstrate how these practices are intricately related to each other in a systemic fashion and how these relationships make change very difficult. Finally, I explore the conceptual and practical issues associated with linking time with value and knowledge in order to address some of the thorniest issues in law firms associated with billable hours, law firm structure, and professional incentives.

It is paradoxical that hourly billing, which was once presented as a solution to difficulties in valuing legal services, has now become an institutional practice that is condemned by lawyers and clients alike. Until the late 1950s, the standard fee arrangement in the legal profession was some version of fixed fee regulated by the minimum fee schedules recommended by state bar associations. Three major historical developments in the past fifty years, however, have caused time-based billing to become the most common practice in the USA. The first is the change of setting in which legal work has been carried out. Large corporate law firms have become mega firms that require more complicated management structures, incentive mechanisms, and employment practices (Gilson and Mnookin 1989; Samuelson 1990). The second is changes in the regulatory landscape in the USA which prohibited the use of fee schedules and expanded the use of pre-trial discovery that was introduced in the 1938 Federal Rules of Civil Procedure (Shepherd and Cloud 1999). These regulatory changes all necessitated a new approach to pricing and billing practices. Finally, in the early 1950s, the combination of the increased costs associated with the growing complexity of law, even in transactional cases, and the declining income of law firms, meant that the management consulting firms and the American Bar Association promoted the idea that law firms would be more successful if they used billable hours in order to stop the declining income of law firms. There was common agreement among experts at the time that in addition to increased revenues, billable hours would help law firms to make better business decisions by knowing which areas of law were more profitable. As a result of these three developments that have changed the landscape of legal practice since the early 1950s, the billable hour has not only become the means of charging clients but also a critical administrative tool in managing large law firms. Firms started to use the number of hours billed to assess their needs for new recruits, to measure the success of their firms, to determine salary levels, and to decide on promotions.

Since corporate law firms today rely on hours as a measure of value of expert labour both internally and externally, the intricate institutional practices that are built around it make it very hard for firms to make radical changes (Calloway and Robertson 2002). Hourly billing survives today and is more common than any other alternative billing and compensation practices because of its presumed simplicity, manageability, and familiarity.

Today, new forces of change—the marketplace, society's perception of legal practice, and regulations in the profession—are demanding that firms revisit these institutionalized practices. I argue that because of these sometimes uncontrollable changes, law firms would be wise to look again at how the value of legal knowledge and service could be determined. While the literature I survey in this essay tends to focus on institutional practices of law firms, it is important to remember that courts and law schools also play an important role in shaping what is acceptable and prudent within the profession (Curtis and Resnik 2002; Rhode 2000).

Professional service firms and the exchange of labour

One of the most controversial issues in the management of professional organizations is how the clients should pay for the services they receive. Within the knowledge economy this issue gains more prominence because different professions, who are responsible for the production and use of their specialized knowledge, use different logic to explain and justify their practices. A second and equally contentious issue is how firms should compensate professionals who provide their services as agents of their firms. Again, different professions provide alternative answers and subscribe to highly institutionalized practices. Both of these issues rest on the question of how labour is exchanged in the economy in general, and in the knowledge industries, in particular.

In investment banking, for example, the fee for the services is based on a percentage of the capital sum involved in a given transaction. The percentage involved often varies according to a sliding scale such that the greater the capital amount, the smaller the percentage becomes. Advertising agencies also work on a percentage basis, but this is based on a cost-plus formula. The fee is determined as a percentage (usually 15%) of the cost of advertising campaign. Physicians, on the other hand, use what is usually called 'tear-off' billing, in which specific activities and their associated prices are set in advance. In the case of law firms, attorneys and their clients are usually presented with three payment methods for the attorneys' labour: an hourly fee for services rendered, a fixed fee for a particular service, or a contingency fee based on the outcomes accomplished by the attorney (Clark 1989). As Figure 6.1 shows, the exchange of labour within professional service firms is a collective product of three core institutional domains of activity: the state and its regulatory agencies, the professions and their associations, and the educational process through which the knowledge workers develop their expertise. They regulate and create context in which the professional

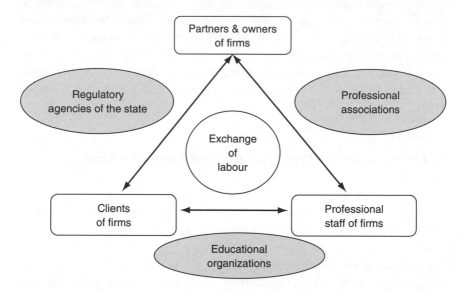

Figure 6.1 Sources of institutionalized practices in corporate law firms

staff, the clients, and the professional service firms enter into exchange relationships.

Since the days of Adam Smith, the concept of labour and the institutional mechanisms developed for its exchange have played a controversial role in the theoretical evolution of economics, sociology, and anthropology. The exchange of labour within professions has been a source of contention, especially in economics, which is dominated by the exchange of commodities. As Commons point out, 'a hundred and fifty years of economic theorizing has puzzled over the problem of giving a decent status to these intangible personal services' (Commons 1934: 181). Smith and his followers contended that services performed by physicians, lawyers, ministers, teachers and housewives were 'unproductive labour' because the usefulness of their labour did not appear in a commodity which could be sold on the market in tons, yards, or litters.

The ambiguity associated with the value of labour, however, is not a peculiar product of economic theory but a product of its own character. Throughout history, different institutional alternatives have been devised to facilitate its exchange, ranging from reciprocal gift-giving and collective farming in primitive societies, to employment contracts in modern economies. A venture capitalist investing in an entrepreneurial activity through partnership, the employment of a manager for a set salary, or even the institution of marriage can be considered particular solutions to the unique problems associate with the exchange of human labour (Stinchcombe 1986). Thus, in order to understand the present conventions adopted within the legal profession for the exchange of labour, it is important to explain how these practices have evolved through history as by-products of unique institutional settings and how actors have chosen among alternatives given the constraints of legitimacy and practical action.

Historical evolution of billing practices in the legal profession

Currently within US legal practice, three billing practices prevail: an hourly fee for services rendered, a fixed fee for a particular service, or a contingency fee based on some outcome. Among these alternatives, the billable hour is the most dominant choice even though it is under constant attack, not only because of market forces but also because of public opinion (Jones and Glover 1998). According to recent surveys, only about ten per cent of the US population believe that they get good value for the fees they pay to their attorneys (Ross 1996).

Complaints about attorneys' fees are not new and have been part of the profession's history since Roman times. For more than two thousand years, efforts have been made to regulate lawyers' fees or to prohibit fees completely. Debates on lawyers' fees were not restricted to how much an attorney should receive, but extended to who should pay for these fees (Kritzer 2002). Every year, journals in the legal profession include numerous articles on the fairness of existing practices which offer new alternatives.

While the billable hour is now commonplace, it is a relatively recent invention. Before the 1960s, few lawyers kept time records and most fees were based on uniform fee schedules approved by the bar associations. If these were not available, the courts assessed the reasonableness of the fee by evaluating a number of different factors specified in the canons of legal ethics. In addition to time and labour involved, courts and bar associations identified several major factors for the evaluation of reasonable fees (Committee on Lawyer Business Ethics 1998). According to the Model Code of Professional Responsibility EC-2-20 (1980), a reasonable fee took into consideration the experience and the reputation of the attorney, the difficulty of the case, the results obtained, the preclusion of alternative work, the client's ability to pay, and the customs of the community (Reed 1989). The assessment of a reasonable fee can be such a difficult matter that even courts are sometimes asked to intervene. For instance, it is the obligation of a bankruptcy judge critically to examine legal fees because they are traditionally paid by the creditors, who have no contractual relationship with the attorney.

Table 6.1 presents a short chronological time line of this historical evolution. During the early stages of the Roman Empire, legal services were rendered free of charge and the honour attached to successful advocacy was considered to be a reasonable reward by itself. Although it gradually became the custom for Romans to pay an honorarium, a statute in 204 BC prohibited anyone from accepting money or a gift for pleading a case (Pound 1953). The prohibition continued for at least two centuries until Emperor Claudius gave recognition to, and established, a fee system. Later on, during the establishment of canon laws, Justinian permitted the enforcement of maximum fees but also prohibited the practice of contingency fees (Ross 1996: 12).

Even after fees for legal services had become acceptable during the last stage of the Roman Empire, these simply represented an honorarium and

Table 6.1 A short chronology of the changes in the compensation of attorneys and legal fees since the Roman Empire

Time period	Common compensation practices
200 BC–AD 50	204 BC statute prohibited any advocate accepting money for legal services.
AD 50–AD 450	Emperor Claudius gave recognition to the existence of fees and established a scale with maximum fees.
AD 450–AD 1200	During the codification of Roman law, Justinian established the enforcement of fee scales with maximum amounts but prohibited contingency fees. Canon laws incorporated the recognition of attorney fees.
1200–1600	During the Medieval period fees were mostly regulated by the state or its courts especially in England.
1600–1750	English legal system accepted the idea of market-based fees. Declared repeatedly that, in calculating attorney fees, one should include not only time but the attorney's education, experience, and the complexity of the dispute itself. In the American colonies, however, there were specific fee schedules that were strictly followed.
1750–1850	In the USA many states enacted fee schedules and penalized lawyers if they charged more than prescribed amounts. Furthermore, the losing party in the case of litigation would pay for legal services (i.e. English rule).
1850–1925	States slowly abolished fee schedules under the pressure from bar associations, which considered them as part of the effort to control the profession by the states. Many firms adopted 'task-based billing'. The elimination of fee schedules encouraged the introduction of contingency fees.
1925–1975	Fee schedules that were determined by the bar associations became more fashionable. At the end of 1950s most state bars had their own minimum fee schedules. Even though these schedules were not enforced, attorneys regularly used them. By the end of 1950s, large law firms also started to keep time records. In 1938 Federal Rules of Civil Procedure implemented the system of broad pre-trial discovery.
1975–Present	In 1975 the US Supreme Court declared minimum fee schedules to be in violation of antitrust laws and hourly billing became the accepted standard among corporate law firms.

the clients were not under any legal obligation to reward their lawyers. The same theory still persists today in England where barristers are not able to sue for recovery of unpaid legal bills.

As Table 6.1 shows, during medieval times, either the state or the courts continued to establish enforceable fee schedules. By the early seventeenth century, the regulated system had slowly developed into a more market-based approach, especially in the British legal system. As the quotation at the beginning of this chapter indicates, many criteria were considered in determining fees, including the oratory ability of the attorney as well as time.

Within the common law countries, the American colonies continued to subscribe to the fee schedule system until the middle of the nineteenth century. During the seventeenth century, for instance, the state of Virginia established fee schedules for attorneys and fixed very low rates payable in tobacco with a heavy penalty for exceeding the permissible maximum. Other colonies, including Massachusetts, New Hampshire, New York, North Carolina, and Pennsylvania, established fee schedules as well (Chroust 1965). Even though these rates were low, popular sentiments towards lawyers and the regulatory powers of the bar associations were very negative in general (Gawalt 1979). The schedules generally governed only litigation fees, which were shifted to the losing party known as the 'English Rule.' Fee schedules also included provisions to penalize those attorneys who charged more than the prescribed amounts. In New York, for example, an 1813 statute prescribed 25 cents for serving a declaration, $1.25 for arguing a special motion, $1.50 for attending a trial of a case, and $3.75 for arguing an appeal (Ross 1996: 11).

Lawyers often opposed this regulation of fees not only because fees were set low, but also because they preferred to determine fees themselves, either through voluntary agreements with clients or through local bar associations. As the nineteenth century approached, many state bar associations started to set up minimum rather than maximum fees in order to reduce competition within the profession and to increase the level of income. These practices were very similar to the pricing or wage systems established by European guilds and the labour unions.

As the nineteenth century progressed, the courts gradually recognized the right of lawyers and the bar associations to regulate their own fees and the states started to repeal their fee statutes. The elimination of the minimum fee schedules was partly the by-product of the more liberal economic thinking at the time but also came from a new understanding that lawyers were not public officers but were acting as private citizens for private purposes (Chroust 1965). Furthermore, attorneys felt uncomfortable defending a practice that was considered to be a working-class device for protecting wages (Gawalt 1979).

As a result of the repeal of fee schedules, there was a period when new and creative billing practices started to appear in the profession during the late nineteenth and early twentieth centuries. Many firms introduced a variety of alternatives such as task-based billing, value billing, or annual retainer fees. They also developed what is called the 'eyeball procedure' and simply billed their clients annually. The repeal of the fee schedules also encouraged the use of contingency fees that were especially popular with lawyers representing poor clients, and the American Bar Association reluctantly approved the use of contingency fees in 1908 (Ross 1996: 14).

Even though there were constant experimentations at the turn of the twentieth century, by the end of the First World War, the state bar associations started to re-adopt the fee schedules. According to a study published in the *Harvard Law Review*, at least thirty-four states and hundreds of local bar associations had established fee schedules at the end of the 1930s (Harvard Law Review Notes 1972). By the end of the 1940s, most state and local bar associations adopted fee schedules because they provided a more legitimate means for attorneys to justify their fees to clients. 'Left to their own devices, many attorneys were uncertain about how to charge clients or were embarrassed to charge for minor work or request reasonable compensation for their services. Fee schedules gave lawyers the courage to charge higher fees' (Ross 1996: 15). Even though the state bar associations repeatedly indicated to their members that they should not charge lower fees in order to avoid price competition, there was always the general perception within the legal community that fee schedules were not helping the economic welfare of their members.

Although the re-emergence of fee schedules was promoted in order to help attorneys to increase their compensation, the bar was worried by the middle of the century that its members were suffering a relative economic decline. During the 1950s and early 1960s, various studies indicated that attorney compensation was failing to keep pace with inflation and was lagging behind that of other professionals, particularly physicians. In a study by the American Bar Association called 'The 1958 Lawyer and His 1938 Dollar', it was claimed that lawyers who recorded their time actually made more money than their counterparts who did not. Management experts recommended that attorneys could raise their income by selecting a target annual salary and dividing that figure by the number of hours that they could bill to a client during a year in order to arrive at an hourly billing rate.

At the outset, large law firms found hourly billing attractive. By the middle of the 1950s, time-keeping was adopted by more than 50 per cent of the lawyers in large metropolitan areas and became standard practice in Wall Street firms by the late 1950s. Between the 1950s and the mid-1970s, management experts continually encouraged their law firm clients to use some form of time-keeping even though they did not specifically recommend their clients to use hourly fees. Consultants were more focused on keeping time records in order to determine whether legal cases were profitable. By the end of the 1960s, the percentage of attorneys who used hourly billing increased steadily and became the standard convention within corporate law firms. Although some firms maintained time records as a way of utilizing fee schedules more effectively, many began to urge the abandonment of the schedules in favour of time-based billing (Ross 1996).

When the US Supreme Court finally declared in 1975 that minimum fee schedules violated the antitrust laws, the landscape had already changed in favour of time-based billing in the profession. By the 1980s, most corporate law firms were keeping time records and were using hourly fees to bill their clients. Most experts in the field agreed that hourly billing made sense for the corporate clients who considered their attorneys similar to their employees who were paid according to the time they spent on the job.

When attorneys first started to use time keeping, the idea was that this was simply one yardstick among many to assess the value of their services. As firms grew in size during the second half of the twentieth century, greater emphasis was paid on recording billable hours as a means of maximizing fee income to pay for the growing numbers of associates.

The increasing emphasis on billable hours naturally required a reassessment of how many hours an associate or a partner should put into their practice. The amount of hours an attorney could reasonably deliver has steadily increased since the adoption of the practice. For instance, the billable hours for the associates climbed from 1500 h to 1700 h in the 1970s and to 1900 h in the 1990s (Fortney 2001). As expected such numbers not only reduced the satisfaction levels of attorneys, particularly the associate members, in large corporate law firms but also led to dissatisfaction on the part of their clients (Kritzer 1994). Based on past historical trends, it is not difficult to predict that the field of law is now ready for new alternative practices that will challenge the billable hour.

Nature of billing practices today

Although hourly billing remains the dominant method of determining fees, its deficiencies have become increasingly apparent, and the bar has offered inadequate responses (Committee on Lawyer Business Ethics 1998). Most state ethical codes require fees to be 'reasonable', and they provide a long list of factors to consider in assessing reasonableness, such

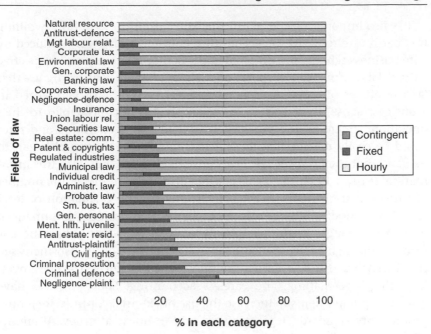

Figure 6.2 Distribution of alternative fee choices in different fields of law

Source: A sample of 972 attorneys in the state of Illinois, 1992.

as the time, labour, and skill involved, results obtained, and the customary charges for similar services. The use of other alternative practices, such as contingency fee arrangements, create their own ethical and legal complications (Rotunda 1999).

A survey conducted in the state of Illinois in the mid-1990s (see Figure 6.2) showed that billing practices varied considerably by practice. In some fields of law, such as negligence or criminal defence, contingency and fixed fees were quite common. Nevertheless the hourly fee prevailed in all twenty-three areas of legal practice surveyed.

While the hourly fee has been criticized extensively for its limitations and potential conflict of interest, there are two basic conventional justifications given for this choice: Lawyers should be paid for their time and effort, and the client is able to control legal costs by specifying who will do the work and at what hourly rate. However, the lawyers themselves argue that there are some serious disadvantages to an hourly billing arrangement. It makes a lawyer focus more on the hours rather than the results of the case, and indirectly penalizes more efficient or experienced lawyers (Clark 1989).

It is also important to point out that the current form of hourly billing was partly the result of the accounting culture, which was produced by elite business schools and dominated the senior management perspective within large American corporations (Kritzer 2002). Kritzer argues that 'as the offices of corporate general counsel became professionalized in a business sense, there was a need to apply business principles to their operation, including the purchase of outside services. Hours and rates could be easily measured and compared, and general counsel began to demand that their outside law firms provide detailed bills with this information' (Kritzer 1994: 187). This is why, ultimately, an increasing number of firms relied on hours as the sole criteria for the calculation of legal fees. Under hourly billing, corporate clients would accept the financial burden of changes in the complexity of legal problems, while the law firms would manage costs. Unfortunately, hourly billing also increased the incentives for law firms to inflate their services through over-lawyering, over-staffing, and careless accounting. Such practices have forced corporate clients to increase the use of external controls, including productivity standards, legal auditors, and in-house attorneys (Kummel 1996).

It should be emphasized here that potential ethical problems do not disappear if one uses the contingency or fixed fee arrangements. For instance, under the customary contingency fee arrangements, an attorney receives a percentage (about one-third) of the client's recovery. No payment is due if the claim is unsuccessful. Although such fee agreements are seen beneficial to a client, they may lead to potential abuse. A lawyer's return may bear no necessary relationship to the amount of work performed or to the risk actually assumed. In many cases where liability is clear and damages are substantial, a standard one-third recovery could provide a windfall for the attorney. If defendants make an early settlement offer, plaintiffs could end up with huge fees for minimal routine services.

All traditional billing systems distribute risk and reward inequitably between law firms and their corporate clients and provide few incentives for efficient legal solutions. In each alternative arrangement, the basic problem arises from the difference in lawyers' and clients' interests. A law firm's objective is to increase return to its partners; a client's goal is to maximize value and minimize costs. If attorneys are charging by the hour and lack other equally profitable uses for their time, they have an incentive to string out profits for as long as possible. And if their billings affect power, promotion, and compensation within firms, those incentives intensify. When hours determine fees and fees determine the careers of lawyers in their firms, efficiency is not going to be a critical factor in decision-making.

Explanations for the choices made by law firms

If the hourly fee system is so detrimental to the relationship between attorneys and their clients, why does it persist? There are various sociological and economic explanations that fall into four major categories. The first is the traditional economic explanation based on agency theory, which emphasizes concepts of moral hazard and adverse selection. Some of the research suggests that the legal profession moved to hourly billing following the introduction of rules that permitted extensive pre-trial discovery. Such costly procedures created uncertainty on the part of the attorneys and prompted them to adopt hourly fees as a means of dealing with this (Shepherd and Cloud 1999).

A second set of explanations is based on power and interest. This approach suggests that institutional practices are maintained and diffused by those whose self-interests are being served and who are willing to invest the necessary resources to protect their interests. As some legal scholars have argued (Davis 1994), the transition to hourly billing during the 1960s was a natural outcome of the explosive growth in the demand for legal services. In a market in which the supply of expert and specialist legal services were relatively scarce and lawyers enjoyed a monopoly, clients lacked bargaining power. They therefore accepted a form of billing that was intended to give lawyers greater control over the size of their profits.

A third explanation, which can be called coercive and normative institutionalization, accounts for the persistence of hourly billing through the coercive powers of the regulatory environment established by the state and the bar. Through deregulation or re-regulation the state (together with professional organizations, such as the bar associations) influenced directly the client–attorney relationship. Similarly, consulting firms specializing in law firm management provided the normative justifications for time-based fee structures in economic terms.

Finally, explanations based on the institutional context suggest changes in practices are constrained by existing practices in related domains. Practices evolve and are institutionalized through both synchronic and diachronic processes. Conventions evolve and are difficult to change because of the spillover effect. Existing conventions in fee structure are a function of other conventions that are followed within the organizational setting of law firms. Thus, the setting within which law is practised makes a difference in choosing a particular practice. As I explain in the following section, the way the legal profession is practised within large corporate law firms has made it very difficult to make any major change in the fee system without any substantial change in the internal practices of these firms.

Institutional explanation for law firm practices—internal focus

In order to understand the constraints the law firms face in changing their billing practices, a set of fundamental questions must be answered that focus on other practices of corporate law firms. Which practices for pricing, billing, compensation, and ownership operate simultaneously in maintaining the existing conventions? What kind of fundamental changes could foster efficient and effective corporate legal services for their clients as well as for the firms themselves?

The period between 1950 and 1990, which is sometimes called the golden age in law practice, brought great prosperity to the practice of corporate law but also a set of intricate practices that are highly institutionalized and very resistant to change in delivering their services and building their professional human capital. Corporate law firms experimented and developed four institutional practices, which I call the four pillars of law practice, involving pricing, compensation, and ownership as well as their billing practices. These practices also represent the business model that evolved within the profession to sustain the viability of corporate law firms. As Table 6.2 points out, in the golden age, certain experiments evolved into institutionalized conventions: cost-plus pricing, hourly billing, deferred compensation through partnership, and tournament-based ownership. While these institutional conventions have some fundamental advantages, they have also imposed substantial disadvantages for clients, law firms, and their attorneys. Both the benefits and the costs are natural products of an internally defined economic model of law firms where pricing and billing practices serve to support internal compensation and ownership requirements (Kummel 1996). Below, I describe each of these practices and how they are closely interconnected.

Table 6.2 The institutional logic of law firm economics

Law firm practices	Dominant practice	Advantages	Disadvantages
Billing practices	Hourly billing	Provides a simple mechanism that resembles an employment contract	Provides opportunities to raise the price of legal services and leads to agency problems
Pricing practices	Cost-plus pricing	Provides simple mechanism that can be linked to attorneys' hours	Ignores market factors and potentially shifts risk to clients
Compensation practices	Deferred compensation to future years based on seniority/ partnership	Reduces the need for extensive monitoring and increases the future commitment of firm's attorneys	Produces rigid labour costs and pricing that cannot take into account market changes
Ownership practices	Tournaments for promotion to partnership	Creates active internal labour markets and promotes internal cohesion among partners	Potentially wastes expensive human capital and creates a vicious circle of growth not responsive to market forces

Billing practices: cost-plus pricing

Cost-plus pricing dominates the market for corporate legal services by offering law firms a supposedly simple and stable source of income. Cost-plus pricing incorporates five elements: (*a*) personnel expense, (*b*) overhead expense, (*c*) partner income, (*d*) realized billing hours, and (*e*) market price (or billing rate). A basic cost-plus price formula to calculate the average billing rate for law firms is:

$$\text{Billing Rate} = \frac{\text{Personnel Expenses} + \text{Overhead Expenses} + \text{Partner Income}}{\text{Realized Hours}}$$

In this formula, the billing rate is the average hourly fee at a target level of realized hours which produces the desired level of partner incomes assuming a specified level of personnel expense and overhead. Billing rates usually vary considerably by geographic market, law firm, practice area, and attorney's expertise and seniority. Realized hours are the hours worked and paid for by clients. Partner income consists of law firms' profit in excess of partners' base compensation. The target level of partner income reflects the number of partners, the base compensation, and related local market factors. Personnel expense consists of the firms' employment costs for partners, associates, paralegals, and staff, including salary, benefits, and other employment costs. Overhead expense includes facilities, equipment, materials, and other operating costs. Under cost-plus pricing, target billing rates are calculated based on the costs and the desired profit. Cost-plus pricing appeals to law firms for three major reasons. First, it is conceptually simple to calculate. Second, it suggests a presumed predictability of income per partner. Third, it implies a growing market for legal services.

Many billing rate formulas similar to the one presented above exist in practice. Altman Weil Inc., one of the most successful consulting firms in the area of law firm management, suggests for instance, the following formula (Bower 2004). In this analysis, all expenses are classified as either personnel or overhead.

Minimum Billing Rate =

$$\frac{\text{Target Revenue for the Lawyer (i.e. Lawyer Salary + Lawyer Overhead + Profit)}}{\text{Realization Rate} \times \text{Expected Hours Worked}}$$

Their research shows that what influences this minimum billing rate is the specialty, experience, firm size, and position (partner or associate). As commonly applies, under this formula, attorneys are expected to generate fees that are equal to three times their compensation (i.e. the rule of thirds) (Samuelson and Jaffe 1990).

Compensation practices: deferred compensation

Research has shown that deferred compensation has been an effective means of long-term sharing of human capital in law firms (Gilson and Mnookin 1985). In order to create an internal balance between risk-sharing and incentives, law firms have traditionally compensated their attorneys through the use of seniority and productivity. Under this institutionalized system, law firms have kept about one-third of the revenues generated by their associates as profits and transferred them to their partners as deferred compensation. In return, the associates received the implicit promise that they would be at the receiving end when they become partners.

In a compensation system based purely on seniority, attorneys' base salary and their share of law firm profits are a function of the seniority level that rises in lockstep to give senior attorneys the full advantage of the system's risk-sharing capability (Gilson and Mnookin 1985). On the other hand, in a compensation system based purely on productivity, attorneys' share of law firm profits reflect their direct contributions to the firm in terms of hours billed by each attorney. Based on his survey of the legal compensation literature, Kummel (1996) reports, 'between 1975 and 1985, large law firms using seniority compensation declined from 75 per cent to 25 per cent. Productive partners, those attracting clients and working long hours, often perceived seniority systems as favouring the least energetic and capable, thereby creating barriers to profit seeking behaviour by partners and associates' (p. 386). Even though market forces have pushed the law firms away from deferred compensation and provided incentives to implement alternative compensation schemes (Cotterman 2001), law firms maintained the basic logic of this institutional practice because it not only facilitated a sense of stability and trust with their clients but also rewarded their most loyal attorneys.

Ownership practices: partnership tournaments

An important component of deferred compensation has been the promotion to partnership through the up-or-out system which rewards merit within the firm. Galanter and Palay (1991), who coined the term 'tournament of lawyers', used the idea to explain why large corporate law firms continue to grow.

The tournament system enables law firms to create an active internal labour market for human capital without expensive monitoring costs. The opportunity of promotion to the partnership offers associates a strong incentive to contribute their labour and create human capital, especially where the firm follows a policy of up-or-out promotion. Consequently, law firms can effectively increase their leverage ratios without increasing their monitoring costs. Furthermore, the system promotes internal cohesion among partners and helps maintain stable relationships with their clients (Heinz and Laumann 1978).

While there is still an ongoing debate about the theoretical logic of partnership tournaments (Rutherglen and Kordana 1998; Spurr and Sueyoshi 1994; Wilkins and Gulati 1998), the probability of becoming a partner has declined considerably in the last three decades. At least among the elite law firms of New York, the probability was about 25 per cent in the 1970s, and in 1990s it was about 19 per cent (Kummel 1996). As shown in

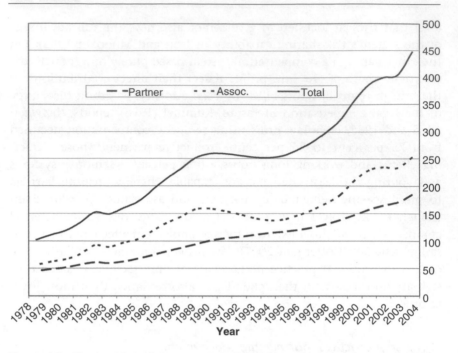

Figure 6.3 The growth in the average size of top 250 corporate law firms in the USA

Figure 6.3, corporate law firms have continued to grow considerably in the last twenty-five years. In the mid-1980s, *BusinessWeek* considered firms with more than 800 lawyers a mega firm (Glaberson 1986). Today the average size of the top ten firms is about 1,780. Most of the economic fluctuations of these decades were buffered by the associates. By changing their leverage ratios, law firms managed to grow their partnership at a steady rate while the associates carried the burden of economic fluctuations.

As presented in Table 6.2, the institutional practices of cost-plus pricing, hourly billing, deferred compensation, and the tournament ownership structure provide a tightly integrated system that is very difficult to untangle. Most of the recent attempts to institute new alternatives to the billable hours have failed partly because of the resilience of this integrated system. As an internally focused business model, the traditional partnership model has been able to sustain itself against most forces (Greenwood and Empson 2003).

It is important to point out here that these institutional practices also impose clear limitations on attempts by law firms to respond to the changes in their economic environment and their relationships with their corporate clients. As shown in Table 6.2, these practices complicate the existing conflict of interest between the law firms, their clients, and their attorneys. Corporate clients seek quick solutions to minimize their transaction costs and legal fees are a cost without any direct revenue benefits. In contrast, law firms seek resource intensive assignments when each activity increases firm profit in a cost-plus pricing system. Finally, attorneys know that each billable hour increases their short-term compensation and long-term partnership status within their firms. Thus, the system produces rigid labour and price structures that are difficult to modify under changing client demands.

Alternatives for the future

Today's corporate law firms are constantly pressured to replace the prevailing institutionalized system of billing practices and to develop a new business model to manage corporate law firms more effectively (Kummel 1996). Corporate clients constantly demand reductions in the cost of legal services, and at the same time, firms' attorneys demand fair compensation for their legal expertise. For the time being, most of the changes proposed have focused on a single aspect of a highly institutionalized system, that is fee structures, rather than on developing new models for the overall management of corporate law firms (Trotter 1997).

With respect to billing practices, numerous new models have been developed within the profession (Calloway and Robertson 2002). Table 6.3 lists a variety of alternative billing practices identified by the Task Force of the Committee on Lawyer Business Ethics Committee (ABA) in 1998. The report by the Committee admits, however, that hourly fee arrangements are still the most dominant model and less than 25 per cent of all corporate legal work uses these alternative arrangements (1999: 188).

These proposals fail to take into account the possible repercussions of alternative fee systems on other elements of a law firm's operations. Although everyone agrees that the traditional hourly billing method is under attack, and that sophisticated corporate clients are not willing to accept traditional methods—it is not possible to establish a more diverse billing system without also rethinking pricing, compensation, and ownership practices. As already explained, the dominant billing practices are a by-product of law practice and law firm structure that have evolved

Table 6.3 Descriptions of common alternative billing practices

Alternative fee arrangements	Description
Based on Modified Hourly Fee	
Blended hourly rate	Rate applies to all hours billed on a matter
Capped fee	Billing based on time but with a maximum total fee
Budgets	Agreed number of hours in advance
Firm estimates	Establishment of a time table and total cost
Discounted hourly rates	Across the board reduction in standard fees
Volume rates	Varying hourly rates depending on the size of engagement
Blended rates	Through negotiations a single hourly rate is established for all attorneys
Contingency-based Rates	Inclusion of success fees on top of reduced hourly charges
Incentive billing	
Value billing	Billing based on the value of services to clients
Cost-plus arrangements	Based on estimated cost of future services rendered
Stock or other investment in clients	Alternative payment arrangements involving stock options
Flat Fee Arrangements	
Task-based flat fees	Charging predetermined amount for each defined task
Percentage fee	Legal fees set as fixed percentage of transaction value
Loaned lawyer	Firm loans a lawyer on the firm's payroll to its client (to work exclusively)
Other Variations	
Mixed billing	Through negotiations different billing mechanisms are used for different stages
Teaming arrangements	Forming teams of in-house and outside counsel who have different specializations

as a logical consequence of internally focused risk-sharing and incentive mechanisms. Unless the totality of the system is taken into account, no creative billing practice could reshape the firms' client relationships and generate sustainable revenues.

Thus, any proposed model should emphasize the ways in which firms can transform themselves from an internally focused structure to a more externally focused one in order to serve their markets. As Kummel argues, many of the costs of the conventional business model are a by-product of firms' internal focus (Kummel 1996: 396). Therefore, any proposed model should be externally rather than internally driven in setting up the incentives and the risk-sharing arrangements. They should be able to provide (*a*) cost efficient legal services for clients with sustainable long term revenues for law firms, and (*b*) cost efficient sources of labour and human capital for law firms with market-based annual incomes for their attorneys.

As with any other professional services, legal services can be divided into four major product groups: brains, experience-based, brand name, and commodity (Maister 1997). A particular service mix has a direct impact on the type of human resources needed, the work arrangements necessary to deliver the service, and the nature of the internal compensation practices to support these choices. This is where pricing of legal services requires more sophistication than simply having differentiated billing rates for various attorneys; it would influence the revenue stream of the firms directly.

Careful attention must also be given to the ways the traditional compensation and ownership practices are reconfigured within an externally focused firm. Law firms usually rely on four distinct types of compensation structures: seniority, productivity, performance, and hybrid. In the past twenty years, a majority of law firms shifted compensation of partners and, to a limited degree, associates from seniority to productivity. Rather than being strictly correlated to tenure, compensation is now correlated to individual performance, mostly in the form of billable hours. The problem with these schemes, however, is that the definition of performance incorporates only a limited view of attorneys' value and contribution to their firms. Attorneys contribute to their firms through finding new clients, minding the business of their clients, and grinding the work for the clients (Nelson 1988). Any sustainable performance measure must take into account the division of labour established within the firm, the career patterns of the associates, and the ownership structure of the firm. Incentive compensation must be available and known to the attorneys of the firm in order to promote their contributions, vital to the success of firm, such as its reputation, the quality of its services, and its brand name. As internally focused entities, law firms have traditionally concentrated on maintaining internal equity in their compensation practices which value seniority and productivity. In today's environment, however, the compensation should be externally competitive and internally transparent.

Equally important is the balancing of the incentives and risk-sharing when it comes to the ownership practices. Law firms end up paying a substantial premium to defer compensation. By design, deferred partner income must be large enough to offset the limited probability of achieving partnership status. With partnership rates of 10 to 20 per cent, a substantial majority of associates do not expect to be partners for a variety of reasons (Wilkins and Gulati 1998). Thus, the lure of future profits from partnership is no longer a potential incentive for all associates (Empson, this volume). For those attorneys who would like to take the partnership track, however, the incentive might not be there if the rewards of partnership were not large enough to assume this risk.

When an external focus is instituted, the cost of promotion to partnership tournaments becomes very apparent for two reasons. First, the up-or-out system of career management results in high training costs as law firms replace productive but unwanted labour. Second, broad ownership participation incurs high costs by distributing large rewards to many partners. Consequently, law firms are forced to consider constant changes in their human capital planning that could be expensive in human capital development and in lost revenue streams.

Many law firms have responded to these concerns by creating new classes of membership such as junior associates, senior associates, permanent associates, of counsel attorneys, non-equity partners, equity partners, senior partners, and managing partners (Galanter and Palay 1994). These changes, however, have not stopped lateral hiring and movement of partners in groups to other law firms. It may be time for law firms to rethink their ownership system and to consider reorganizing themselves as professional corporations. This would make it possible for the firms to have a much broader ownership distribution with different ownership interests. Some practitioners as well as law firm consultants have been arguing that the partnership has lost its purpose and must be replaced with a risk-management mechanism based on the principles of strictly limited participation, and substantial capital investment (Ehrlich 1993). These recommendations are based on the assumption that while many attorneys are competent to manage the legal work of their law firms, only a limited number of them need to be owners or managers (Kummel 1996). In addition, when there is a fair market non-deferred compensation system established within the firm, the economic appeal of ownership would diminish and only those senior attorneys, who are willing and able to exchange their own financial and human capital for a diversified portfolio of legal investments, would participate in the ownership system. Such an ownership structure would eventually reorganize the financial rewards within law firms away from legal ownership and towards legal employment.

Conclusions: the future of law firm practices

The historical narrative and the theoretical arguments presented in this chapter point to one inevitable conclusion. Today's corporate law firms are going through major transformations not only in their billing practices but also in their internal structure and in their pricing strategies. As in any transition period, we expect to see a lot of experimentation and the introduction of diverse new practices within the highly institutionalized field of law. Ultimately, these experimentations should produce a new stable equilibrium for the profession, for the corporate law firms, and for the careers of attorneys. In some sense, the corporate law firms, as well as their clients, have a unique opportunity to be involved in an ongoing experiment that will shape the future of law practice for the years to come.

In order to be successful, however, these new practices must be accompanied by three fundamental developments: first, a renewed managerial focus on revenue generation rather than billable hours; second, a better understanding of the role of pricing and branding in revenue generation; and third, a critical examination of the organizational capabilities needed for revenue generation within law firms. In a world where there is growing sophistication on the part of client firms in planning, managing, and controlling legal costs, law firms need to understand how to price the value of their services independently of the tenure of their lawyers working on a case, or the billing rates set through a traditional budgeting process. This can only be done if law firms reduce their focus on billable hours and distinguish revenue generation from partners' profits and associates' compensation.

In 2004, *The American Lawyer* (AMLAW) magazine asked some of the most influential people in the legal profession to look ahead twenty-five years and predict some of the most important developments in the profession or business of law. Mark Chandler (Vice President of legal services and General Counsel of Cisco Systems) and Joseph Dilg (Managing Partner, Vinson & Elkins) emphasized the evolution of the law firm business model and the need for 'reducing the role of the billable hour as the organizing principle of the law firm.'

Such a shift requires an intimate understanding of how the clients assess the value of legal services and how their clients' businesses actually work. As John Carroll, Regional Managing Partner of the Americas at Clifford Chance states in the same article, 'The greatest area of dysfunction in the current practice of law is the degree to which the interests of law firms and the interests of clients are in competition. In the next quarter-century, we should expect that clients and law firms mature their relationships to a point of far greater alignment.' The development of such a new compact, however, requires a new business model of revenue generation within law firms. Corporate law firms need to have a fresh look at how their firms produce revenues, and the importance of price and brand in this process, in addition to the management of attorney costs. We need to learn from other businesses how these are successfully managed. The business world has learnt the hard way that revenue generation is an intricate by-product of managing pricing, brands, and service development. Senior management of corporate law firms need to have a similar focus on what influences their clients' value propositions and the price drivers that influence their decisions.

Finally, corporate law firms must establish new revenue building capabilities within their firms. These capabilities require the development of a supporting organization and related managerial practices. One important lesson the corporate world has learnt about pricing is that developing the right pricing strategy for higher revenues requires the effective integration of different functions such as marketing, finance, operations, and research and development (Docters et al. 2004). This is also true for corporate law firms. It is imperative that different practice areas or units within firms learn to work together in developing service portfolios, new service pricing and new managerial routines to coordinate these activities.

The way these fundamental issues are debated and the solutions proposed will ultimately have a profound impact on the lives of individual lawyers, law firms in general and the legal profession as a whole.

7

Your capital

Building sustainable value: a capital idea

Stephen Mayson
Nottingham Law School, The Nottingham Trent University

Introduction

Historically, lawyers have not needed to think very much, or in a very sophisticated way, about the value of their businesses. Equity partners in professional partnerships have usually invested capital in the firm, and may look to banks and other lenders for help with financing premises, equipment, and working capital. There has been a predominantly internal focus on investment and valuation, with most partners expecting only the return of their contributed capital and any undrawn profits. The disappearance of goodwill from the vast majority of law firm balance sheets has removed the prospect of capital appreciation that can be realized by a departing partner. Further, external ownership has generally not been permitted, and only limited external investment has been allowed (if at all) by the professional rules in most jurisdictions. There has therefore been little reason to look at law firms as outside investors might.

But pressures are mounting in the world of legal practice. Competition has become more acute and less localized. Markets have segmented as clients and competitors have become more sophisticated. Greater size, specialization, practice diversity, geographic reach, consolidation through merger and acquisition, and reliance on technology, have combined to increase the need for finance in the legal sector. At the same time, increasing attention to productivity and profitability has curtailed the number of partnership opportunities in many firms as they have focused on managing for profit and performance and have taken more active steps to control their equity base (see Leblebici, this volume). Further, where once partners in law firms might have come from families with personal wealth, now partners are likely to come from more varied backgrounds and may need to borrow to invest. Finally, limits on borrowing capability could well require some law firms in the future to seek external funding. For example, more firms might follow the example of Clifford Chance, which, in December 2002, raised (and later repaid) US$150 million in the US private placement market—the largest amount ever borrowed in the capital markets by a law firm. Some might even be tempted by an IPO.

In the UK, the implementation of the Clementi Review (Clementi 2004; Department for Constitutional Affairs 2005) heralds more extensive external investment and ownership. Already, private equity funds are showing an active interest in investing in law firms as soon as they are able to do so, and there are conversations about possible IPOs. External ownership has been possible in South Africa and Australia for some time. Such initiatives encourage a more sophisticated understanding of the value of law firms— particularly if ownership shares are eventually to be traded in private or public markets.

There are three circumstances in which the value of a law firm as a going concern should be explored (ignoring non-business-related issues, such as divorce settlements): (a) the admission of new partners, either by promotion or lateral recruitment—the new owners should be interested in understanding what it is they are moving into and investing in, (b) the merger and acquisition of law firms—the relative value and fit of the respective firms should be explored, and (c) the possibility of external ownership or investment—where this is possible the new owners or investors need to understand in depth what it is they are acquiring or investing in.

Some professional service firms, such as investment banks, surveyors and advertising agencies, may have a valuation derived from their position as quoted companies. In this chapter, I explore what drives the value of law firms where presently there is no market. What makes them an attractive proposition for investment or ownership? Why are some firms seen to be worth more than others? Would partners in law firms benefit from adopting a different perspective on their businesses?

This chapter adopts the viewpoint of a prospective investor or owner of a law firm. The objective is to investigate what might drive their perception of the firm's value in order to gain insights that are of value to the current owners. As professional regulators explore the potential competitive benefits of new and wider opportunities for ownership and investment, now is an appropriate time to explore ways in which lawyers can manage the value of their businesses and convince others of that value.

My contention is that, even if the current owners of a law firm cannot or do not intend to seek external ownership or financing, the discipline of structuring or running their business from the standpoint of an outside investor will, first, improve the business for themselves and others who follow and, second, position the firm favourably if the rules are amended in their jurisdiction or if they change their minds.

In this chapter, I present a framework for analysing the value and sustainability of law firms. I suspect that many partners in law firms are already intuitively aware of many of the dimensions explored here; and those who might consider investing in a law firm will also be conscious of many relevant issues. The key to value lies in creating a sustainable firm—in which all owners and investors (current and future, external or internal) should be interested. The framework discussed here provides a structure and language for analysing and assessing that sustainability, which both supports and goes beyond intuition and instinct. It provides a basis for investigation and action.

A capital viewpoint

It is trite to say that law firms are 'people businesses'. Of course they are, but they are also much more than that. Financiers, accountants, and economists often think in terms of 'capital': a law firm's balance sheet is a statement of its financial and physical capital. These concepts are well developed and understood. But although they provide a starting point in assessing value, they say nothing about the firm's people, its client relationships, its reputation or brand value, or many other things that contribute directly to its success, competitive advantage, profit, and value.

To adopt and pursue the capital viewpoint, in this chapter I identify three further forms of capital that, taken together, encapsulate these intangibles: human, social, and organizational capital. All law firms have these types of capital which, combined with financial and physical capital, provide the basis of their competitive advantage, profitability, longevity, and value. Of course, different firms have them to different degrees, in different combinations, and develop and manage them with varying levels of success. Understanding these forms of capital better, and learning how they work together, will provide insights into what exactly underpins the firm's competitive and financial success, and so allow partners in law firms to position the firm more attractively for either expanded ownership or investment.

Valuation

Rather than the somewhat narrow view of value that law firms have traditionally adopted, valuation theory relevant to unquoted professional service firms (see, e.g., Pratt, Reilly, and Schweihs 1998) suggests many different possible bases of valuation—including a multiple of revenues and the discounted cash flow method. On closer examination, however, all of them fundamentally turn on just two dimensions: the volume of the firm's 'economic income', and the perceived sustainability of that income. The evaluation of sustainability will be manifest, for example, in the multiple of revenues, or in the discount rate used—in both cases reflecting the assessed degree of risk or uncertainty in the persistence of the firm's economic income. Valuation theory thus potentially shifts attention away from simply generating maximum economic income to an equal interest in its sustainability—that is, to both short-term and long-term issues.

When those on the outside of a business assess its financial success by reference to its profitability, they assume that the various stakeholders in the firm have been appropriately rewarded and that there is residual income that belongs to the entity of 'the firm'—that is, to its owners. In many businesses, the owners, investors, and workers are different people; in the traditional partnership structure of law firms, they are not. It is therefore important to distinguish the different roles of the same people. In this sense, it is illuminating to divide up net profit and allocate returns to the different roles of equity partners. There are three roles or stakes to be rewarded out of net profit: (a) investors—as part of net profit distribution, some firms allocate interest at the market rate on partners' contributed financial capital as representing a reasonable measure of the return on that capital, (b) workers—partners' stakes as working lawyers can be recognized as the market rate of salary that would be needed to replace them with appropriately experienced employed lawyers, and (c) owners, entrepreneurs or risk-takers—after the allocations to the finance and labour stakes, the residual amount of net profit (or loss) represents the return to the equity partners for their stake as owners of the business. Those on the outside of the firm would normally regard this as its true 'profit'—in other words, as *the firm*'s income due to its owners as a return on the risk of being in business.

Many current approaches to profit-sharing in law firms confuse these rewards. Unless they are operating a pure eat-what-you-kill model, most partners tend to see all of the firm's net profit as theirs without considering how much was generated by collective effort rather than purely personal contribution; indeed a pure lockstep model promotes and celebrates this attitude. Whatever model is used it is often difficult to see which of the various stakes a partner has in the firm is being rewarded and in what proportions. For as long as the partners retain all three roles, there will be no real incentive to distinguish the allocation of rewards. However, if partners claim too much remuneration as working lawyers, they will reduce the firm's true profit and potentially its valuation and attractiveness as an investment.

The relative ability of the firm or individuals to claim the economic returns is based on the degree of dependence that each has on the other. If the firm is too dependent on its partners and staff, this will either reduce its economic income, or negatively affect its perceived sustainability (or both). The key point here is not that firms cannot exist without individuals: it is self-evident that they cannot. What matters is the extent to which a law firm is more than the sum of its parts—whether it can be seen as a separate, continuing entity with its own income independent of the individuals who currently constitute it.

In some law firms contributions to productivity and value are based on the personal knowledge, contacts, and effort of individual partners. There may be little commitment of individuals to, or recognition of, the firm as a separate entity. In some firms, partners may feel that they *are* the firm—that there is nothing which is greater than the sum of the parts. Identification with the firm may be minimal. This is a psychological issue that is not necessarily related to the size of the firm—even the largest law firms have partners who behave individualistically without recognizing a larger entity that is the firm whose interests take precedence over personal preferences. This is the outcome of failing, or not feeling the need, to distinguish the different roles or stakes that the same individual has in the business (a theme explored by Empson, this volume).

I referred above to the variable meaning of economic income. What is treated as the measure of the firm's economic income varies with the method of valuation. In the popular legal press, a law firm's success tends to be based on its profitability—particularly net profit per partner.

However, in a valuation, net profit will rarely be the appropriate measure of economic income and, indeed, a firm's economic income may be a significantly different amount from its accounting net profit. For example, a valuation based on a multiple of revenues would treat fee income as the appropriate measure of economic income. For a discounted cash flow valuation, the firm's 'true profit' will be used, but further adjusted to reflect cash movements. This will involve, for example, adding back depreciation (an accounting entry that does not use cash) and deducting net capital expenditure (outgoings of cash that are not accounted for in the firm's profit and loss statement), and perhaps adjusting for the payment or receipt of exceptional or non-recurring items such as damages awarded in legal actions or insurance receipts.

Valuation, then, turns on two dimensions: the volume of economic income and its perceived sustainability. The volume can be optimized by achieving more economic income compared with rivals. The perceived sustainability of that income is related to the perceived stability and endurance of the firm itself, its key people, and its work flow. Put another way, potential owners or investors make a risk assessment. Their key concern should be how long it might take to recoup their investment: the lower the firm's economic income or the less sustainable it seems to be, the longer it will take and so the higher the risk. If the risk is higher, a new investor will either expect a high return quickly, or will take a larger ownership share for the investment in order to exercise more control and to claim a higher share of the return.

Underlying tension

Valuation has the potential to expose an underlying tension between individuals on the one hand and the firm as a collective entity on the other (see also Empson, this volume). As already discussed, a firm will be judged to be more valuable if its economic income is high and that income is perceived to be sustainable. The perceived sustainability of the firm's income results from either building a flow of work (from tied-in client relationships and reputation) or building an 'organization' that is perceived as a continuing entity, separate from those individuals who at any given time comprise it (or from both). So, if the firm is perceived to be dependent on key partners who could leave the firm, taking relationships and client work with them, the sustainability of the firm's income could be doubted and its value depressed.

Investors should therefore be concerned about the security of the firm's revenue flow, and about who has the greater claim to it (the firm or individuals). Within a partnership the partners may not be too concerned about the distinction between the firm's and individuals' income. Subject only to internal profit-sharing disputes, all income will be regarded as belonging to individuals. However, where external ownership is or may become a possibility, it is illuminating to understand what is attractive to the external market. From conversations with private equity houses, it has become clear that their initial preference could well be for law firms with the following features: they have contracts for work (to suggest a flow of fee income and perhaps to reduce its volatility), they have no or minimal dependence on 'prima donna' partners (to increase stability), they have plans for expansion and succession (to demonstrate sustainability), and they have effective leadership and management (to encourage follow-through and continuity). These features are thought to increase the funds' chances of a viable exit route, and would probably favour larger firms whose work relies more on processes and routines than professional virtuosity.

This view may change over time as external investors become more attuned to the spectrum of legal practice. At one end, we find those practice areas based more on repeated transactions executed through predefined processes (e.g. volume transfers of real estate); at the other end are those practice areas that are inherently based on the individual input of specialist lawyers (e.g. corporate tax advice). Certainly, process-driven practices might find it easier to deliver relatively stable (and possibly contracted) income, minimal dependence on individuals, effective management, and demonstrated succession through the substitutability of process operators over time. But the necessary dependence of expertise-driven practices on technical specialists should not inevitably disadvantage them. Sustainability for this type of practice could be built on the demonstrated ability of the firm to 'tie' its specialists to the firm (by creating an attractive and supportive working environment) and by developing a firm reputation or brand that enhances the prospects of these specialists' being able to develop and maintain client relationships and interesting work.

What valuation theory suggests, then, is that three dimensions of the business are potentially very important: individuals (with their expertise, experience, and personal reputation), relationships (with clients and referral sources, and in the wider business and social community), and the firm itself as an organization (with its collective reputation, management, systems, processes, and the like). Adopting the terminology of capital, these three dimensions can in turn be referred to as human, social, and organizational capital.

Five types of capital

There are, therefore, five forms of capital relevant to the value of a law firm: financial, physical, human, social (Coleman 1990), and organizational (Tomer 1987). No form of capital is an island: the interrelationships among them are a vital part of the dynamics of competition and valuation.

Capital and ownership

Generally, if a firm owns capital, it can be valued and included in a transfer of ownership. But for valuation purposes, it is important not to take an unduly literal or legalistic view of 'ownership'. Not all of the forms of capital discussed can be owned—even though one might say that they 'belonged' to someone. For example, we can say that an individual or a law firm 'has a reputation' and that this reputation belongs to them, but it is stretching the point to say that they 'own' it. In fact, much of what is important to a law firm's productivity, profitability, and sustainability may belong to others. So, critical legal knowledge, or the experience of dealing with certain transactions, might belong to an individual partner, rather than the firm. A firm's value may therefore depend on capital that it does not (and cannot) own.

Fortunately perhaps, the essential issue for valuation is not so much ownership as whether the relevant resources are *embedded* in the firm in some way that gives the firm access to them. This might include, but is not limited to, ownership, and incorporates other ways of associating the capital with the firm (such as contractual rights of access, or knowledge embedded in know-how systems, or as organizational routines).

Where ownership is not possible, then, firms need *access* to capital belonging to others. For example, an individual's knowledge, skills, experience, and reputation belong to the individual concerned. Consequently, a firm's structural and contractual arrangements will need to confer as secure an access to those resources as possible (bearing in mind that contracts and restrictions will still not prevent key people from leaving, and that the best way of securing continuing access may be to create an environment that motivates them and to which they feel committed).

This has been graphically illustrated over the years. Recently, for example, the advertising agency Lowe Worldwide lost Tesco as a client. Tesco had been a client of the agency for more than fifteen years, and was believed to be the agency's largest account (indeed it is one of the largest advertisers in the UK). In a situation reminiscent of Saatchi & Saatchi ten years earlier, one of Lowe Worldwide's founders left to form a new agency, and the retailer decided to follow. These illustrations highlight one of the challenges that pervades professional service firms, and that may have significant consequences for valuation; both economic income and perceived sustainability can be jeopardized by the departure of key people.

For the most part, what has been recorded on firms' balance sheets and subject to valuation has been assets (capable of ownership and transfer)— particularly financial and physical capital. However, as already discussed, much of the value of a law firm is derived from other types of capital which are not all capable of being owned in the legal sense and are not recorded on its balance sheet. Consequently, both balance sheet capital and off-balance sheet capital are important to the firm, but there are significant differences between them. These off-balance sheet forms of capital play a vital role in demonstrating the sustainability of the firm's income and of the firm itself. That they cannot be precisely measured and accounted for does not make them less important—and certainly no less valuable.

Human capital

The notion of 'human capital' has long been used to refer to a broad range of knowledge, skills, and other attributes vested in an individual. The unit of analysis for human capital is the individual: human capital is always embedded in and belonging to individuals. However, much of what staff in a law firm learn and do is specific to the firm and its clients. So, although human capital can never belong to the firm, it is often in the collective interest of the firm for it to invest in encouraging staff to develop their human capital either more deeply through specialization or more broadly into new areas of expertise. Indeed, from a competitive point of view, the better or deeper the know-how of the firm's staff, the more likely the firm is to have an advantage over its rivals.

Given the nature of human capital, dependence on individuals is inevitable if knowledge and experience are to be applied in the delivery of the firm's advice and services. The fundamental issues for the firm and its value are the development, retention, and replication of that knowledge and experience, and its distribution (i.e. the extent to which it remains proprietary to individuals, or has been disseminated and embedded within the firm and so has become more widely accessible).

Social capital

Whereas human capital is embedded in individuals, social capital is embedded in relationships (a point explored by Uzzi, Lancaster, and Dunlap more fully in this volume). We cannot say that a relationship belongs to an individual or a firm because all relationships are at least two way. A partner might claim that he or she has a relationship with a client, but the client might see things differently. Social capital is not therefore within the sole control of either a firm or an individual. This is the principal reason why it is a separate form of capital rather than part of human or organizational capital.

Social networks are important to legal practice. They determine the nature and extent of client relationships, they give us access to contacts outside the firm; social dealings allow us to build up 'credit-slips' of favours that we have given to others that we might reasonably expect to be returned, give us access to information and business opportunities that might offer a competitive edge, they are vital to the development of common values and of trust. Uzzi, Lancaster, and Dunlap (this volume) demonstrate how economically valuable such external relationships can be to a law firm.

Relationships can be both *external* and *internal* to the firm. Internal social capital is therefore the network of relationships that partners and staff have with each other: the strength and effectiveness of this capital will determine how pleasant and efficient internal dealings are, who is able to influence others more easily or successfully, and who is trustworthy. The process of socialization described by Empson (this volume) leads to the creation of internal social capital. External social capital refers to relationships that those on the inside have with clients, suppliers, the community, and so on. Those partners with more extensive social networks or closer relationships may be more effective in developing business, gathering information, and harnessing support when it is needed, and are thus potentially more valuable to the business.

Social capital is important to a law firm's competitive advantage, efficiency, profitability, and sustainability: it oils the wheels of business (internally and externally), and is the foundation of the expression 'it's not what you know, but who you know'. It is important to valuation because the mobilization of social capital can increase economic income (by raising revenue or improving efficiency and profitability) and underpin a more sustainable business based on continuing relationships, common values, and trust. A firm with stronger, better, and more extensive social capital should be more valuable. Like human capital, a law firm cannot own social capital; but it can encourage or inhibit its development and use. Social capital does not just happen: as with any capital, it requires investment (time and effort) and should give a return (such as information, a returned favour, an opportunity, trust, or organizational efficiency).

In forming networks, lawyers can act either personally or on behalf of their firm—that is, they can develop and then call on relationships either in an individual or representative capacity (although one may lead to the other). Contacts that existed before they joined the firm are likely to be regarded as personal, and are perhaps more likely to survive any subsequent departure from the firm. Those that are formed as a result of being part of the firm may be regarded as representative, and may or may not survive departure.

Given that relationships can be formed and sustained in both personal and representative capacities, a critical issue for the firm to consider is what will motivate an individual to mobilize personal social capital for the benefit of the firm, and to channel the benefits of representative social capital to the firm rather than the individual. For example, Catherine, a corporate partner, may have spent time with a client as an in-house lawyer. The relationships that she develops become part of her social capital. When Catherine returns to the firm, she can choose whether or not to call on those relationships to secure work from a variety of sources within the client firm for, say, the real estate lawyers and litigators in the firm. Similarly, Peter, an employed personal tax lawyer, may have been introduced to a local accountant by a partner in the firm. When the accountant approaches Peter with potential client work relating to a corporate tax problem, he must decide whether to take it on personally (and increase his chances of meeting his targets) or to refer it to a partner for allocation to a more appropriate fee-earner.

A firm that encourages internal competition runs the risk of inhibiting the joint activity and mutual help that is crucial to the development of both internal and external social capital. In this context, Peter might therefore be tempted to make a decision for personal rather than collective benefit. Likewise, a firm that focuses unduly on chargeable time at the expense of marketing and networking activities, or restricts the costs that can be reclaimed from the firm for engaging in such activities, runs the risk that individuals will see their networking time as more for personal benefit than for the firm, and may be less inclined to mobilize those relationships in the firm's favour. Catherine might similarly make a decision based on personal interest. By keeping their relationships to themselves and being unwilling to share the benefits or products of their contacts with others inside the firm, Catherine and Peter would be doing nothing to contribute to the entity of the firm that is so important to increasing its value. Their firm then risks failing to persuade any new owners and investors that its continuing income is not disproportionately dependent on individuals and their personal networks.

Organizational capital

A valuation perspective requires a shift of emphasis from the personal to the collective, from the individual to the organization. The fifth form of capital therefore emphasizes the idea that there are resources that belong to the firm itself as a collective entity. Organizational capital is thus distinct from both human capital (which is embedded in individuals) and social capital (which is embedded in the relationships between individuals).

Some lawyers simply do not accept that there is anything that can be identified and characterized as the firm's as opposed to 'theirs'. Where this is the dominant view within a firm, the adopted measures of performance are likely to be those that emphasize personal or localized productivity and relationships.

Those who have difficulty with the concept of organizational capital usually regard their own individual performance and contacts as key to the firm's productivity and competitive success. For example, Tessa, a trust and estates practitioner, has built her practice on very close personal relationships with a local clientele and a significant degree of personal specialization in trusts, estates and tax law. She regards—perhaps with some justification—her human and social capital as being the real sources of new and continuing instructions. Nevertheless, unless Tessa is a sole practitioner, a firm still provides the context for her activity. The firm will have its own structure, culture, and reputation: they will make it easier for Tessa to continue to attract work and to deliver a good service to her clients. Though unarguably derived from the interaction and endeavours of individuals, the firm's structure, culture, and reputation cannot be said to belong to any entity other than to the firm itself.

Organizational capital can be identified in all law firms and does not belong to the firm's owners in any individual capacity. Investment in it can contribute to a firm's success, stability, and sustainability in different ways; what I described earlier as the firm's income (its true profit) is the return on that investment. Organizational capital can be regarded as relating to either or both of: (*a*) the *method* of delivering legal services (such as teams, knowledge management systems and routines), or (*b*) the *context* for that delivery (such as reputation and brand, culture, contracts, structure, and strategy).

Depending on where the firm's work falls on the spectrum from the inherently individual (expertise-driven) to the collective (collaborative or process-driven), certain aspects of organizational capital may be more or less important. Both method and context are influential in all types of practice. But for process-driven firms (e.g. those that focus on volume debt collection, residential real estate, and mortgage repossession cases supplied by bulk providers—particularly banks and other financial institutions—under medium-term contracts), method will focus more on standard documentation, routines, and possibly automated document assembly, and all aspects of context will be important. In these firms, there is evidently investment in physical capital (technology), human capital (fee-earners), and social capital (networking and relationships). But it is also easier to see in this type of practice the nature of the collective investments being made in the organization itself and in the coordination of its service delivery: contracts (for the supplies of case work and employed labour); systems and processes (to make more consistent, effective, and efficient use of the technology and people to deliver both quality and profit); structure (teams of fee-earners to handle the work appropriate to their processing specialization); and strategy and policies (to target and distribute new business).

These elements of organizational capital all increase the perceived stability and sustainability of the business; they are supplemented by two other elements—the firm's reputation and its culture—which add to that stability and sustainability. None of this capital can be said to belong to any individual: it is embedded in collective, cooperative, coordinated activity. In the case of such a 'process-driven' firm, its stock of organizational capital creates something that a potential owner or investor could assess and use to reach a judgement about the potential security of any investment. There is something which is distinct from and exceeds the sum of the human parts.

On the other hand, expertise-driven firms will focus their methods more on informal teams and communication as well as know-how and work product systems, and on the reputation and culture elements of context. These firms are often major commercial law firms handling a small number of large transactions. They might need to devote a significant number of partners and fee-earners to one deal, but all the issues of reputation, culture, organizational structure, teams and teamwork, processes, and business strategy, are equally relevant. In this instance, the processes will relate more to case or project management supported by good know-how and work product retrieval systems than to volume processing. In other words, they still have and need organizational capital. The question is not whether organizational capital exists or is necessary; rather, it is the difference of emphasis required to improve the firm's economic income or sustainability given the nature of its practice.

In the expertise firm, the emphasis is less on formal structure, contracts, volume processing, and knowledge systems, and more on teamwork and knowledge-sharing. Although teams can be formally designed as part of the firm's organizational structure (say, as departments or practice groups), informal teams can be just as effective—and often more so. Lawyers with common practices, clients, interests, or experiences may gravitate towards each other and create their own social group and, in a sense, their own knowledge management system (they are often referred to as 'communities of practice': see Wenger 1998; and Wenger, McDermott, and Snyder 2002). In other words, the management may be less structured and 'tight' than for the process-driven firm, but organizational capital is still required, embedded in the firm, and necessary to secure the effective and profitable delivery of legal services to clients.

The objective of the firm's managers in an expertise firm may well be to seek sustainability by investing in the emergence of a sympathetic structure and organizational culture, and of communities of practice, that are attractive even to 'maverick' performers—an environment that allows them considerable freedom and autonomy while providing mutual support and the sharing of know-how. In this way, the firm may, over time, build a strong reputation for serving such stars well and providing a positive and supportive environment: this may also increase the degree of commitment that the individualists have to the firm. This culture may then become a source of the firm's competitive advantage.

Lawyers can be particularly dismissive of organizational structure, regarding it as 'bureaucracy' and creating unnecessary costs. Certainly, creating and maintaining internal structures (such as departments and practice groups) carry both direct and opportunity costs. These structures are part of the division of labour and in law firms are usually intended to encourage, or reflect, specialization by service, client, market, or geography. They are also directly instrumental in the development and mobilization of internal social capital.

However, with specialization comes the need for across-the-firm coordination, and many of the costs of organization are attributable to coordinating mechanisms, such as managerial positions (e.g. head of department, group leader), procedures and standardization (e.g. standard form precedents), training and supervision, committees, meetings, and management information systems (e.g. client databases). Thus, the larger and more diverse the firm's business, the more complex—and therefore more costly—the firm's structure is likely to be (Mayson 1997; Mintzberg 1993). To a significant extent, these costs cannot be avoided. Changes of structure may also bear 'adjustment costs' as some of the human capital embodied in the firm's managers becomes obsolete, or management tasks change; and the firm may be forced to develop or recruit new managerial know-how to implement a new structure.

Further, teamwork, collective effort, and organizational efficiency do not just happen. Where there are a number of other people in the firm, serving a number of clients, there will be competing claims on resources as well as the prospect of overlap or gaps in the provision of advice and services. This will particularly be the case where different specialists need to serve the same clients—for example, the property or divorce needs of Tessa's high net-worth individuals or the corporate tax needs of Peter's clients. Organization—in the form of strategies, policies, and structures—remains at least desirable (if not inevitable and necessary) in order to coordinate the investment in resources and the provision of professional services. It is a distortion for Tessa or Peter to regard themselves as islands unconnected to others within the archipelago of the law firm.

Lawyers are right to be sceptical, but mistaken if they think that all structure and organization is unnecessary. Good structure and management results from investment, even though the direct costs inevitably

155

reduce profits: if this investment is not reflected in higher revenues or an improvement in perceived sustainability, economic income and the firm's value will be depressed.

Relationships between the forms of capital

There are relationships between the five forms of capital; one or more may be used to acquire, create, or gain access to another. For example, financial capital is used to acquire physical capital (cash or borrowings to acquire equipment), secure and develop human capital (agency fees and salaries to attract people, and training costs), provide access to social capital (usually through human capital, but possibly in the form of investments in relationships), and to create organizational capital (mainly by investing in systems, the firm's reputation, and the working environment).

Similarly, organizational capital will be created from the interaction of the other forms of capital. For instance, financial, physical, and human capital can create routines and organizational structures; human and social capital will create a culture, and will play a significant role in developing the firm's reputation; technology (physical capital) and system design and implementation (human capital) may also be needed to create, say, document assembly or know-how systems.

Organizational capital also provides access to all other forms of capital—including financial capital where a lender or investor may be swayed by the strength of the firm's reputation. It will also be influential in the development of new human capital (e.g. through training, manuals, and know-how systems, or through engagement in organizational routines) and social capital (e.g. through the creation of departments, teams, and communities of practice that encourage people to work together and communicate, or provision of networking opportunities based on the strength of the firm's reputation).

Making choices

As we have seen, valuation theory identifies two principal dimensions of valuation: the volume of the firm's economic income, and the perceived sustainability of that income. We should expect a firm with high-economic income and high-perceived sustainability to have the highest value. Valuation is thus influenced by the balance between these two factors. This balance should reflect the firm's strategy, as well as the attitude of the owners (particularly their preference for the short-term generation of income or longer-term investment), and will have implications for its capital-building activities.

The premise of this chapter is that an external standpoint would not focus just on maximizing income but would also require us to examine the entity of the firm and the sustainability of the firm and its income. Organizational capital is essential to this perspective: whatever the nature of the firm's practice, organizational capital plays a part (even though the emphasis on its components necessarily changes to reflect the requirements of a particular practice). From the outside, the strength of organizational capital holds the key to how strong and how well tied-in the other forms of capital are—particularly human and social capital.

But would external owners and investors evaluate organizational capital, and how would a firm demonstrate that it has it? I believe that both external and internal owners and investors do look at organizational capital—but do so intuitively. They do not have a name for it. They seek to understand the firm's dependence—on people, clients, suppliers, and so on; and they assess the degree of risk facing the firm resulting from those dependencies. Using the framework and language of organizational capital might make an investigation more rigorous.

Computing economic income is a tried and tested process. Assessing sustainability is less clear-cut. For many quoted businesses, the difference between market value and book value is the perceived value of the business' intangible assets and is represented by 'goodwill'. This additional value is an accounting entry arising from the exercising of business judgement and assigning a monetary amount to an opinion: it is a matter of judgement more than mathematics. The concept of organizational capital creates a potential typology for the elements of goodwill: it provides a basis for enquiry and risk assessment, and creates a structure for exercising judgement.

Organizational capital points to those factors that can assess dependence, longevity, and reputation. It concerns the extent to which human and social capital are embedded in and supported by the firm through culture, collective reputation, communities of practice, strategic context, motivation, structure, contracts, routines, knowledge management, and systems. If there is significant evidence of embedding, then there is something which can truly be called 'a firm' that is worth investing in; if there is not, the organization is a more or less empty, fragile, and less valuable shell. Organizational capital goes to the very heart of the firm's sustainability.

On this basis, it would be prudent to analyse a firm's organizational capital as the foundation for evaluating its goodwill. Over time, appropriate metrics may be developed to demonstrate and quantify the elements of organizational capital. In the meantime, enquiry and proxies may—and may have to—suffice. For example, league tables, market research, and client surveys may act as proxies for reputation or brand strength; personnel turnover, internal staff questionnaires, and associate surveys (such as those in *AMLAW* and *Legal Business*) may give insights into culture, staff stability, and motivation. There is still much work to be done on this, though the process started some time ago for some quoted companies with the idea of an 'invisible' balance sheet (see, e.g., Edvinsson and Malone 1997).

In principle, therefore, owners, investors, and managers would need to make choices about which dimensions of valuation—economic income, or perceived sustainability (or both)—promise the best route to a favourable valuation. They should then take the appropriate steps to accumulate, develop, or retain the different forms of capital that advance the firm's strategy and lead to, or preserve, that valuation.

Most law firms recognize human capital, but perhaps spend less time and attention building and managing social and organizational capital on behalf of the firm and for its benefit. Organizational capital will be a significant part of the capital structure of a firm because its effects are crucial to:

1. *Culture.* In general, an individualistic culture is less likely to be interested in the sustainability of the business, and more interested in securing maximum personal income and power based on the dependency of the firm on them. A collective culture will tend to manifest more elements and more depth of organizational capital.

2. *Rewards.* Individuals will always play a pivotal role in the context of a law firm as a know-how and relationship business: they bring and continue to develop human and social capital that can be applied for their own and the firm's benefit. But the key issue in the context of valuation becomes: who has the greater claim to the income generated—the individuals whose human capital was influential in productivity, or the firm whose organizational capital provided the context and support for the productivity of that human capital (see Gilson and Mnookin 1985; Leblebici, this volume)? The question is important because if the emphasis falls on human capital, then the

greater rewards will be claimed by the human repositories of that capital; whereas if the emphasis falls on organizational capital, then the rewards will be claimed by the firm for distribution among a number of stakeholders. If this is the case, there will be an entity to invest in.

3. *Strategy.* The firm's strategy must be consistent with its culture and the nature of its practice, and must be designed to deliver competitive advantage that secures its economic income and sustainability. However, the inherent nature of some forms of capital may not allow firms a free choice in meeting all competitive aspirations. For example, the so-called 'Magic Circle' firms in London and 'Charmed Circle' firms in New York enjoy a capital endowment built up over many years. Their ability to attract many of the best lawyers to work on the best deals for the best clients is the result of a particular combination of capital (especially human, social, and organizational) accumulated over time. It is now probably impossible for other firms to replicate the 'path through history' that these firms have taken and the ties that have bound one generation to another. As a result, these firms occupy a privileged and dominant position in the marketplace for legal services which their domestic rivals—however much they are able to invest—cannot now match. Put another way, the strategic groups or clusters identified by Sherer (this volume) have their own capital endowments that allow them to maintain their differences from other groups and clusters. Having made the right decisions at the right time (if only serendipitously), these firms have created barriers to entry for aspirant competitors: the forms of capital and the combination of them are critical to competitive advantage and future value.

4. *Mergers, laterals, and retention.* The rationale for many firms taking in lateral hires is the prospect of gaining access to the clients of the new recruits. However, experience also shows that, very often, the promised relationships fail to materialize as clients decide to stay with the recruit's original firm or take the opportunity to instruct a completely new firm and not follow the recruit. In a similar vein, law firm mergers can also fail to deliver the expected client benefits. In the language of this chapter, what clients do is attach significance to both the human capital of the individuals who move, and to the respective organizational capital of the old and new firms. If they find the new firm lacking or less credible, they will not always

follow the individual—however good their human capital. Similarly, if partners and staff currently within a firm feel that its organizational capital is weak or declining, or does not fit with the nature of their practice and aspirations, they may decide to move to another firm which they perceive to have stronger organizational capital (better strategy, reputation, culture, structure, and so on). Such an analysis may explain why over forty media and intellectual property lawyers left Denton Wilde Sapte in 2005 to join DLA Piper—the largest ever lateral movement in the UK.

Conclusions

Valuation theory identifies two principal dimensions of valuation: the volume of the firm's economic income and the perceived sustainability of that income. Five forms of capital play a role in driving both a relatively higher income and a perception of sustainability. For those who want a return of capital greater than that which they initially invested in the firm, there are two possible routes to realizing value.

The first is internal and more traditional. It relies on the admission of new partners (through promotion, lateral recruitment, or merger) who are willing to invest capital that reflects more than the book value of the business because they expect eventually to receive a direct benefit. This requires something akin to additional goodwill value (and is in turn likely to intensify the need for external funding). This chapter shows that the key to that additional value is an understanding of organizational capital that reduces dependence on individuals, and generates income and value for the firm itself as a separate entity. A firm that is disproportionately dependent on one or more key individuals who might leave, hold the firm to ransom, or claim too much of the firm's income as personal remuneration is inherently a less secure investment. Although law firms will remain necessarily dependent to some (often differing) degree on the human and social capital of its partners and staff, the perception of sustainability can be enhanced by demonstrating that the firm has developed, or is developing, its organizational capital. However, this can be undermined by individualized measurement and reward systems. Thus, for individuals with strong reputations and client followings to 'relinquish' income to the firm, they will need to see some value or benefit from organizational capital: the whole must exceed the sum of the parts. This is most likely to come from the strength of the collective reputation or brand, or its network of contacts and relationships, or possibly its work processes and support.

This leads to a second route to realizing value: attracting external ownership or investment. Although not universally possible, there are signs that governments and regulatory authorities are increasingly willing to regard legal practice as essentially a business service that needs to be freed (as they see it) from the anti-competitive shackles of self-regulation and professional restrictions on business models. In this sense, the customer network, infrastructure, brand value, and investment capability of a major consumer business (such as a retail bank, supermarket, insurance company, or membership organization) could yet prove sufficiently attractive to partners in some law firms to encourage them to accept external ownership or investment in their businesses in return for relinquishing some or all of their current equity ownership and rewards. As this happens, the external viewpoint explored in this chapter will become a reality. The same conclusions hold: external owners and investors will want to see law firms that are not dependent on individuals, but that generate income and value for the firm itself as a separate entity. They will be concerned to secure their investment through knowing that they have an exit route based on the attractiveness and 'marketability' of the firm as a sustainable entity independent of those who currently work in it.

Organizational capital is distinct from both human capital and social capital. Given that neither human nor social capital can be owned by the firm, organizational capital becomes an important (but often neglected or underestimated) contributor to sustainability and value. It provides either, or both of, a context (reputation, culture, contracts, structure, and strategy) or a method (teams, knowledge management, routines) for delivering legal services. These elements are all features of the organization rather than of any one or more individuals, and reduce the dependence of the firm on those individuals. Building this form of capital is a principal means of generating and preserving sustainable value.

8

Your competitors

Mapping the competitive space of large US law firms: a strategic group perspective

Peter D. Sherer
Haskayne School of Business, University of Calgary

Introduction

Strategists search out information to understand their rivals with the aim of defending and strengthening their firms' competitive positioning. In industries with numerous firms and many actual and potential rivals, gaining an understanding of rivalry presents a formidable challenge. The legal sector represents a prime example of this. To meet the challenge, I advocate using the theoretical insights and statistical tools that are found in the academic field of business strategy, specifically the approach known as the strategic group perspective. This approach to mapping the competitive space of large US law firms provides guidance on understanding the rivalry that exists among firms at a point in time and over time.

A strategic group represents a group of firms that resemble each other (Porter 1979). Members of a group share defining qualities and differ from other groups on those same attributes. Research that takes a strategic group perspective involves grouping firms on the basis of their likeness and then comparing firms within and across the differing groups. This research raises important theoretical questions and provides insights into such concerns as: what constitutes a strategic group, how strategic groups are measured, how firms 'behave' in a group, and what explains the stability or movement of firms across groups over time (McGee and Thomas 1986).

The literature on strategic groups is tied to a class of statistical tool known as cluster analysis. Cluster analysis procedures generally use simple mathematical measures of distance or likeness to group individual firms on the basis of how similar or dissimilar they are to one another (Aldenderfer and Blashfield 1984). The average numerical values on the attributes for the different groupings are then used to infer what the different clusters represent. While findings from cluster analysis often mirror views held in the field, a benefit of cluster analysis is that it can simultaneously analyse information on multiple dimensions of firms. It can, therefore, generate results that more fully capture the complexity of the competitive space in ways that might not have been expected. Firms which are commonly viewed as key competitors may, in fact, turn out to occupy a different competitive space and firms which are deemed very different may in fact be located within the same strategic group.

I demonstrate the value of a strategic group perspective by conducting cluster analysis on approximately 200 large US law firms for 1999 and 2003, thereby enabling me to examine trends during this important historical time. The data used in the cluster analysis are from *The American Lawyer* (*AMLAW*) 100 and 200 and *The National Law Journal* (*NLJ*) 250.

A number of the findings mirror observations held in the field, yet other findings are less expected and perhaps even surprising. The findings document the stability that occurs among what I label the 'circle of highly elite firms', firms like Cravath and Davis Polk. These firms almost all have their principal office in New York and a modest international presence. Very few firms are able to break through the barriers needed to enter into this elite group. The findings capture too what many in the field say: Baker & McKenzie is a unique firm. It gets its own cluster in both years. Its distinctiveness is reflected in its massive size, by law firm standards, and sizeable international presence. The findings also show that only a few firms have much of an international presence. Many large US law firms are regional or specialized players—relatively smaller firms with minimal international presence. Other firms occupy a potentially vulnerable position—they are neither small and specialized enough or large and powerful enough to stand still.

The strategic group analysis additionally reveals the important role that internationalization played among US law firms from 1999 to 2003. In 1999, a strong international presence (in addition to Baker & McKenzie) was reserved for a cluster of firms that included the international pioneers Altheimer & Gray, Cleary Gottlieb, Coudert Brothers, Shearman &

Sterling, and White & Case. These early internationalizers had almost 40 per cent of their lawyers overseas. By 2003, they had almost 50 per cent of their lawyers overseas, and the majority of their offices were outside the USA. By 2003, a group of later internationalizers had emerged that included the likes of Skadden and Jones Day. The firms in this cluster were larger in size than the early internationalizers yet had only about 20 per cent of their lawyers and half of their offices overseas. As a group, the later internationalizers aggressively acquired lateral partners and made mergers and acquisitions. They operated as 'second movers', following in the footsteps of the early internationalizers. The dissolution in 2003 of Altheimer & Gray and the break-up in 2005 of Coudert Brothers, juxtaposed with the strength of other early internationalizers such as Cleary Gottlieb, provide insights into what were first-mover disadvantages, what was required to gain first-mover advantages, and what were second-mover advantages for such firms as Skadden and Jones Day.

The strategic group perspective guides us in understanding rivalry at a particular point in time and the potential threat of new rivalries that occurs over time. Using this perspective, my analysis generates the following questions that are explored in more detail in the conclusion. How does a firm break the barriers to enter the circle of elite US firms? How do mergers and/or acquisitions affect the trajectory of firms? Why do many of the elite US firms have a limited international presence? What separates successful from unsuccessful early US internationalizers? Does it 'pay' to be a later US internationalizer? Why is New York such an important platform for internationalizing activities? Where might we expect movement of firms across strategic groups to occur? What additional internal characteristics of law firms (e.g. compensation system) help to explain their strategic positioning?

Before turning to the results of the analysis and addressing the above questions, I will first explain the concept of strategic group analysis in more depth, review what cluster analysis entails more fully, and show what is needed to conduct a strategic group analysis on large law firms.

Strategic group perspective

Understanding rivalry among firms has long been a paramount activity of academics in the field of business strategy. Contemporary thought on the matter owes a great deal to the pioneering efforts of Richard Caves and Michael Porter (Caves and Porter 1977; Porter 1979, 1980). Caves and Porter, whose intellectual origins were in the field of economics, were responding to the view that, under conditions of perfect competition, industries are composed of homogeneous firms. This conventional economic perspective argued that, in the world of perfect competition, firms in equilibrium resembled each other in terms of their key input variables and had the same profitability. Firm differences either did not exist or were simply idiosyncratic and deemed to be inconsequential. With this view of the world, there was no need to understand rivalry beyond knowing that every firm was a rival to every other firm but no firm could unduly influence an industry.

Caves and Porter, however, believed competition was often imperfect and that there were groups of firms within industries that competed amongst themselves. While the term 'strategic group' originates with Hunt (1972), it was Caves and Porter who developed the notion. They argued that between the industry and the individual firm, there was an intermediate level of analysis, the strategic group. Firms within a strategic group were homogeneous and across strategic groups differed. In their view, strategic groups were something more than an artifact of statistical homogeneity. Members of a strategic group behaved like a group, not just a collection of individual firms located in the same competitive space. They interacted with one another, closely watched one another, and, in the end, came to know each other well.

The notion of strategic groups provides seemingly competing predictions for understanding the rivalry that occurs within and across groups. Using arguments from economics on behaviour in oligopolies, Caves and Porter argued that firms in a strategic group not only resemble each other, but signal and imitate one another to limit their rivalry. Such notions of rivalry are reflected, for example, in the implicit, if not explicit, gentleman's agreements that allegedly occurred in the past among large US law firms in setting associate pay. Competition existed among firms in recruiting talent, but was constrained or limited in nature. However, the fact that members of a strategic group share attributes means that they might face similar, if not identical, pressures and are competing directly. For example, law firms that comprise a group primarily based on their clientele (e.g. corporations that pay for high-end legal services) are likely to be in direct competition with one another. We would then expect firms within that strategic group to have strong rivalries. Intense rivalry of this sort typically does not last as it is self-destructive. Even so, there is no way to know a priori whether rivalry will be heightened or constrained at any point in time. This only comes from empirically assessing, and arriving at an understanding of, the competitive dynamics of an industry and its strategic groups at a particular point in time.

Rivalry across firms in different strategic groups also operates in seemingly different ways. One way is in terms of non-competing groups—groups that do not compete among themselves. The notion underlying non-competing groups is simply that firms in different strategic groups are distinct from one another and, therefore, do not compete directly. For example, it is widely recognized that firms in a group that primarily provide mid-market services to corporations would not be seen as in direct competition with firms in a cluster that provides high-end services. The other side to the argument is less apparent. Although firms are in different groups, they still might be vying for the same competitive space. This extended view of rivalry often requires taking a dynamic rather than static view of an industry in that it points to the potential for new entrants into a group. This extended view of rivalry is in line with Porter's argument (1980) that competition goes beyond immediate or direct competitors to include potential new entrants.

Porter (1979) argued that, just as there are barriers to entering an industry (i.e. entry barriers), there are mobility barriers to moving from one strategic group to another. The notion of mobility barriers meant that switching groups was conditioned by the cost of moving. A small firm, for example, often had to acquire another firm at a premium in order to increase its size. When mobility barriers are low, we would expect that firms can move readily from one strategic group to another. When mobility barriers are high, as is often the case in a firm moving from being small to being large or from being a low- to high-price service provider, there is often relatively little movement across strategic groups. The notion of mobility barriers is used to explain the temporal stability that is found for strategic groups in a number of industries (Fiegenbaum and Thomas 1993).

The notion of mobility barriers can alternatively be conceived of in terms of mobility 'drivers' that help to explain the dynamics of an industry. For example, if size acts as a mobility barrier that limits firms from moving to another cluster, it alternatively acts as a mobility driver when a firm gains size, allowing it to move from one cluster to another. Thus, while mobility barriers help to explain stability, we see that mobility drivers help to explain industry dynamics.

The attributes of firms that serve as mobility barriers or drivers are the same factors that differentiate firms among groups. The most visible difference between firms is their size. Some firms are simply bigger than others, for example in their numbers of employees or revenues. It is, therefore, no surprise that the first studies on strategic groups, such as Porter's (1979), used size to group firms.

Most researchers, however, believe strategy is multidimensional and that grouping firms, therefore, should be done on multiple attributes (Thomas and Venkatraman 1988). Firms can differ on an enormous variety of attributes from their geographical coverage, operational approaches and organizational structures, to their financial position. There is not, however, consensus on which attributes of firms to examine, nor is it always possible or even wise to use the same attributes across industries. Different industries will have attributes specific to the industry context and the same attributes will hold more or less importance.

McGee and Thomas (1986) discuss the main sets of attributes used to differentiate firms into strategic groups. One set of attributes centres around various measures of firm size, like the number of lawyers or total revenues. Typically, these attributes are readily accessible. A second set of attributes has to do with internal characteristics of organizations, such as their operational procedures or organizational structure. Such measures are more difficult to access and might signal information on a firm's strategy and management as sources of competitive advantage. A third set of attributes is geographical or spatial in nature, like the extent of internationalization. Measures of internationalization are often based on where employees are located, where facilities are placed, or where sales are generated. A fourth set of attributes is financial and includes measures like return on investment. Studies often treat such measures as outcomes to be assessed based on group membership, with the view that they are the consequence of firms' strategies, not attributes of them. However, such measures can provide valuable information in differentiating firms into groups in terms of, for example, whether they operate in higher-, middle-, or lower-end service or product markets. A final set of attributes has to do with the price of goods and services or market share as an indicator of where in the market the firm is selling its good or services.

These attributes are not, however, exhaustive; there are many others and, most importantly, there are others that are potentially important to the specific industry context. Nor are the attributes mutually exclusive. Studies find that attributes are often redundant in that they are highly correlated. For example, firm size (even in terms of employees) and market share are often highly correlated: bigger firms have greater market share. Efforts are typically made to include a range of attributes to include those that capture the specific industry context, and to avoid using redundant information by employing statistical tools for reducing the number of attributes.

The strategic group perspective provides us with an understanding of the rivalries that exist in an industry composed of numerous competitors, like the large US law firm industry. By helping us to focus on actual and potential rivalries, a strategic group perspective complements the resource-based view of the firm (Barney 1991; Grant 2002; Wernerfelt 1984), which argues that certain valued and inimitable firm differences, such as a firm's culture, lead to sustained competitive advantage. The strategic group perspective guides us in comparing individual firms and their differences by enabling us to define more clearly the firms that operate as actual or potential rivals. Before presenting the findings from the analysis of strategic groups, I explain briefly the preliminary process that was conducted in order to obtain the results.

Preliminary process for cluster analysis of large US law firms in 1999 and 2003

Caves' and Porter's arguments on strategic groups have been the basis for numerous studies in diverse industries that range from airlines, banking, brewing, home appliances, insurance, MBA programmes, pharmaceuticals, petroleum, and retailing. The studies typically use cluster analysis to group firms (Thomas and Venkatraman 1988). Cluster analysis is a set of procedures that share the aim of using mathematical measures of distance (or similarity) to group firms (Aldenderfer and Blashfield 1984).

Cluster analysis is not simply a statistical technique that eliminates the need to make judgements (Aldenderfer and Blashfield 1984). The researcher using cluster analysis has to determine the number of clusters to 'extract'. While statistical procedures are available to help with the extraction, the richness and verisimilitude of the groupings often depend on just how many groups are selected. This is an issue because, a priori, it is often unclear just how many strategic groups there are in an industry and this has implications for the number that is selected. Extracting too many clusters gives the impression that the industry is highly differentiated while extracting too few clusters gives the impression that the industry is homogeneous.

I conducted cluster analysis on large US law firms using information from the *AMLAW* 100 and 200 and *NLJ* 250 for 1999 and 2003. Four key attributes of law firms were used in the analysis. The first attribute, firm size, was measured from the *AMLAW* 100 and 200. Firm size was measured as the number of lawyers that are partners or associates in a firm. The second attribute, profit per partner (PPP), was based on figures from the *AMLAW* 100 and 200. I used PPP as a proxy to identify where a firm stood in the market for legal services. Firms with higher PPP typically have higher billing rates and have higher-end clients. The third attribute, leverage, is defined as the ratio of associates to partners (associates/partners). Firms in this analysis show considerable range in their leverage ratios, with some firms having roughly one to two associates per partner and other firms having three, and even four associates per partner. The fourth attribute, percentage international, is measured as the percentage of lawyers in a firm that are located outside the USA. It is highly correlated with the number of international offices that a firm has but is a clearer measure of the extent to which a firm is international, as offices can vary substantially in their number of lawyers.[1]

Cluster analysis is influenced by differences in the magnitude and variance of attributes. A variable such as PPP varies from approximately US$300,000 to almost US$3.5 million while the percentage international varies from approximately 0 to 90 per cent. These differences in what are termed the 'elevation' of attributes can lead to those taller or more dispersed attributes having undue influence on the results of the cluster analysis. Therefore, I standardized the attributes using a commonly accepted procedure to create what is known as a *z* score. Standardizing in this way ensures that simple differences in the metrics did not lead to certain attributes overwhelming others and potentially masking differences among firms.

Since cluster analysis does not have a rule for extracting the number of clusters, I sought a set of clusters that was (*a*) parsimonious, that is, clusters were not fragmented or small, and (*b*) captured differences among groups of firms. The 1999 data were particularly susceptible to fragmentation in the number of clusters because profits in 1999 rose sharply for a number of firms. In particular, Wachtell, Lipton, Rosen & Katz (Wachtell) and Robins, Kaplan, Miller & Ciresi (Robins) had banner PPP which exceeded even that of highly prestigious firms like Cravath (reaching over US$3 million in PPP). This leads to these firms forming their own cluster. A six-cluster solution masked critical differences among firms in 1999, so I ran the analysis with a seven-cluster solution. The seven-cluster solution provides what I believe to be a clear representation of the firms in 1999.

169

The cluster analysis of the 2003 data revealed clear differences among firms using just six clusters. By that time, Wachtell had joined other elite New York firms that operated as a cluster in 1999 and again in 2003. Robins received banner profits in 1999 for its litigation of the tobacco companies but its PPP had dropped by 2003, leading it to being grouped in another cluster.

Strategic groups within the US legal sector

Key results for 1999 and 2003 mirror observations that have been made in the field: first, the group of highly prestigious firms referred to as the 'circle of elite', including Cravath and Davis Polk, were the basis of clusters in both 1999 and 2003. Most of these firms appear annually at the top of *AMLAW* 100 rankings. Second, Baker & McKenzie is clearly a unique firm. It formed its own cluster in both 1999 and 2003. No other firm had that distinction. It is both massive in size, by law firms' standards, and sizeable in its international presence, while being relatively modest in PPP. Third, there were clusters of relatively smaller firms with little international presence in both 1999 and 2003. These firms comprise a large and majority group of US law firms. Fourth, despite the low rates of internationalization among US law firms, in addition to Baker & McKenzie, there was a cluster of firms in 1999 and two clusters in 2003 that had a significant international presence. Taken together, these very basic findings capture groupings of firms that mirror observations made in the field. Moreover, they show that there was substantial temporal stability among firms in the strategic groups. This stability reassures us that the groupings have a solid foundation and are not temporally fleeting.

The seven-cluster solution shown in Table 8.1 for 1999 serves as the basis from which to examine trends. Several points are clear from the clusters. The thirteen firms, comprising the circle of elite, including Cravath and Davis Polk, are moderately sized, located almost exclusively in New York, have very high PPP, and a modest international presence with 9 per cent of their lawyers located overseas. The five firms in the cluster labelled early internationalizers, Altheimer & Gray, Cleary Gottlieb, Coudert Brothers, Shearman & Sterling, and White & Case, are moderate- to larger-sized and have a significant international presence. The twenty-one firms in the cluster labelled 'big domestic firms' are large, have relatively high PPP and lower leverage ratios, and a modest international presence. The cluster includes well-known firms such as Jones Day, Latham &

Table 8.1 Seven-cluster analysis, 1999

	Cluster 1 Circle of elite	Cluster 2 Early internationalizers	Cluster 3 Big domestic firms	Cluster 4 Small domestic firms	Cluster 5 Small domestic leveragers	Cluster 6 Baker & McKenzie	Cluster 7 Banner firms
Firm size	441	565	774	274	336	2,477	178
PPP ($)	1,372,692	804,000	656,904	400,613	578,000	485,000	3,220,000
Leverage (ratio of associates to partners)	3.2	3.1	2.2	1.6	3.2	3.4	1.7
% International	9	38.4	5.5	12	1.9	78.7	0
Number of firms	13	5	21	106	50	1	2
Representative firms[a] (up to five)	Cravath; Cahill Gordon; Davis Polk; Milbank Tweed; Sullivan Cromwell	Althaimer & Gray; Clear Gottlieb; Coudert Brothers; Shearman & Sterling; White & Case	Jones Day; Latham & Watkins; O'Melveny & Myers; Sidley Austin; Skadden	Arnold & Porter; Dickstein Shapiro; Fish & Richardson; Greenberg Traurig; Hale & Dorr	Bingham Dana; Cadwalader Wickersham; Fish & Neave; Schulte Roth; Testa Hurwitz	Baker & McKenzie	Wachtell; Robins

[a] A complete list is available from the author on request.

Watkins, and O'Melveny & Myers. The 106 firms in the cluster labelled 'small domestic firms' are small in size, have the lowest PPP, leverage at the lowest rate, and almost no international presence. These firms are focused either regionally or in particular legal specialities. The fifty firms in the sixth cluster have many of the same qualities as the small firms in the fifth, but their leverage ratio is double that of the smaller players, and so they are labelled as 'small domestic leveragers'. There is also a cluster for Baker & McKenzie. Its vast size at almost 2,500 lawyers and its overwhelming international presence at almost 80 per cent in 1999 made it truly distinct and, therefore, set it apart from the other firms. Its PPP were the second lowest among the groups. Finally, the firms of Wachtell and Robins emerged as a cluster, which is entitled 'Banner Firms', in light of the banner year that both firms had.

The results from 1999 highlight several points. First, the firms with the highest PPP do not have the most significant international presence. Second, size alone does not predict the international presence of a firm. The large firms have a modest international presence while the early internationalizers are significantly smaller but have a much greater international presence. Third, Baker & McKenzie is clearly an outlier at 78.7 per cent international and 2,500 lawyers. Fourth, the PPP of Wachtell and Robins make these two firms outliers. The data for these last two firms demonstrate why caution should be exercised in viewing data from any one year as more than simply a snapshot of that year. It is important to compare the findings from 1999 to the findings for 2003 for this reason.

As shown in Table 8.2, several key findings emerged from the 2003 cluster analysis. First, the circle of elite strategic group, now with fifteen firms, includes most of the firms in 2003 that it did in 1999. It now additionally includes Wachtell and is joined by Boies Schiller, Quinn Emanuel, Schulte Roth, and Dickstein Shapiro. Boies Schiller's penetration into the circle of elite comes a short time after its founding in 1997 by David Boies, formerly of Cravath. Similar to Boies Schiller, Quinn Emanuel, a highly regarded Los Angeles firm, does plaintiff litigation work. The majority of firms in the circle of elite, in contrast, have substantial corporate and banking practices.

The dominance of the circle of elite firms has increased since 1999. With PPP at almost US$2 million, they generate almost double the PPP of the nearest cluster of firms. These firms as a cluster have also reduced their international presence, with the number of lawyers located outside the US falling from 9 to 7 per cent. Their increased profitability coupled

Table 8.2 Six-cluster analysis, 2003

	Cluster 1 Circle of elite	Cluster 2 Early internationalizes	Cluster 3 Later internationalizers	Cluster 4 In the middle	Cluster 5 Small domestic firms	Cluster 6 Baker & McKenzie
Firm size	430	982	1,470	609	325	3,053
PPP ($)	1,903,333	1,022,500	1,121,667	816,636	524,189	595,500
Leverage	3.5	3.95	3.5	3.34	1.9	4.0
% International	7.0	49.3	19	5.7	1.3	83
Number of firms	15	4	6	55	111	1
Representative firms[a]	Cravath; Cahill Gordon; Davis Polk; Milbank Tweed; Sullivan Cromwell	Cleary Gottlieb; Coudert Brothers; Shearman & Sterling; White & Case	Jones Day; Latham & Watkins; Mayer Brown; Skadden; Weil Gotshal	Greenberg Traurig; Hale & Dorr; Hogan & Hartson; Morgan Lewis; O'Melveny & Myers	Arnold & Porter; Baker & Daniels; Fish & Neave; Robins; Wolf Block	Baker & McKenzie

[a] A complete list of firms is available from the author on request.

with their reduced international presence raises questions on the value of internationalization, which I explore further in the concluding section.

Second, as might be expected, Baker & McKenzie continued its internationalization with 83 per cent of its lawyers being located outside the USA. It continued to be so distinctive that it again formed its own cluster. Its PPP were again the second lowest among the strategic groups.

A third development was the emergence of a cluster in which firms were neither large nor small. This fourth cluster is referred to as 'in the middle'. The firms stuck in the middle (see Porter 1980) are not in an enviable position. They are not small enough to operate as regional or specialist players, but they are not large enough to compete directly with large firms. Firms in this strategic position often take action to grow, particularly through mergers and acquisitions.

A fourth important development was the increased international presence of the firms across the sector as a whole. The firms in 2003 had, on average, an international presence of 4.97 per cent lawyers working overseas whereas in 1999 the figure was 3.68 per cent (these weighted averages are derived from the figures on the clusters in Table 8.2). While the increase might appear small, the actual number of lawyers working overseas for these US firms rose by almost 2,000 over this period. It is also constrained by the vast number of large US law firms that had virtually no presence overseas. The small reduction in the percentage from nine to seven by the elite firms in Cluster 1 is therefore particularly significant given the aggregate trend for firms to increase their international presence.

A final and related development was the rise of an additional cluster of firms with a strong international presence. The cluster is referred to as 'later internationalizers' and includes firms like Skadden and Jones Day. The later internationalizers have a moderate yet significant international presence representing approximately 20 per cent of a firm's lawyers in 2003 (these same firms, on average, had only about 9 per cent of their lawyers outside the USA in 1999). The firms are quite large at a mean value of almost 1,500 lawyers.

The early internationalizers in Table 8.2 include again Coudert Brothers, Cleary Gottlieb, Shearman & Sterling, and White & Case (Altheimer & Gray dropped out of the analysis because it was dissolved). Firms in this cluster increased their international presence to almost 50 per cent, a percentage change of roughly 25 per cent since 1999.

Table 8.3 provides further information on the clusters for 2003 that extend beyond the data reported in Table 8.2. Data are reported for 2003

Table 8.3 Key differences for 2003 six-cluster analysis

	Cluster 1 Circle of elite	Cluster 2 Eary internationalizers	Cluster 3 Later internationalizers	Cluster 4 In the middle	Cluster 5 Small domestic firms	Cluster 6 Baker & McKenzie
PPP change in $ (2003–1999)	429,231	145,000	189,167	234,100	95,670	110,000
Firm-size change (2003–1999)	99	338	514	136	61	576
Gross revenues in $ (2003)	394,066,670	595,875,000	989,666,670	364,563,640	162,108,110	1,134,000,000
Gross revenues change in $ (2003–1999)	138,884,600	223,125,000	397,833,300	143,400,000	54,123,700	316,000,000
Revenue per lawyer (RPL) in $ (2003)	942,333	611,250	684,167	594,091	499,640	370,000
RPL change in $ (2003–1999)	135,385	31,250	70,000	124,800	82,062	40,000
% International change (%International$_{2003}$– %International$_{1999}$)	2%	9.3%	10.5%	2.4%	0.7%	4.9%
International offices (2003)	3.3	18.75	10	2.7	0.62	59
Domestic offices (2003)	3.4	4.25	9.3	8.5	6.3	9
Laterals per year 2000–2003 (average for four years)	2.8	12.9	21.3	15.6	7.0	25.5
Merger/acquisition (percentage of firms that had one or more during the four years)	0%	0%	33%	15%	5%	0%

on gross revenues, revenues per lawyer, the number of domestic and international offices, the number of laterals averaged over the years 2000–3 (based on data from *The American Lawyer*—see Braverman 2001a), and the percentage of firms over the years 1999–2003 that were involved in a merger and acquisition (based on information gleaned from *The American Lawyer*). I also used the clusters for 2003 to compare firms on their changes from 1999 to 2003 on PPP, firm size, revenues, revenues per lawyer, and the percentage of international offices. The numbers on Table 8.3 cannot be calculated by subtracting cluster data reported in Table 8.1 from Table 8.2 for 1999 and 2003 as there are typically different clusters for the two years, and even when a cluster has the same name, there are different firms in it. Nevertheless, the additional data on Table 8.3, which is calculated by comparing the data for the firms in the clusters in 2003 with the data for those same individual firms in 1999, allows us to see more fully the differences among firms in the different clusters and the changes that occurred during the period 1999 to 2003.

As shown in Table 8.3, the later internationalizers average almost US$1 billion in gross revenues (Skadden, in 1999, was the first to achieve that distinction). The firms have a modest number of international offices at ten and almost the same number of US offices. Their offices are located in the major financial centres of the world and other highly competitive markets. The firms that comprise the early internationalizers are large but smaller than the later internationalizers. They have gross revenues of almost US$600 million in 2003 and have a substantial number of international offices—with an average of 18.75, almost double that of the later internationalizers. They also have few US offices relative to their international offices, with an average of only 4.25 whereas the later internationalizers have roughly the same number of US and international offices.

Table 8.3 shows that the later internationalizers as compared with the early internationalizers made greater use of lateral partner hires and were involved in more mergers and acquisitions. The later internationalizers acquired, on average, 21.3 lateral partners per year from 2000 to 2003. During the period from 1999 to 2003, one-third of the firms in this cluster were involved in a merger or acquisition. The early internationalizers acquired on average approximately thirteen laterals per year. There was no merger and acquisition activity among these firms from 1999 to 2003. Even accounting for the differences in size between the early and later internationalizers, the latter firms still made considerably more lateral hires and mergers and acquisitions. Viewed as a make or buy decision (internally develop talent versus acquire talent externally), the later internationalizers are buying talent more than the early internationalizers.

The financial data in Tables 8.2 and 8.3 shed further light on the early and later internationalizers. First, the firms in these clusters have roughly equal PPP in 2003, with the later internationalizers averaging approximately US$1.1 million and the early internationalizers averaging approximately US$1 million. Second, the firms that constitute the later internationalizers have seen their revenues grow by approximately 67 per cent from 1999 to 2003 while the firms that now constitute the early internationalizers have seen their revenues grow by approximately 60 per cent during this time. This percentage difference represents an absolute difference of over US$170 million in average revenue gain per firm during this period. Third, the change in revenues per lawyer in dollars from 1999 to 2003 for the later internationalizers was US$70,000 versus US$31,250 for the early internationalizers. Thus, the data suggest that the later internationalizers as compared to the early internationalizers have higher revenue growth and greater efficiency. The data further suggest that the later internationalizers are better positioned to move forward in competing internationally. Their resources and financial position presumably also helped them to acquire lateral partners and make mergers and acquisitions.

The reality of the situation is more complex, however, once we examine individual firms in these two clusters. Among the later internationalizers, Jones Day has been particularly aggressive in using mergers and acquisitions and lateral hires to internationalize. Skadden, however, has taken a conservative approach to internationalizing by largely avoiding lateral hires and not making mergers and acquisitions. In this way, Skadden's approach resembles early internationalizers such as Cleary Gottlieb, acquiring outside talent only as a last resort and in small numbers in its international operations (Braverman 2001a). Altheimer & Gray and Coudert Brothers, given their relatively lower PPP and, as discussed below, limited presence in key major legal markets, might simply have lacked the ability to acquire key laterals or make major mergers and acquisitions.

Table 8.4 provides further information on the number of lawyers in major US cities for the early and later internationalizers and for Baker & McKenzie. What the data reveal is that firms like Altheimer & Gray and Coudert Brothers did not have a substantial platform in the USA, defined here as having a large number of lawyers (200 or more) in a office that is one of the four major legal centres in the USA. The largest US office for Altheimer & Gray was in Chicago, where it had 191 lawyers in 1999. The

Table 8.4 Number of lawyers in four major US cities for early and later international-izers and Baker & McKenzie in 2003 (with 1999 in parentheses)

Firm name	New York	Washington, DC	Chicago	Los Angeles
Early Internationalizers				
Altheimer & Gray	NA (0)	NA (0)	NA (191)	NA (0)
Coudert Brothers	142 (161)	39 (28)	0 (0)	32 (22)
Cleary Gottlieb	428 (310)	97 (76)	0 (0)	0 (0)
Shearman & Sterling	551 (517)	81 (42)	0 (0)	0 (0)
White & Case	401 (336)	105 (75)	0 (0)	59 (40)
Later Internationalizers				
Jones Day	226 (128)	250 (115)	161 (130)	142 (115)
Latham & Watkins	275 (187)	188 (149)	135 (107)	314 (226)
Mayer Brown	219 (157)	114 (96)	507 (461)	69 (53)
Sidley Austin	434 (106)	224 (135)	513 (433)	149 (112)
Skadden	873 (669)	227 (195)	197 (125)	122 (140)
Weil Gotshal	591 (406)	60 (47)	0 (0)	0 (0)
Baker & McKenzie	56 (59)	56 (51)	204 (190)	0 (0)

NA. Information not available as firm was dissolved.

largest US office for Coudert Brothers was in New York, where it had 161 lawyers in 1999. Similarly, Baker & McKenzie, despite is vast size, had its largest US presence in Chicago, with 204 lawyers in 2003, and just 56 in New York in 2003 (to address this deficiency, Baker & McKenzie acquired Coudert Brothers' office in New York in 2005 along with seventy or so of its partners—See Longstreth 2005a). What the data further reveal is that Skadden has built a very strong US platform. In 2003, Skadden had 873 lawyers in New York, 227 lawyers in Washington, DC, and even 197 in Chicago. The data for Jones Day reveal it has built more of a platform in New York and Washington, DC over the period from 1999 to 2003.

Table 8.5 provides data on the number of lawyers in major international cities for the early and later internationalizers and for Baker & McKenzie. The data reveal that Altheimer & Gray largely stayed out of the major international cities and that Coudert Brothers had a relatively modest presence in each of these cities. However, Shearman & Sterling shows a strong presence in London and Paris, two of the more hotly contested markets. Cleary Gottlieb has a moderate presence in London and Paris and a relatively strong presence in Brussels. Baker & McKenzie has a significant presence in the highly competitive London market and also in Hong Kong. Skadden has taken a fairly conservative internationaliza-tion strategy, with its largest number of lawyers in London. Jones Day, White & Case, and Latham & Watkins are building European strongholds around London and Paris. Mayer Brown now has a strong presence in

Table 8.5 Number of international lawyers in major international cities in 2003 for early and later internationalizers and Baker & McKenzie (with numbers from 1999 in parentheses)

Firm name	London	Paris	Brussels	Frankfurt	Tokyo	Hong Kong
Early internationalizers						
Altheimer & Gray	NA (8)	NA (0)	NA (0)	NA (0)	NA (0)	NA (0)
Cleary Gottlieb	61 (39)	80 (57)	59 (50)	35 (27)	9 (5)	20 (12)
Coudert Brothers	34 (27)	57 (55)	51 (12)	36 (12)	4 (2)	22 (26)
Shearman & Sterling	121 (82)	95 (55)	5 (0)	41 (24)	6 (5)	18 (19)
White & Case	171 (42)	87 (53)	34 (25)	62 (4)	35 (24)	31 (22)
Later Internationalizers						
Jones Day	178 (28)	80 (37)	23 (15)	41 (26)	20 (3)	31 (7)
Latham & Watkins	80 (22)	96 (0)	12 (0)	24 (0)	10 (4)	10 (3)
Mayer Brown	284 (37)	27 (0)	2 (0)	55 (0)	0 (0)	0 (0)
Sidley Austin	87 (45)	0 (0)	6 (0)	0 (0)	10 (1)	49 (45)
Skadden	64 (31)	25 (16)	18 (7)	16 (4)	19 (2)	16 (16)
Weil Gotshal	108 (78)	25 (0)	7 (10)	31 (0)	0 (0)	0 (0)
Baker & McKenzie	265 (216)	98 (60)	52 (36)	101 (69)	79(47)	166 (158)

NA. Information not available as firm was dissolved.

London, attributable to its merger in 2002 with the UK's Rowe & Maw (Goldhaber 2002).

Conclusions

The strategic group perspective guides us to a series of important questions about large US law firms through the theoretical issues it raises and the statistical tools it employs. In this section, I draw on the prior parts of the paper to address six questions.

Question 1: Where should we expect to find stability in clusters and, where should we expect to find movement across strategic groups?

The most visible stability occurred among the circle of elite. The firms in this cluster, including Cravath, Wachtell, and Davis Polk, have been able to maintain their status as elite firms since at least the early 1980s (based on law firm profitability data that were first made available by *The American Lawyer*). Movement in and out of this circle occurred most often among firms that did plaintiff litigation work and in which there were large payouts from suits. Boies Schiller and Quinn Emanuel have managed to stay atop the *AMLAW* rankings on PPP. Robins, however, has not.

Nonetheless, a firm that focuses on plaintiff litigation work is vulnerable to vagaries in its profitability. Plaintiff litigation suits often take several years before a payout, with a jump in PPP once a suit is settled. Moreover, a strong presence in plaintiff litigation work arguably locks out, or at least makes it more difficult for, a firm to have a strong corporate practice. Suits are typically targeted at just the clients that a corporate practice services, namely large corporations.

Merger and acquisition activity was another key element that was linked to the movement of firms. Mergers and acquisitions placed firms on different trajectories from their past. For example, in 2001, Sidley Austin merged with Brown & Wood, catapulting the firm into the later internationalizers. Similarly, in 2002, Mayer Brown merged with the UK's Rowe & Maw, making it into a later internationalizer.

How successful these and other mergers and acquisitions are depends critically on their implementation. The strategic management literature does not offer us great hope (Jemison and Sitkin 1986). Research has consistently shown that mergers and acquisitions among publicly held corporations do not lead, on average, to value (King et al. 2004; Zollo and Singh 2004). There are firms that succeed and others that lose through mergers and acquisitions. Research suggests that firms do a reasonably good job of selecting merger and acquisition candidates that are a strategic fit, but do a much poorer job of selecting partners that are good organizational or cultural fits. Moreover, research suggests firms critically underestimate how much is involved in integrating merger and/or acquisition partners.

Question 2: Does a firm need to be international to compete?

The circle of elite firms defies the notion that a highly successful firm needs to be international. These firms have the highest PPP and, as the data show, they have retrenched on their internationalization efforts. Indeed, despite the growing presence of US firms in China, Cravath recently closed its office there (Goldhaber 2005).

A major cost of internationalizing for the circle of elite firms has to do with the benefits that accrue to them through their limited size. They have remained smaller and that has arguably made them more governable, manageable, and focused in terms of their competencies. Moreover, international clients can avail themselves of these firms' services even if they do not have international offices. In fact, the firms provide legal services overseas. For example, according to *The American Lawyer* (Griffiths 2003), Cravath was eighth in the number of M&A deals in Germany. However, full internationalization, by taking on local law capabilities, would mean adding lawyers and offices overseas, which could potentially dilute the firms' governance and management systems, and competencies. Moreover, for many of these firms it would mean breaking from a policy of avoiding the hiring of laterals or only doing this as a last resort and in small numbers (Braverman 2001a; Sherer 2005). These changes could add expenses, decrease revenues, and ultimately erode profitability.

The circle of elite firms might, however, be missing very significant opportunities to exploit their competencies and explore new ones without great costs (March 1991). The experiences of Skadden demonstrate the point. It is engaged in a focused international strategy built around its capabilities in M&A and financial transactions. There appear to be real advantages to its strategy. Skadden gains further entry to client firms that are international in their business. Skadden also engages in learning *in vivo* overseas in ways and in content that could not have taken place otherwise. By not internationalizing, firms like Cravath would appear to lose out on clients and explicit and tacit knowledge and ultimately to limit their profitability.

Question 3: Does it cost to be a 'first mover' and what are the advantages of being a second mover?

The dissolution of Altheimer & Gray and the break-up of Coudert Brothers suggest that being the pioneer or first-mover internationally was not necessarily advantageous. Reviews of the literature on the effects of early market entry on profitability (Lieberman and Montgomery 1988, 1998; Vanderwerf and Mahon 1997) do not find evidence that first-movers, on average, enjoy a superior level of profitability. The first mover has an opportunity to grab market share. Whether that translates into profits depends on the costs of being a first-mover, the ease in which competitors can enter the market, and the extent to which second-movers can free-ride by learning and gaining from the experiences of the first-movers (Glazer 1985; Lieberman and Montgomery 1988).

Several of the firms that pioneered international practices appear to have taken actions that reduced profits. They had many international locations and in some locations their reason for being there was speculative in nature. Moreover, many offices were relatively thin in numbers and presumably thin in the depth of legal specialization. What these firms appeared to be doing is trying to gain beachheads with the notion that, as business grew in a particular city, they would be the ones that could cash in on it.

Second-movers like Skadden appear to have learned from the early movers' actions. They located themselves in the major financial capitals in the world and their offices were built to compete in the depth of their specializations or the extent of their practices' global integration. They have built themselves up largely through having a strong New York platform and have not spread themselves out in their number of locations, or they are thin in the number of lawyers they have in each location.

The second movers might have been guided by some of the early internationalizers that took a fairly conservative approach to growth and internationalizing. Cleary Gottlieb was founded in 1946 and established its first international office in Paris in 1949. In 2003, it had a strong presence in New York with 428 lawyers, a moderate presence in Europe, and a limited presence in Tokyo and Hong Kong. Shearman & Sterling also had an international presence in the immediate post second World War–era, with its work in rebuilding the international banking system. In 2003, it had a very strong presence in New York and strong presences in London, Paris, and Frankfurt, but very limited presences in Hong Kong and Tokyo. These two firms appear to have built a strong platform in New York and have carefully leveraged it. They now have significant history and capabilities in running international operations.

Question 4: Which US cities serve as platforms for internationalizing?

Building a strong presence in New York with high-end legal work requires competing against circle of elite members such as Cravath, large and resourceful firms like Skadden, and other strong firms. For a firm to succeed in New York, it must either become as strong as these firms or find distinctive competencies that the competing firms do not have. Either way, it is a struggle. As Longstreth (2005b: 92), states: 'New York is still a very high hill. It's the financial capital of the world, a beehive of commercial litigation, and the first stop of the best foreign clients when they're searching for lawyers in the United States. Any firm with global ambitions must have a presence in New York. 'Without one', says O'Melveny & Myers chair A. B. Culvahouse, Jr., articulating a widely held sentiment, 'it just doesn't work'. But it is a struggle that places a firm on a hill with an arguably higher vantage point—one from which it can presumably be more competitive in its entry point into international markets.

Latham & Watkins is an example of a firm which has made a strong presence in New York as a part of its long-term strategy. As Table 8.4 shows, Latham & Watkins added almost 100 lawyers to its New York office between 1999 and 2003 to put it roughly on a par with its Los Angeles office. William Voge, leader of Latham & Watkins' New York practice was quoted by Longstreth (2005b: 94) as saying: 'Our view twenty years ago was that if we wanted to succeed in New York we [had to] play on the same playing field as Cravath, Davis Polk, Sullivan & Cromwell, Skadden, Simpson Thatcher... that we had to be sharing in their market share and on the next level down—that was unequivocal.' Today, the New York office is Latham & Watkins' largest (Longstreth 2005b). By contrast, Latham & Watkins catapulted from twenty-two lawyers in London in 1999 to eighty in 2003 and from no lawyers in Paris in 1999 to ninety-six in 2003.

The question remains whether other cities can serve as platforms for international operations. Among the later internationalizers, only Mayer Brown treated Chicago as its main platform. Nonetheless, several firms including Skadden have a significant presence there. The value of an office in Chicago is suggested by the managing partner of Skadden's Chicago office, as quoted by Fleischer-Black (2005: 104): 'It's got a window to the world that's quite a bit different than either New York or the West Coast... many of our transactions have a non-US player in them.'

Question 5: Where should we expect movement in the future?

The 1999 data tell us that large firms looked for new markets presumably because they had begun to saturate their existing ones or because they had competencies that leveraged readily. Where we can especially expect movement in the future is among those firms that are now labelled as 'in the middle'. As a group of firms, they have neither the size of the later internationalizers, nor the prestige and distinctive competencies of the circle of elite, nor the narrower focus or regional nature of the specialized players. It is perhaps no surprise that firms like Greenberg Traurig and Squire Sanders have made moves in recent years to bolster their size and hence change their positioning (Pearlman 2002). If the past is a guide, we can track these firms' development by seeing whether they build strong platforms in New York or even Chicago. There is the possibility, however, that they will take different routes to internationalizing. Greenberg Traurig could, for example, take a South American route to internationalizing, effectively avoiding competition with many of the early and later internationalizers.

Question 6: What additional internal characteristics of firms (e.g. compensation system, organizational structure) help explain their strategic positioning?

The above discussion has focused on those explanations of firms' strategic positioning that can be substantiated with readily observable data. But there are explanations on which there are less data, many of which are internal characteristics in the way in which firms are managed. As the resource-based view of the firm (Barney 1991) suggests, these internal characteristics have significant implications for how firms are strategically positioned, and for their competitive success.

A recent article in *The American Lawyer* (Koppel 2005) brings to light the implications of internal characteristics on strategic positioning. As the article notes, Baker & McKenzie has a partner compensation ratio that far exceeds that of Cleary Gottlieb. Baker & McKenzie uses an eat-what-you-kill pay system in that lawyers get paid largely for what they service directly. Cleary Gottlieb uses a lockstep system in that partners at particular seniority levels are paid relatively equally. Thus, Baker & McKenzie pays a partner in a city in a developing country where billing rates are relatively low a much lower salary than it does partners in those cities in countries where they command higher billing rates. This allows the firm a degree of freedom to expand readily since it does not have to be concerned about subsidizing the lawyers that generate less in fees. Cleary Gottlieb does not, however, have the same degree of freedom. Its constraints guide its strategic actions and act as brakes. With its compensation system, Cleary Gottlieb is apt to open only those offices that can generate revenues and PPP equivalent to its other offices and accept into partnership only those lawyers who can earn at least as much as existing partners. Thus, it is likely to avoid anything but the most controlled expansion.

The examples of Baker & McKenzie and Cleary Gottlieb highlight that other attributes, many of them mechanisms inside the firms, come into play in further understanding rivalry among firms. Gathering such information often requires going beyond the type of quantitative data that was examined here to find qualitative information on firms.

As these six questions and the discussion of them suggest, the strategic group perspective provides both theoretical insights and statistical tools for more clearly understanding current and future rivalry among firms in an industry. The strategic group perspective thus provides a way of meeting the law firm strategist's formidable challenge of mapping the competitive space in the increasingly complex and rapidly changing legal marketplace.

Note

1. A fifth set of measures that was examined and subsequently omitted from the analysis concerned the practice portfolio of the firms (i.e. in what areas of law a firm practised and to what degree their practice was specialized). Using a categorization developed by Sherer (1995), data were categorized from the *NLJ* and the NALP on the percentage of lawyers in nine practice areas (e.g. corporate and banking, employment, litigation, intellectual property, property, tax). Neither measure of the practice portfolio differentiated clearly among firms in the different groups.

9

Your ethics

Redefining professionalism? The impact of management change

Royston Greenwood
School of Business, University of Alberta

Introduction

Law firms are not philanthropic organizations. Nor should they be. Like all enterprises within a market system, law firms strive for commercial success. In fact, the very best of them are as successful as the more high-profile publicly traded corporations. Yet, law firms are also supposed to temper pursuit of commercial goals by observance of a code of ethical principles that defines 'professional' and 'unprofessional' behaviour. In common with other professional service firms, law firms are expected to embrace a commitment beyond the commercial interests of any single firm, to the 'profession' at large. This notion may be idealized and has been challenged (as noted below), but it is distinctive of how lawyers talk about their work. In this chapter, I argue that the balance ('tension' might be a more appropriate term) between commercial and professional values may have been disturbed by the organizational and managerial changes described in this book, to the detriment of professional behaviour.

The importance of the legal profession in contemporary society and the role of corporate and or commercial law firms in facilitating economic exchange has long attracted academic attention. Early work emphasized two research themes. One theme emphasized law as a profession and sought to understand the *place of 'professions' in society* (e.g. Abbott 1988; Freidson 1970). This 'sociology of the professions' literature explores the implicit contract between the state and the professions, whereby the former gives state-sanctioned jurisdictional exclusivity to the latter in exchange for guarantees that self-regulation will ensure appropriate technical competence and commitment to a code of ethical behaviour by the profession's members. A second research theme explores the *relationship between forms of organization and professional behaviour* (e.g. Raelin 1989; Scott 1965). This research examines whether particular organizational forms enable or repress the ability of professionals to evoke their profession's ethical principles. A common interest of both research streams has been the nature of professional behaviour and the organizational and regulatory circumstances under which it is enabled.

Both of these research themes have received reduced attention in the past decade. In their place, a third research stream has evolved focusing upon the *internal functioning of law firms*, that is upon how law firms are organized, governed, and managed. Early examples (e.g. Galanter and Palay 1991; Nelson 1988) analysed patterns of behaviour such as the dynamics underlying law firm growth and patterns of demographic stratification within the firm. More recent work has taken an explicitly managerial stance, querying how firms are or might be managed (e.g. Lorsch and Tierney 2002; Lowendahl 2000). This book falls squarely within this latter tradition. That is, it examines the internal management practices of law firms.

My central point is that the changes taking place in the management of law firms draw renewed attention to the central questions of the two earlier research streams. That is, I raise the implications for professional behaviour of changes in governance and management practices.

The changing context of law

Contemporary law firms face very different circumstances from those experienced by predecessor firms of earlier decades. Three changes in particular stand out. Firms are much larger. They are geographically more dispersed. They face stiffer competition. As a consequence, law firms are experiencing new and sometimes daunting managerial and organizational challenges.

The first of these changes—increase in size—will be familiar to practising lawyers and yet the scale of the change is worth restating. Leblebici (this volume) notes that a 'mega' law firm in the mid-1980s would have approximately 800 professionals. Today, the average size of the world's ten largest law firms is over 2,000: Baker & McKenzie, the largest (in number of lawyers) has 3,067 lawyers compared with only 752 twenty years ago. By the standards of the accounting industry, of course, these figures are modest—in 2006, for example, PricewaterhouseCoopers had approximately 103,000 professionals and 27,000 support staff—but for law firms such growth has brought with it unfamiliar problems of organization and management.

The second change—increase in geographical complexity—has been driven by the need to service clients who are increasingly international in scope. Only a relatively short time ago, law firms would have few, if any, overseas offices, relying instead upon referral agreements with foreign firms. Now, as Sherer's chapter in this book has demonstrated, many US law firms have merged or opened overseas offices, but most of the largest international law firms have their origins in the UK. Clifford Chance, for example, has twenty-eight offices in nineteen countries. (Again, accounting firms put these figures into perspective; PricewaterhouseCoopers has 769 offices in 144 countries, making them one of the world's most geographically dispersed commercial enterprises.) But geographical dispersion has raised novel managerial challenges for law firms.

The third change—enhanced competition—has steadily increased over the past two decades. Firms have taken advantage of changes in regulatory frameworks to market their services more openly and aggressively. Clients are more prepared than in earlier decades to switch their business from firm to firm, forcing law firms to take competition seriously. Foreign firms have entered domestic markets. And, perhaps most worryingly, other professional firms, notably accounting firms, have encroached upon the jurisdiction traditionally serviced by law firms.

Law firm responses

Taken together, these contextual changes, not surprisingly, have affected and are still affecting the way that firms are approaching issues of strategy, management, and organization. Law firms are struggling to understand and resolve new stresses and tensions, seeking to reconcile or adapt traditional practices with contemporary demands. Much experimentation and learning is underway.

Practitioners are thus in need of the insights provided by serious academic research—hence the motivation for this book, which introduces the work of research-oriented academics to practitioners grappling with change. As such, the chapters represent the application of theory and systematic analysis rather than the anecdotal reflection often characteristic of writings by consultants. Throughout, there is attention to the importance of systematic analysis and a cautious reluctance to go beyond the data or to be definitive rather than suggestive. As such, there is no attempt to be didactic, to offer lawyers authoritative-sounding prescriptions. Instead, lawyers are offered frameworks of analysis constructed from data, in order to provoke reflection.

Inevitably, there are topics not addressed in this book. We are not told how firms are developing formal knowledge management systems, or about the rising importance of lifestyle issues, the obdurate problem of the gender glass ceiling, of the range of alternative approaches being developed for determining compensation, how some firms are hiring non-legal professionals to occupy critical managerial positions, the growth of lateral hires, and the willingness of partners to change firms. These and other issues are outside the scope of this volume and await future attention. One of the contributions of this book is that it will stimulate work in these hitherto neglected areas as academics continue to see law firms as an important site for empirical investigation.

Rather than elaborate on these possible additional research topics, I want to comment upon an issue which is touched upon in several of the chapters but which does not receive explicit treatment. It is an issue that seems to me to be fundamental for the continued success of law firms. Moreover, it is an issue that connects the research represented in this book to the earlier research traditions outlined above. I ask a simple question: *Has the growth in the size, complexity, and competitiveness of law firms affected the professional behaviour of their members?*

Conclusions: implications for professional behaviour

Running through much of this book is a recognition and acceptance of the need for greater rationalization of law firm structures and procedures. The same observation has been made for other professional service firms (see Brock, Powell, and Hinings 1999). Firms have to be better and more formally managed because they face aggressive competition and because they are large and complex. Reliance on face-to-face inter-action, collegial monitoring, and often part-time management no longer suffice.

In place of the less formal approaches characteristic of smaller firms, large firms have adopted more formal structures of management and organization. They now have formal departments with formal managers. There are COOs, CEOs, marketing directors, and public relations directors. These posts are often occupied by specialists who are not lawyers. Formal strategic management systems are in place. The performances of partners and non-partners are systematically measured and assessed. Compensa-tion practices based upon lockstep seniority are giving way to productiv-ity and performance-based assessments, in which the ability to generate revenues, rather than technical excellence, dominate. Accountability is strong and explicit. The very language used in these firms has changed: law is a *business* and has to be explicitly *managed*, 'practice development' is 'marketing', 'professional development' is 'training', and so on. From being a necessary and unpopular evil, management is now acknowledged (albeit often grudgingly) not only as essential but as requiring full-time and skilled incumbents. Along with full-time managers has come a shift in authority away from the full partnership towards those occupants of managerial positions—although the latter are still formally dependent upon the former, giving the relationship an element of negotiation less evident in corporate settings. Some professional service firms have even abandoned the legal form of partnership per se (Empson, this volume). Law firms in the majority of jurisdictions are still prohibited from taking such steps, but many observers believe that these prohibitions will soon be removed.

The shift towards more formal managerial practices is not entirely new, nor do they entirely replace traditional structures. Leblebici (this volume) notes how adoption in the 1960s of billable hours as the pre-ferred method of calculating lawyers' fees reflected the introduction of principles of business. Cooper et al.'s study of large Canadian law firms (1996) found that new arrangements are layered (sedimented) upon the old. Nevertheless, the shift to more formal structures has become much more pronounced in the past decade because of the contextual changes outlined above: competition, size, and geographic complexity. Critically, the shift has potentially major implications for professional behaviour and the self-regulating status of law firms because it is disturbing the balance between competing definitions of professionalism inherent in law (and all professional service) firms.

An early approach to the study of the professions saw the professions as *necessary* within modern social systems and *benign* in their consequences (e.g. Goode 1957; Parsons 1954). Fundamental to this perspective is the belief that the complexities of modern society require expertise for the pursuance of some occupations, creating an asymmetry of knowledge between practitioner and client. This asymmetry opens up a serious opportunity for the former to exploit the latter. Professionals refrain from doing so because they are guided by an ethical code of behaviour, embodying values such as peer vocation, public service, self-regulation, and autonomy. Brint (1994) suggests that this perspective embodies a *social trustee* ideal of professional behaviour, linking command of an esoteric body of knowledge with wider social purposes. That is, claims to professional status are legitimate to the extent that they 'serve important functions for the broader community and... meet high standards in the performance of intellectually demanding work' (Brint 1994: 16). Critically, the social trustee definition of professionalism subordinates self-interest and commercial gain in favour of ideals of service and public welfare.

In its nineteenth-century formulation, the model drew upon the aristocratic values of gentlemanly service (Leblebici, this volume). More important than command of knowledge (i.e. expertise) were values of trustworthiness and service. 'Gentleman' professionals, moreover, were not in need of remuneration; therefore, denial of self-interest was not significant. Later, the need for high levels of remuneration to compensate for the time taken to acquire complex knowledge was recognized and the values of social trusteeship were protected through such arrangements as the setting of fixed rates for services (in order to avoid competition for work compromising service standards), bans on advertising, and norms of respect between professionals (e.g. avoidance of poaching clients).

An alternative approach to the study of the professions saw the claim to professional status as a *rhetorical strategy designed to legitimate privileges* to an occupation rather than as a necessary response to societal complexity (Freidson 1970; Johnson 1972; Larson 1977). Claims to high ethical standards and public service were reinterpreted as myths aimed at protecting privilege. That is, the rewards of professional life were viewed as a product of conscious attempts by professionals or their patrons to extract economic and social 'rents' from consumers or to exercise social control by obtaining preferential market institutions. This labour market shelter perspective is clearly much more attentive to issues of power and privilege and early expressions of this perspective came close to portraying the concepts of professional and profession as rationalized myths.

More recent discussions have been more nuanced, avoiding the relative one-sidedness of both of the above portrayals. A particularly insightful approach is Brint's reformulation (1994) of the labour market shelter perspective. Brint put forward an *expertise-based* definition of market-focused professionalism, in which claims to professional status are predicated on command of an abstract body of knowledge (superior to others in its application to a given set of activities and tasks) and which is allocated through mechanisms of the marketplace. Notions of disinterested service and commitment to broader notions of public welfare (the emphasis of the trustee perspective) are minimized, but not entirely.

Redefining the professional as 'expert', rather than 'trustee', has three consequences. First, professional success is related to profitability and serving those who pay, not to serving clients in need. Second, clients are paymasters and therefore should have a powerful voice. Third, technical competence is downgraded because other attributes, that is managerial and entrepreneurial skills, are given equal status.

The distinction between the trustee and the expert definitions of professionalism is useful because it suggests definitions of professional and unprofessional behaviour. For example, under the trusteeship definition, marketing would be regarded as unprofessional, especially if it involved 'poaching' clients. The expertise definition, on the other hand, would tolerate rather more overt marketing. Similarly, whereas both definitions would regard misrepresentation of competence as unprofessional, the expertise definition, with its emphasis upon the market, would contain a stronger tone of *caveat emptor*. Under the trustee definition, promotion to partnership in a law firm would be on the basis of technical competence and service, whereas under the expertise definition it would be more on the basis of an ability to generate new business and successfully manage clients. In short, the expertise definition legitimates a more commercial approach to the conduct of law firms.

Brint argues that recent decades have seen a shift towards the logic of expertise. How far this is the case is not clear, but there are signs that he might be correct. Leblebici (this volume) for example, notes that the trend from the regulation of fees by professional associations towards more firm-level determination of appropriate billing, reflected a new understanding of the profession. Lawyers were no longer seen as public officers but were acting as private citizens for private purposes. In effect, this new understanding recognizes the right of lawyers to *sell* their expertise. More recently, concerns have been expressed that law firms prefer to serve the very largest corporations because doing so is especially profitable. Serving a particular category of clients is not inevitably antithetical to the principles of trusteeship. Yet, evidence from recent, well-publicized failures raises cause for concern. The Enron affair is a stark example of how prestigious professional service firms (including law firms) were alleged to have behaved inappropriately.

The argument that I want to put forward is that *these breakdowns in professional behaviour are directly linked to the increasing rates of competition, size, and complexity and the associated adoption of more formal management structures*. These dynamics have tilted law firms towards celebration of the logic of expertise and weakened the impulse to think of themselves as trustees of a higher set of principles. That is, I propose that increasing competition, size, and complexity have led to the adoption of structures and processes that have (possibly unintentionally) enabled a shift in how professionals think about 'professionalism'.

Professional behaviour is shaped by four 'agents of socialization': educational institutions (such as law schools), professional associations (law societies, bar associations), clients (especially large clients), and employing organizations (law firms). These agencies have different *relative* commitments to the two definitions of professionalism. Thus, clients are more committed to seeing professionals as experts, expecting that lawyers will provide *technical* excellence focused upon their (the clients') interests. Professional associations profess the ideal of trusteeship because they interface with the state and society. They are (possibly) more aware of and concerned about risks to the profession's monopoly should their members be seen to adopt commercial success as the primary (or exclusive) criterion of appropriate conduct. Educational institutions have been little studied but, at face value, are also likely to promote the ideals of trusteeship. Law firms contain both definitions. On the one hand, they are commercial entities seeking business success. On the other, they are, supposedly, professional-friendly environments, nurturing the ideals of trusteeship.

Each of the three contextual shifts raised earlier can be argued to have affected the balance between the relative influence of the four socializing agents. First, the structural developments within law firms described in this volume reinforce and reproduce the importance of commercial success. Managing law firms as businesses highlights the importance of commercialism. The development of corporate structures and systems in response to greater competition has amplified attention to commercial criteria. In other words, the balance of emphasis within large law firms has shifted away from the notion of trusteeship towards that of expertise. Further, law firms are more vulnerable to 'client capture' and thus to adopting their clients' definition of professionalism. Finally, the sheer scale and geographical scope of modern law firms has weakened the regulatory ability of their professional associations. Law firms have outgrown the boundaries of existing regulatory agencies. The preference of large firms for in-house training means that lawyers are less exposed to the moderating influence of law societies. Taken together, all these factors suggest that large law firms will define professionalism as a commitment to commercially focused expertise.

Empson (Chapter 2) offers a more optimistic picture. For her, the legal form of partnership could be displaced without fundamentally undermining collegial relationships (the 'ethos' of partnership) provided that particular attributes are in place. I do not deny this possibility. Nevertheless, I am less sanguine. What matters is not only whether the ethos of partnership can be protected in the large, complex law firm (I fully accept that this is important), but also how far, and whether, the ethos of partnership is hitched to the logic of expertise and/or trusteeship. Arguably, a powerful ethos of partnership solely focused upon a definition of professionalism as market-driven expertise, would be the worst of all worlds. I suggest, therefore, that recent changes in the management structures and systems of law firms (and of other professional service firms) have contributed to the ascendancy of a more commercial imagery of the law firm, and that this could adversely affect professional behaviour.

These changes to the values of a professional service firm are neither irrevocable nor inevitable. Empson suggests how values of partnership might be sustained by particular structures. The same argument is probably applicable to my concern with professional values. The key point, however, is that acknowledgement of the problem, namely the *risk to the balance between the two value systems, has to be recognized*. This is not easy to achieve. Moore et al. (2006) convincingly describe how large professional service firms (in their case, accounting firms) are vulnerable to 'moral seduction' because of incremental dynamics that gently direct a firm unwittingly in a direction that they would normally try to avoid.

Therefore academic and practitioner attention needs to turn to the possible implications for professional conduct of the changes analysed in this volume. The professions are highly privileged. It is time, once again, to scrutinize more carefully the forces determining the relative priorities which lawyers give to professional and commercial values and to consider whose interests they serve. In other words, *cui bono*?

10

Your challenge

Sustaining partnership in the twenty-first century: the global law firm experience

Tony Angel
Linklaters LLP

Introduction

The emergence of global law firms over the past decade has been one of the most remarkable developments in the history of the legal profession. It reflects those firms' decisions to align themselves with the world's emerging global corporates and financial institutions and their ambition to build worldwide relationships with them. As such it also reflects a very different approach to the practice of law, and one which has catapulted law firms onto a global stage.

This is not to underestimate pioneering international networks established in the past by firms such as Baker & McKenzie, Coudert Brothers, and others; but these were not amongst the elite law firms in the market. Nor did the early international networks established by US and UK firms create global organizations; they were—and most international firms remain—overwhelmingly based in their home jurisdictions and dominated by their home law heritage and home-based clients.

The global law firms are increasingly different. They initially emerged mainly from the UK rather than the USA, and it is still the case that four out of the five largest firms in the world by number of lawyers, and four out of six by gross revenue, are headquartered in the UK.[1] These firms have had to face some unique business challenges as they have extended their size and geographic reach. The question often asked is: at what cost?

In meeting these challenges, have they moved so far beyond their roots as professional partnerships as to become global international businesses? Picking up on the issue raised by Laura Empson's earlier chapter, is it really possible for global law firms to retain the core elements of professionalism and partnership, as well as the collegial culture, so prized by lawyers? Or have they reached a scale when they are simply legal machines, where the individualism, entrepreneurial flair, collegiality and partnership ethos that exists within smaller firms has given way to corporatism, stultification of initiative, commercialism and a new kind of culture?

In short, have the global law firms sold their souls to the corporate devil?

Certainly, global law firms have in a short space of time developed from relatively small national partnerships to giant global businesses. In doing so, they have had to adopt some of the techniques and systems of much bigger organizations and to adapt some time-honoured partnership practices. Some critics argue that in making this transition they have lost some of the core aspects of the partnership ethos. I would argue the contrary; that, in fact, the success of the strategies of the global law firms depends on them maintaining the essence of the partnership model.

These firms have had to think hard about the challenges—cultural, organizational, and strategic—posed by increasing scale and geographic reach, and about how to sustain a partnership ethos in a multi-office, multi-practice, worldwide firm.

In this chapter, I outline the history of these firms and the factors that drove them to globalize; I describe the strategy they have adopted to meet the challenges of globalization; and I explore some critical aspects of the partnership ethos in a global law firm and explain how it is maintained. In doing so, I touch on some of the criticisms that are made of global law firms and challenge the 'corporate myth' that has emerged.

I speak essentially from my own experience as Managing Partner of Linklaters from November 1998 to date. During this time we underwent a transformation from being an English law firm to becoming a global one—although I expect the experiences will have been pretty similar in other globalizing magic circle firms and in firms seeking to emulate them. In retrospect, when we embarked on the journey, we underestimated the scale and intricacy of the challenge we faced, especially as the period of transition coincided with a period of recession. I suspect all the global law firms have learned, and continue to learn, a great deal about how effectively to harness the scale, power, and complexity of their global firms for the benefit of clients whilst maintaining the motivations, values, and approach that made them successful partnerships in the first place.

I can only describe what global law firms have done and why they have done it: others must judge whether in their view they have in consequence moved from a 'partnership' to a 'corporate' culture.

A little bit of history

It is first necessary to understand something of the history of these firms, how they emerged and the process of globalization that transformed them.

We do not have to go back far in time to recall an age of national law firms using overseas correspondents. Senior partners of leading national firms from across the world established informal, often personal, networks at yearly conferences of the International Bar Association. Firms developed 'good' or even 'best' friend relationships but operated entirely independently. With one or two exceptions, international firms did not really come into existence until the 1970s. It was then that a few law firms, including what came to be known as the magic circle law firms in the UK, started to move beyond their premium position in the domestic market to expand overseas.

Throughout the 1970s, that expansion, for UK-based firms at least, involved the establishment of small offices in financial centres around the world, made possible by the standing and perceived neutrality of English law and by the Eurodollar market that came into existence when US regulation and taxes drove dollar fund-raising outside the USA. Magic circle firms were able to set up overseas branches focused around international financings as well as the use of English language and English law in international trade and cross-border transactions. Once established, these offices also acted as convenient locations for domestic English law advice for overseas clients in an age of less advanced communications.

It is not clear whether any of these operations were ever profitable; the financial systems did not exist to find out and, on the whole, English law firms were pretty relaxed then about the profitability of individual practices and offices. The driver for the establishment of many overseas offices was the personal inclination of a particular partner to spend a few years in a pleasant foreign capital, so business plans were often pretty rudimentary; individual enthusiasm played a large part in the decision-making process.

By the 1980s the position was changing. The large, mainly Anglo-Saxon, clients of magic circle firms found it puzzling that when they went, say, to the Paris office of their favourite firm they could not get a transaction done under French law. They had grown to like the way in which magic circle firms handled transactions and dealt with client relationships, and were more used to their solution-orientated approach than to the rather academic approach that then existed in Continental Europe. This client demand led the magic circle firms to establish small domestic law operations in key jurisdictions alongside their English law operations.

The picture changed dramatically in the 1990s. First, the advance of technology broke down barriers of time and space; secondly, deregulation reduced tariff barriers, led to the abolition of exchange controls, and drove a step change in international trade. The combination in the financial arena, when coupled with rapidly integrating global markets, led to the emergence of financial super-conglomerates of huge scale and financial muscle. In the corporate sector, global companies emerged; major technology and telecommunications companies grew out of nothing as the internet, mobile technology, and e-mail took hold; and industrial production was transformed by the transfer of manufacturing to new and rapidly developing low cost centres. In Europe, the growth of the single market was also a compelling driver of change: nationally based companies started to see the entire EU, and not just one country within it, as their home market.

In comparison with their globalizing clients, at first the legal profession remained fragmented and most firms continued to be essentially national. But, as the dramatic change in their clients continued, a number of firms saw a developing threat to their existing relationships if they did not respond to their clients' changing business needs, as well as the opportunity to follow and help their clients around the world. Hence, increasingly over the course of the 1990s, most of the magic circle firms grew their non-UK–based operations and expanded their 'foreign law' footprint. By the early years of the new millennium, four of the five UK magic circle firms had effectively made the decision, often with continental European firms as merged partners, to transform themselves from internationally minded English law partnerships into global law firms.

Globalization

What did the process of globalization mean for a law firm? To us it meant aligning Linklaters around a target client base of the world's major corporations and financial institutions—putting ourselves in a position to undertake for those clients their most complex, challenging, and important transactions across the globe. To do that we needed a firm which had sufficient strength and depth to establish close relationships in the jurisdictions where target clients were headquartered, and the broader execution capability necessary to effect their most important transactions around the world.

This is not the place to describe the different approaches that the four globalizing magic circle firms took to establishing their global networks, nor to contrast their approaches with those of most of the US-headquartered international firms. But it is worth speculating on why most US firms took a different route. Whilst one or two mainly regional US firms emerged with a similar globalization strategy to the magic circle, the major New York–based firms that ventured overseas more commonly focused on an 'enhanced internationalization' strategy, similar to the magic circle firms in the 1980s.

The USA is a hugely larger economy than the UK, the home to many more global companies and a more litigious society. Even when US corporates and banks expand overseas, the US domestic market generally remains extremely important to them; and New York is the world's leading financial centre. These factors create a huge and profitable domestic market for US law firms and lessen their immediate need—and appetite—to expand abroad. This is especially so for the ultra-profitable elite New York firms—the natural competitors to the magic circle in the finance area—who culturally have also tended to eschew size. The result has been a much more cautious approach to practising non-US law.

In contrast, the UK domestic economy is relatively small, extremely open, and internationally oriented. The result is a domestic legal market that cannot support large numbers of big law firms, but has a significant number of UK-headquartered clients with global aspirations. Coupled with an internationally acceptable legal system and the benefit of the English language, UK firms were thus compelled to expand out of the UK market to grow and flourish, and they were able to do so—at least initially—by following their clients.

There is a tendency to underestimate what the UK-headquartered firms achieved over a mere five-year period, driven by the restrictions of their domestic market and the globalization of their clients. In terms of Peter

Sherer's cluster analysis (Chapter 8), the four global magic circle firms are more profitable than all but the elite US firms—despite an investment in their global networks that has run to hundreds of millions of pounds in a short space of time. They do this at a scale several times that of the elite US firms and significantly greater even than that of the later internationalizers, and with hugely greater geographic spread. Many of the US elite pride themselves on their relationships with the US investment and commercial banks; the global magic circle firms will typically bill those clients alone hundreds of millions of dollars, with Clifford Chance and Allen & Overy in particular having huge banking practices. In 2005, as in previous years, the global magic circle firms dominated the European and Asian M&A league tables;[2] and despite their relatively weak US M&A practices, they took four of the top twelve places in the global M&A league tables.[3] The banks and corporates using the global law firms on this work are amongst the world's most sophisticated organizations and extraordinarily demanding clients; the success of the global magic circle firms is a tribute to their quality of service even more than to their scale.

As to what they look like, the UK-headquartered global law firms are rapidly becoming truly global professional service firms. They are single integrated global partnerships with hundreds of partners sharing a single profit pool and, largely, a single lockstep remuneration structure across practices and offices. Although UK-headquartered, all now have more fee earners overseas than in the UK and, increasingly, international management: Freshfields, for example, now has joint German and British Senior Partners and a US Managing Partner; and Linklaters' International Board includes partners of seven different nationalities. The firms undertake transactions that frequently require cross-practice and cross-office teams working on deals involving multiple laws, and they operate complex matrix management systems across dimensions such as client, practice, sector, and office as they seek better to integrate their worldwide networks and serve their global clients. Contrast this with the international accountancy firms which, now Arthur Andersen has gone, are essentially federations of separate firms still striving for global integration. Most of the management consulting firms ceased to be partnerships long ago and, even when they operate as if they were, essentially the same skill and product is sold in different markets. None have had to face the pace of change the global law firms have faced.

Strategy and alignment

So what is the basic strategy of a global law firm and what is needed to align the firm behind that strategy?

Competitive advantage for a global law firm lies in its ability to put together teams across practices and across offices to manage global client relationships and to undertake complex transactions more effectively than can be achieved by independent firms working alone or together. Realizing that competitive advantage requires both a very clear strategy for the firm and the alignment of the entire organization behind it. The partners of the firm must live and breathe it so that, instinctively, their entrepreneurial efforts, marketing, working practices and approach all pull in the same direction, towards achieving the firm's strategy. Within a decentralized organization, as any successful law firm must be if it is to be responsive to clients, it is the implementation of the strategy through the individual actions of partners every day that defines the firm—not what 'central management' says.

Strategy in a global firm

Within Linklaters, and, I expect, other global firms, strategy starts with identifying our target clients—the world's major corporations and financial institutions. These are the clients around which we are seeking to align the firm. They are large, complex organizations and are more likely than other clients to undertake complex transactions across practices and across offices. These clients, and the financial institutions in particular, often have multiple decision-makers in different locations and different functional areas within their organizations, each of whom may instruct law firms. If global firms have sufficiently effective client relationship management systems they can leverage their global reach. By managing the relationship effectively across their networks, they can deliver better value to the client—through better knowledge of the client, its systems, its approach and its global business needs—than their competitors.

That is not to say that global firms do not act for many other organizations, some of which are entirely domestic. In those instances, however, competitive advantage derives more from the quality of lawyers whom global law firms are able to recruit, the training they are given, and the global experience, systems, and scale they can bring to bear.

The position changes on cross-border transactions, and in particular when global firms act for their target clients on their most complex transactions across borders and across practices. Here their competitive advantage comes into play most forcibly. Our own internal evidence is clear. The more of our offices are involved in a transaction, the higher our average billing rates—from wherever in the world that matter is managed and well over 50 per cent of our income now comes from transactions that involve more than one office to a significant extent.

The increase in billing rates with geographic spread is not surprising: multi-office transactions are often a proxy for complexity. On those sorts of deals we, like other global firms, have fewer competitors and are better able to leverage our global experience, practices, systems, and infrastructure, to deliver a superior service for our clients.

Achieving strategic alignment

A strategy which focuses on the most complex cross-practice, cross-jurisdictional work for the world's leading companies and banks, is extraordinarily demanding. In my judgement, it requires:

1. a clear agreement across the firm of who our target clients are and what our target work is, so as to minimize conflicts, maximize efforts towards institutionalizing global relationships across the network, and best to leverage competitive advantage;

2. the highest level of quality and expertise across the firm, delivered in a coherent and consistent way across practices and across offices;

3. an ability and willingness rapidly to form teams across practices and across offices to work together effectively on transactions—without the inhibitions generated by questions about the allocation of credit for the deal or arguments about who will be leading and managing it;

4. a common firm culture, and so a recognizable 'look and feel' for the client wherever they deal with the firm, even if there may well be a local accent in any particular jurisdiction;

5. an infrastructure that supports global client relationships, integrated cross-border working and a global organization;

6. an entrepreneurial approach by partners to the development of the firm's business, and a sense of ownership that makes partners willing to take the necessary action to maintain the alignment of the firm behind its strategic objectives.

It also requires the entire firm to be aligned behind the strategy. Even in a global law firm, both legal advice and management (of clients, transactions, and people) are highly decentralized; every part of the firm needs to be fully aligned behind the firm's objectives, so that it naturally responds in an integrated way with the rest of the network, if the strategy is to succeed fully.

Getting to this degree of alignment is a journey, and a challenging one given the background from which global law firms have come. They grew rapidly domestically, and largely organically, in the late 1980s and early 1990s, but their international expansion in recent years has made them much bigger again as a result of organic growth, team hires, lateral hires and mergers. These have made the cultural and management challenges of integration especially hard.

The pace at which this move to alignment has occurred, the approaches adopted and the distance so far travelled has been different in different firms. However, one particularly striking driver has been the more managed approach to lockstep and decisions about which partners and practices fit within a global firm. Whilst it is wrong to focus too much on lockstep, it does attract continuing attention, and much of the negative impression of global law firms that has emerged in recent years is, I suspect, the result of this managed approach.

All the UK-headquartered global firms are lockstep firms, with partner take based solely on seniority. Historically, lockstep was seen as a benign system. The automatic increase in remuneration, coupled with a lack of accountability for performance by individual partners to the firm as a whole, meant that wide divergences in both practice alignment and contribution were tolerated. With the advent of globalization this changed and lockstep came to be seen as a powerful driver of integration and alignment. It encourages referrals within the network, sharing of work, institutionalizing of clients, a global approach to client relationship management, and teamwork on transactions. It is irrelevant to the remuneration of individual partners who actually introduces or works on any particular deal—the only way to improve individual remuneration is to improve overall profitability.

But, for lockstep to drive alignment it needs to be managed. If global lockstep firms are to compete effectively in the global market they must be sufficiently profitable to retain their stars; taken with the strong sense of fairness prevalent in partnerships this requires all partners to make an overall contribution (as part of a practice or office team) broadly in line with their lockstep remuneration. Where over time this is not achieved, a partner has to cease to be an equity partner as, within a strict lockstep system, there is simply no mechanism for reducing remuneration to bring take back into line with contribution. This drives alignment with the firm's strategy: partners in practices and offices that are insufficiently aligned in terms of clients or work will find it increasingly hard to make an adequate contribution. The most complex and challenging work for the best clients is, on the whole, the most profitable work. Partners in practices who act for lower level clients and on less demanding work (and who therefore are not aligned with the firm's strategy) are not able to keep up. Neither are those who do not have the skills required to do this work. Over the past five years global law firms have parted company with many of them.

Could these firms have retained these partners and/or practices at a lower level of remuneration where pay and contribution were in line? In my judgment, only at immense cost to the strategic alignment and focus of the firm.[4]

Some say this sort of determined action in support of a strategic objective illustrates the loss by global law firms of partnership values. Certainly the firms themselves recognize the dangers of managing performance within a lockstep firm too aggressively: if partners have concerns over their future, they may cease to adopt the very behaviours lockstep is designed to encourage. But partnership is a two-way street: firms must be fair to partners, and partners must also make a fair contribution to the firm.

The partnership ethos

The continued existence of lockstep within the magic circle global law firms is a strong driver not just of a partnership ethos but of the behaviours outlined above as key to the success of the firms' strategies. However it is certainly not sufficient. A number of other key factors are necessary:

1. *teamwork*: to form teams across practices and offices;
2. *management*: to maintain focus on target work and clients, to enforce quality and to deliver infrastructure;
3. *sense of ownership*: to encourage an entrepreneurial approach and active involvement by partners in delivering the firm's strategy;

4. *cultural alignment and collegiality*: to ensure a consistency of experience for global clients and to reinforce teamwork and firm values; and

5. *profitability and public good*: to attract and retain the best.

It seems to me that all of these are entirely consistent with partnership. It is curious then that it is precisely these five areas that critics focus on when they say that global law firms have lost their partnership ethos and now have more of the scale and culture of corporations. The criticisms tend to be around the same five areas:

1. *teamwork—or autonomy*: a focused firm strategy reduces a partner's freedom of choice as to whether a client or matter is taken on, how it is carried out and the underlying professional independence or autonomy that is seen as the essence of being a partner in a professional partnership;

2. *management*: professionals hate to be 'managed'. Within a global law firm, it is perceived that lawyers have to fit within a hierarchical management structure and are subject to unnecessary systems and processes that inhibit individual preferences;

3. *sense of ownership*: it is of the essence of partnership that a partner should have the rights of an owner of the business. Within a global firm it is perceived that this sense of ownership has disappeared and that partners have become mere employees;

4. *culture and collegiality*: in a partnership there is a sense of 'clubbiness', a collegiality that is palpable in many firms. The view is that this sense of collegiality cannot operate on a global scale across hundreds of partners;

5. *profitability and public good*: lawyers pride themselves on being in a unique profession and on being driven by more than the mere motive of profit. Individual partners must be able to decide in any particular case what trade-offs they wish to make between taking on work for the public good and achieving acceptable levels of profitability. The ability to make that choice is constrained if certain kinds of work are 'out of bounds' or insufficiently profitable.

So, the above five key success factors and criticisms of global law firms are the flipside of the same coin. Does the debate matter? I think it does. These are five critically important challenges global law firms must address if they are to remain attractive places for professionals to make a career and if they are to maintain their ability to attract and retain the best recruits. I see the approach of the global law firms to each of these five factors as entirely conducive to a partnership ethos. The criticisms seem to confuse a partnership with a collection of sole practitioners—they reflect a vision of law firms stuck in the ethos of the barristers' chambers or two-partner law firms of the nineteenth century.

Teamwork or autonomy?

Teamwork is core to aligning a global firm behind its strategy and delivering an effective service to clients. Global law firms target clients which cannot be looked after by a single partner but are served by many partners in multiple areas, so cooperation between partners in managing the client relationship is critical. So too in doing the work: lawyers from many practices and offices have to work together if they are to deliver an exceptional result in an integrated way on transactions across practices and offices for these institutional clients.

So, global law firms need to invest heavily to build teamwork—with regular practice and office meetings, cross-practice and office training sessions (not just for technical knowledge but in soft skills and creating common values), secondments between offices, and similar activities. They need to establish the ability to operate to common standards across the world through common training, the use of common precedents, and the adoption of common motivations and values.

This kind of teamwork requires, first and foremost, buy-in to a common goal; a common appreciation of which clients and transactions are important to the firm. To the extent that partners cannot then have different aims and objectives, yes they lose autonomy. But there is, in my judgement, something better than autonomy—its antithesis, partnership, or as the UK Partnership Act of 1891 defines it, 'carrying on business in common with a view of profit'.

To the extent that autonomy requires multiple individual partner objectives to be accommodated within a single firm, it is not possible to present the integrated and coherent approach that global law firms strive to achieve, servicing their core clients on their core transactions. In a firm where partners have different priorities and different aspirations, different clients will be important to different people within the firm. The system may work well for smaller transactions and national clients, where effectively one partner delivers the service, perhaps with support from a couple of specialists, but it is not effective to manage a multi-jurisdictional client relationship or the delivery of a complex service to a global bank. Autonomy can thrive within a collegial environment where the collegiality allows partners to support each other where necessary and accommodate differences of approach, but collegiality that does not foster teamwork, however much it involves friendship, is not the kind of collegiality that global firms need. For a global firm, teamwork is key.

Management: always a bad thing?

The scale of global law firms, their challenging strategy and the need to achieve a high degree of alignment around that strategy, makes management essential. But, given the extremely negative way in which professionals respond to management of any kind, it is perhaps worth explaining in more detail what management means in this context.

Essentially, within a global law firm, management has three main tasks:

1. to obtain partner buy-in to the firm's goals and objectives;
2. to maintain alignment of the firm behind them; and
3. to provide the infrastructure and support that enables the firm to achieve them.

Obtaining partner buy-in to the firm's goals and objectives is obviously key. I have outlined above how, within a professional service firm, it is the individual behaviours of partners on the ground that define the firm's strategy and culture; and unless there is substantial buy-in from partners to the firm's goals and objectives, no amount of management will achieve them.

Even where there is a substantial buy-in, maintaining alignment behind those objectives is a challenge. The firm will need to make numerous choices as to which clients to target, what work to do, what practices and offices to grow, how to prioritize limited resources, and so on, if it is to make real progress towards achieving its strategy. All of these choices may impact adversely on some partners. Maintaining buy-in will then, in effect, require management to be able to rely on peer pressure amongst partners so that the consensus in favour of maintaining alignment with the firm's objectives will override individual objections. This remains feasible only so long as management has credibility and there is broad agreement on the firm's strategic objectives.

Within Linklaters, the partnership long ago determined that, if we are to achieve our strategic objectives, when it comes to the management of the firm there must be a greater sense of direction; it is the Firmwide Managing Partner (FMP) who is responsible for ensuring the firm's strategy is implemented. The FMP appoints the National Managing Partners (NMPs) (grouped into regions) and Global Practice Heads (GPHs) (grouped into three divisions) who head up the countries and practices within our matrix system and who are responsible for ensuring that each practice and each office achieves the goals set for it. Although the appointment is after consultation and subject to approval by the International Board (see below), the aim is to minimize the tendency for NMPs and GPHs to act simply as shop stewards for their partners—that would give a bottom-up degree of control which would lead to a significant lack of focus within the firm. In practice, the process works well at regional and divisional level, but a different approach is needed at lower levels. Within smaller groups of partners the strong ethos of partnership means partners tend to operate more as peers rather than in a hierarchical way. So, the smaller the unit, the greater the need for consensus. With larger units, it is accepted that consultation rather than consensus is sufficient.

But, describing the system in terms of its hierarchy is to miss the most critical part of the management process. In practice, management spends, and rightly spends, a significant amount of time consulting, communicating with and persuading the partnership. On the biggest governance issues, the International Board may play a role, but in relation to most management issues this process is undertaken through the management hierarchy. As it is what partners do every day on the ground that really counts, it is important to win hearts and minds if real progress is to be made. The key difference today is that decisions are no longer taken by consensus; they are taken by management if, after consultation, they are still thought to be right and if sufficient support has been won, whether or not there is consensus (or, sometimes, even a majority). Partners generally accept that subtle but important shift, that management must be allowed to manage—so long as they have had a fair opportunity to have their voice heard.

Finally, management plays an essential role in providing the infrastructure and support that the firm needs to achieve its goals. Generally, in any firm it is accepted that physical infrastructure is provided by management, but to obtain alignment in a global firm more is required. The need for consistency of quality across the firm, a common approach to handling transactions, the effective management of client relationships, and so forth, means that, increasingly, over time, a consistent global firm

209

approach is required to recruitment, training, client relationship management and much else, and that the infrastructure to achieve that needs to be both delivered across the firm and consistently utilized. This is, I suspect, work in progress in many global firms, and certainly in Linklaters. The pace at which changes are introduced needs to match the pace of partner buy-in to these systems and processes and the acceptance of their value—a difficult balance to achieve as their impact affects an increasingly wide range of partner activity.

So, management does operate to restrict a partner's freedom of action in some key respects. Partners are guided towards the clients the firm wants to serve and the work it wants to do; they are asked to follow best practice guidelines in relation to client relationship and people management; they are expected to exhibit the firm's motivations and live the firm's values.

However, management does not mean central management of work. That always remains within the sphere of the partners running the practice teams, the clients and the matters. Global law firms, like any others, ultimately depend on the skill and professionalism of the lawyers on the deal to deliver for clients.

Furthermore, management depends ultimately on the consent of the managed. Global law firms are still partnerships and management is accountable to partners for its actions. Difficult management actions are only feasible where there is general buy-in to the firm's strategy and to the goals and objectives that have been set. It is to the credit of partners that they are now prepared to delegate the management of the firm to others to achieve its strategy even though the consequences may sometimes be uncomfortable. However, if management gets too far away from partners, it will fail.

Essentially, therefore, management within a global firm is ultimately linked to the need—and the desire of partners as a whole—to maintain strategic alignment and the firm's culture. The larger and more diverse a firm becomes, the greater the risk that the bonds of a common goal and culture will be weakened. What happened naturally in a one-office firm needs to be actively managed in a global firm. Protecting the bonds of a common goal and culture means that you need the explicit expression of a common vision and values. The management team leading a global firm essentially become the stewards of that common vision and those values; partners accept the logic that, if the firm is to be successful, this is a vital role.

Ownership: partner or employee?

But what of ownership? Surely within global law firms today partners have become mere employees? That is indeed a challenge. It is critically important in a global law firm that partners maintain both the entrepreneurial approach to the development of the business, and the sense of proprietorship, that makes the highly decentralized management of the firm's business effective. This only comes with a sense of ownership.

I think we need to disentangle here the three roles of partners. First, they do the work—they bring to clients a degree of experience and technical expertise which is their professional skill. Second, they are managers— of client relationships, of people working on the job, and of transactions. Finally, partners have a role as owners of the business. They put up capital for the firm alongside their time and their career and are entitled to know that the organization into which they have committed that capital and from which they derive their livelihood is operating as effectively as possible.

There are different ways of approaching this ownership right. One is certainly to say that on becoming a partner you gain the right to determine whether something does or does not occur. That certainly remains the attitude within some partnerships, and if that is regarded as the essence of being a partner then, indeed, the global firms have lost it. However, if the essence of being a partner is to 'carry on business in common with others with a view to profit' then, despite—and because of—being a part owner, each partner owes to the others an obligation to work effectively towards the benefit of the organization as a whole and towards achieving its goals. Giving a right of veto is to confuse ownership and management rights.

For that very reason, individual partners at times have to bow to the greater good: the majority vote counts, and where the majority have delegated decision-making to a management structure then its decision counts. If a firm is to be effective, when it has under a properly authorized process reached a decision on a way forward, individual objections cannot be allowed to upset that decision. The partners in global law firms long ago relinquished their right to object to the colour of the carpet.

So, how do the global firms maintain the important sense of ownership amongst partners? Fundamentally it comes from two almost contradictory dynamics. First, management needs to be given the authority and power to manage, but is accountable to partners as a whole as owners of the firm for its actions. Second, even for decisions within its authority and power, a sensible global law firm management will—as noted earlier—think carefully about how to get partner buy-in, and on big decisions will consult extensively. Where this occurs, it is generally possible to get acceptance of decisions even from those with an opposite view.

Within Linklaters we have a two-tier board structure. At the top of the firm, the International Board is the ultimate governance authority of the firm. It is to the International Board that the FMP is responsible and accountable for delivering the strategy of the firm. The FMP reports regularly to the International Board as to the firm's progress, and seeks support and approval from the International Board for major initiatives—the most major of which (such as the election of new partners) may need approval by vote of partners as a whole. Plainly it is critical to that process that the Board comprises partners of stature within the firm who represent the full range of constituencies and the Board is elected by partners as a whole by secret ballot.

It is through the governance structure that partners exercise their 'rights' as owners, directly on the most major issues and otherwise indirectly through the International Board. If partners are concerned about the management of the firm, they can raise issues with the International Board and the FMP can be held to account. The Board effectively acts as the partnership in miniature.

But, whilst important, this governance structure and the accountability of management alone are not enough. Partners need to be treated as owners of the business in other ways too. Generally, involvement and consultation on key decisions, widespread dissemination of information and good communication is also important, as are tangible privileges of ownership.

Even with all this, however, maintaining a sense of ownership with increasing scale is an ever more formidable challenge. It is one that global law firms need to meet if they are to maintain the engagement of partners.

Culture: collegial or not?

Most partnerships have their own distinct culture and global law firms are no different in this respect. The difference between them and most smaller firms is the way in which culture is nurtured, protected, and passed on.

When firms are sufficiently small, and especially where they are substantially located in a single place, a common culture is achieved by regular contact amongst partners, who then set the tone for the firm as a whole and socialize new entrants into the partnership. On the whole, relatively little positive action to identify and promulgate the culture is felt to be necessary; indeed in some cases the culture is actually homogenized by ensuring partners come from a particular school, class or background: this is the backbone to their collegiality.

As firms grow, at first they can achieve a similar degree of cultural alignment by working at it hard enough—seconding partners from one office to another, holding regular partner and team meetings and maintaining a 'dominant' group. As they get even bigger they may define common goals. But, eventually, firms reach a scale where something more needs to be done to maintain that common culture and collegiality between partners.

Within a global law firm there is plainly a need for a common culture and collegiality: every lawyer a client deals with anywhere in the world is a representative of the firm and needs to exhibit common values. The teamwork which is critical to a global firm strategy is based on a collegial approach.

So, achieving and then maintaining a common culture is a major task for a global law firm and one to which huge effort is applied. It requires not just the definition of common goals to which all partners in the firm subscribe, but a clearly articulated set of motivations and values. We, and I expect other global firms, struggle with getting buy-in to this as a concept, but partners clearly recognize and value the common culture we are trying to build. More than that they also seek collegiality across the firm. Given the diversity of nationalities and cultures represented in a global firm, there is not the uniform background amongst partners that appears in many national partnerships, but are global firms necessarily any the less collegiate for that?

As I see it, global law firms differ from national firms in the way in which collegiality is built and operates.

Within a single office, collegiality is built by contact. Partners bump into each other in the corridor, are often friends as well as colleagues, and mix socially. Within a global firm collegiality by contact still operates within individual offices or practices, but across the firm collegiality has to be created by aligning partners behind common objectives, common goals, and common aspirations. It is then nurtured and grows as global firms build a common culture. When a partner knows that whoever they deal with across the firm, whether they know them or not, is trying to achieve the same goal and is driven by the same motivations and holds the same values, then collegiality will exist even between partners who rarely meet.

This effect, though hard to describe, is commonly seen in other contexts. If you travel abroad and meet a member of some society of which you are a member, or a fellow alumnus from university or school, there is often a strong sense of connection based on little more than a common experience. If, within a global law firm, that can be coupled with common motivations and values, a common purpose and common objectives, a strong sense of collegiality can be generated.

Building that common culture means first articulating the goals, motivations and values and then ensuring that they are lived and nurtured. At first they may be seen as woolly and irrelevant. It takes time and clear signals of their importance to make them real and meaningful. They need to be continually reinforced, and the sense of collegiality can certainly be helped by contact—in cross-office practice groups, common training and working together. With increasing volumes of work requiring teams across practices and across offices, the opportunities to reinforce collegiality by personal contact grow all the time. Whilst many global law firms are only part of the way along this journey, what is being built is very different, and I would say ultimately much more powerful, than collegiality based on sitting down the corridor from someone for twenty years.

Profitability and public good

One argument levelled at global law firms is that they are driven by commercial rather than professional considerations. The assumption is that the drive to profitability is incompatible with the highest professional standards. If that is the case, a number of things are striking about global law firms, at least those in the magic circle.

First, they all have strong and growing corporate social responsibility programmes. These extend well beyond traditional *pro bono* activities to encompass community activities more widely, and best practice in relation to the workplace, the environment and dealing with clients and suppliers. The firms as major and growing institutions recognize their responsibility to society as a whole. Global law firms consciously measure and control their efforts in this area, as much to ensure an appropriately high level of contribution is made as to limit it—what gets measured gets done. Given the allocation of a defined amount of resource, proper management processes exist to direct that effort in the most effective way, not simply according to the whims of individual partners.

Second, one of the reasons 'profitability' is seen as a dirty word relates to the position of trust that lawyers have in relation to their clients. Given the specialist knowledge a lawyer may have, he or she is perceived to be in a position where that trust may be abused if profit is a dominant motive. There is a different dynamic in a global law firm. Generally, their target clients are extremely knowledgeable about the transactions on which they seek help. Often in-house lawyers are heavily involved in reviewing advice received and make regular comparisons between the professionalism and approach of different firms. Hence, there is a very small risk of a disparity in knowledge leading to problems.

Third, global law firms are heavily dependent on their reputations. Loss of reputation by a global law firm would be devastating—witness what happened to Arthur Andersen. Hence the effort they put into maintaining the highest level of professional standards is huge, and certainly not affected by profitability issues. Generally every aspect of training, and the values global law firms seek to instil, give issues of integrity the greatest possible weight.

Conclusions: partnerships or corporations?

I think that there are two key areas of confusion amongst critics of global law firms. The first is to assume that partnership is coincident with independence rather than cooperation. The second is to look at the 'corporate' model as an alternative to partnership.

For these increasingly large law firms to function, they need a high degree of cooperation and professionalism coupled with systems and techniques that may be borrowed from corporates.

Many lawyers think of the corporate model as highly structured and organized with multiple layers of management, a lack of autonomy and strict controls. That may once have been true but it is certainly not the way corporations are going today. A recent survey in *The Economist*[5] quoted from the latest Annual Report of Toyota: 'Senior managing directors do not focus exclusively on management. They also serve as the highest authorities in the specific operational functions.' In other words, specialists have become leaders. This system, says the company, 'helps closely co-ordinate decision-making with actual operations'.

So, Toyota is moving to the same system that is essential within a law firm—of having producer managers steeped not in management but in the profession of being a lawyer.

Furthermore, the corporate model that lawyers have in their mind is an historic one based on multi-layered corporations where knowledge management played a small part. Now, they are much leaner, and knowledge workers represent a large and growing percentage of the employees of the world's biggest corporations.

Even a cursory glance at the management literature illustrates the increasing attention being given to the rise of knowledge workers and the need for corporations to find more effective ways of using them. Indeed, many are now trying to replicate the professional service firm partnership within a corporate structure. Far from law firms becoming more like corporations, in this respect corporations are struggling to become more like law firms.

This is because, in my judgement, global law firms do an extraordinarily good job of enabling their 'knowledge workers' to achieve their potential. They organize partners into teams and then set those teams very clear but high-level goals (aligned around the vision and strategy for the firm) of the sort of clients to go for and the sort of work to be achieved. They also set high-level profitability targets as, at least within a lockstep firm, wide divergences in profitability cannot easily be tolerated. But, they then largely leave those teams to get on with achieving their target objectives in whatever way they think fit. They support them with the right processes and systems to enable a coordinated approach and to create a common culture. They provide IT and business development and marketing support. They provide the training across offices and across practices that allows those national practice areas to work effectively with other national practice areas on major complex transactions. They provide systems and processes to attract and retain the best people and encourage partners to mentor associates and to bring them on in the way they should. Does this sound idealistic? In some ways yes: global law firms have a long way to go—but look how far they have come in just half a decade.

Have they come so far they can no longer be regarded as professional partnerships and have aligned themselves with the 'corporate' world? That depends on your own definition. Fundamentally, I think that, within a global law firm, the partnership ethos remains both essential and intrinsic to the organization. It is no longer simply an unspoken but shared cultural understanding; partners now share something more clearly enunciated but much more challenging—a common vision, a common goal, and common values—and are prepared to work together to achieve that. With a scale of 500 partners or so, that is not easy.

When partners do feel 'managed' and subject to the pressures of 'corporatism' (and that is a comment that does sometimes come from within these firms), what is actually happening is that the interests of the firm's broader partnership are being brought to bear on them through its governance and management structures. Achieving alignment around a vision means identifying, transitioning, and realigning those practices which threaten the achievement of that vision; whether it is by getting the firm into conflict situations, by undermining the quality of the brand, by affecting the consistency of performance, or by undermining profitability and so effectively damaging the firm's bargaining power in the recruitment market.

Management also means constantly re-evaluating the vision and resetting the goals. But bear in mind that the people who ultimately control the governance and management structure are the partners themselves: we all often recognize something we ought to be doing but find it difficult to do without being 'pushed' a little. The appointment and empowerment of the right people in the governance and management structure ensures that partners are subject to the right amount of push, and that the firm remains on the 'straight and narrow'.

So, the partnership ethos and the collegiality that comes with partnership, is no longer the automatic result of being two doors down a corridor from a colleague for twenty years. Within a global law firm it is actually much more important than that; it is part of their unique selling proposition. The culture they are building—reflected in the ability of their partners to work together in teams across practices and offices, to build and manage global client relationships, to trade their independence of action for the greater good of achieving the firm's objectives, and to communicate and work effectively in situations they just would not have been in twenty years ago—is the fundamental product that the clients of global law firms are buying. And increasingly, clients are valuing it highly.

Notes

1. *The Lawyer*, Global 100, 2005.
2. Mergermarket Tables of Legal Advisers 2005.
3. Thomson Financial Mergers & Acquisition Review Fourth Quarter 2005 (by value and volume).
4. Some global firms do have some mechanisms for dealing with differences in contribution, for example, using salaried partnerships or country-based adjustments, but these techniques are limited.
5. The New Organization: *The Economist*, 21 January 2006.

Bibliography

Abbott, A. (1988). *The System of Professions*. Chicago, IL: University of Chicago Press.

Abel, R. L. (1989). *American Lawyers*. Los Angeles: University of California Press.

—— (2003). *English Lawyers between Market and State: The Politics of Professionalism*. Oxford: Oxford University Press.

Aldenderfer, M. S. and Blashfield, R. K. (1984). *Cluster Analysis*. Beverly Hills, CA: Sage.

Alvesson, M. (2001). 'Knowledge Work: Ambiguity, Image and Identity', *Human Relations*, 54(7): 863–86.

American Bar Association (1980). *Model Rules of Professional Conduct*. Chicago, IL: American Bar Association.

American Bar Foundation (2004). *After The JD: A Ten Year Longitudinal Study of Lawyers' Careers. A Preliminary Report*. Chicago, IL: American Bar Foundation.

American Lawyer Editorial (2004). 'The Next 25 Years', *The American Lawyer*, 26(5): 25–6.

Anderson-Gough, F., Grey, C., and Robson, K. (1998). *Making Up Accountants: The Organizational and Professional Socialization of Trainee Chartered Accountants*. Aldershot, UK: Ashgate.

Augur, P. (2000). *The Death of Gentlemanly Capitalism*. London: Penguin.

Baker, W. E. (1990). 'Market Networks and Corporate Behavior', *American Journal of Sociology*, 96(3): 589–625.

Bar Council (2004). *Equality and Diversity Code for the Bar*. London: Bar Council.

Barney, J. (1991). 'Firm Resources and Sustained Competitive Advantage', *Journal of Management*, 17: 99–120.

Barrett, P. (1999). *The Good Black: A True Story of Race in America*. New York: Dutton Press.

Baxter, M. (1998). 'Black Bay Street Lawyers', *Canadian Business L. J.*, 30: 267.

Bower, M. (1997). *Will to Lead: Running a Business with a Network of Leaders*. Boston, MA: Harvard Business School Press.

Bower, W. (2004). 'Pricing Legal Services', in Altman Weil, Inc., *Report to Legal Management*. Milwaukee, WI: Altman Weil, Inc., May.

Braverman, P. (2001a). 'In Motion: Lateral Moves by Attorneys in Top 200 US Law Firms', *The American Lawyer*, February: 88–91, 93.

——— (2001b). 'Firm Anxiety: Greenberg Traurig Opens Los Angeles Office', *The American Lawyer*, July: 98–105.

Brint, S. (1994). *In An Age of Experts: The Changing Role of Professionals in Politics and Public Life*. Princeton, NJ: Princeton University Press.

Brock, D., Powell, M., and Hinings, C. R. (1999). *Restructuring the Professional Organization*. London and New York: Routledge.

Calloway, J. A. and Robertson, M. A. (2002). *Winning Alternatives to the Billable Hour: Strategies That Work*, 2nd edn. Chicago, IL: American Bar Association.

Carbado, D. and Gulati, G. M. (2000). 'Working Identity', *Cornell Law Review*, 85: 1259.

Catalyst (2001). *Women in the Law: Making the Case*. New York: Catalyst.

Caves, R. E. and Porter, M. E. (1977). 'From Entry Carriers to Mobility Barriers: Conjectural Decisions and Contrived Deterrence to New Competition', *Quarterly Journal of Economics*, 91: 24–262.

Chambliss, E. (2004). *Miles to Go: 2004: Progress of Minorities in the Legal Profession*. Chicago, IL: American Bar Association.

Chapman, C. and Empson, L. (2005). *Performance Measures, Pay, and Accountabilty: A Comparison of Two Professional Service Firms*. Gothenberg, Sweden: European Accounting Association.

Chroust, A-H. (1965). *The Rise of the Legal Profession in America*. New York: Norman.

Clark, E. T. J. (1989). 'Getting Out of the Hourly Rate Quagmire—Other Billing Alternatives', in R. C. Reed (ed.), *Beyond the Billable Hour: An Anthology of Alternative Billing Methods*. Chicago, IL: American Bar Association, pp. 183–6.

Clark, K. (2000). 'The Coming Together of the Common Law and Civil Law', in A. Kaufman and D. B. Wilkins (eds.), *Problems in Professional Responsibility for a Changing Profession*. Durham, NC: Carolina Academic Press.

Clementi, D. (2004). *Review of the Regulatory Framework for Legal Services in England and Wales*. London.

Coleman, J. S. (1988). 'Social Capital and the Creation of Human Capital', *American Journal of Sociology*, 94: S95–S120.

——— (1990). *Foundations of Social Theory*. Cambridge, MA: Belknap Press of Harvard University Press.

Committee on Lawyer Business Ethics (1998). 'Business and Ethics Implications of Alternative Billing Practices: Report on Alternative Billing Arrangements', *The Business Lawyer*, 54, November: 175–207.

Commons, J. R. (1934). *Institutional Economics*. Madison, WI: University of Wisconsin Press.

Cooper, D. J., Hinings, C. R., Greenwood, R., and Brown, J. L. (1996). 'Sedimentation and Transformation in Organizational Change: The Case of Canadian Law firms', *Organization Studies*, 17(4): 623–47.

Corporate Legal Times (2003). 'The Color Barrier: Minority Corporate Counsel Make Diversity a Top Priority', November: 42.

Coser, L. (1974). *Greedy Institutions: Patterns of Undivided Commitment*. New York: Free Press.

Cotterman, J. D. (2001). *Compensation Plans for Law Firms*, 3rd edn. Chicago, IL: American Bar Association.

Curtis, D. and Resnik, J. (2002). 'Teaching Billing: Metrics of Value in Law Firms and Law Schools', *Stanford Law Review*, 54: 1409–25.

Davis, L. F. (1994). 'Back to the Future: The Buyer's Market and the Need for Law Firm Leadership, Creativity and Innovation', *Campbell Law Review*, 16: 147–90.

Deger, R. (2003). 'Strength In Numbers', *San Francisco Recorder*, March 18.

Department for Constitutional Affairs (2005). *The Future of Legal Services: Putting Consumers First* (Cm 6679). London: The Stationery Office.

Dirsmith, M., Heian, J., and Covaleski, M. (1997). 'Structure and Agency in an Institutionalised Setting: The Application and Social Transformation of Control in the Big 6', *Accounting, Organizations and Society*, 22(1): 1–27.

DiversityInc (2003). The Business Case For Diversity, 4th edn.

Docters, R. G., Reopel, M. R., Sun, J. M., and Tanny, S. M. (2004). *Winning the Profit Game: Smarter Pricing & Smarter Branding*. New York: McGraw-Hill.

Edelman, L. B, Fuller, S. R., and Mara-Drita, I. (2001). 'Diversity Rhetoric and the Managerialization of Law', *American Journal of Sociology*, 106: 1589.

Edvinsson, L. and Malone, M. S. (1997). *Intellectual Capital*. London: Piatkus.

Ehrlich, C. (1993). 'A New Law Firm Structure for the '90s: In Tough Times, Old Partner-Associate System Is Becoming Outdated', *Legal Times*, January 18: S37–S40.

Ellemers, N., Spears, R., and Doosje, B. (1997). 'Sticking Together or Falling Apart: Ingroup Identification as a Psychological Determinant of Group Commitment Versus Individual Mobility, *Journal of Personality and Social Psychology*, 72: 617–26.

Ely, R. J. and Thomas, D. A. (2001). 'Cultural Diversity at Work: The Effects of Diversity Perspectives on Work Group Processes and Outcomes', *Administrative Science Quarterly*, 46: 229.

—— —— (2003). 'Learning From Diversity: The Effect of Learning on Performance', Harvard Business School Working Paper.

Empson, L. (2004). 'Organizational Identity Change: Managerial Regulation and Member Identification in an Accounting Firm Acquisition', *Accounting Organizations and Society*, 29: 759–81.

—— and Chapman, C. (2006). 'Partnership Versus Corporation: Implications of Alternative Forms of Governance in Professional Service Firms', *Research in the Sociology of Organizations*, 24: 145–76.

Epstein, C. F., Saute, R., Oglensky, B., and Gever, M. (1995). 'Glass Ceilings and Open Doors: Women's Advancement in the Legal Profession', *Fordham Law Review*, 64: 291.

Fama, E. and Jensen, M. (1983). 'Separation of Ownership and Control', *Journal of Law and Economics*, 26: 301–25.

Fiegenbaum, A. and Thomas, H. (1993). 'Industry and Strategic Group Dynamics: Competitive Strategy in the Insurance Industry, 1970–1984', *Journal of Management Studies*, 30: 69–105.

Fleischer-Black, M. (2005). 'Coming to Chicago: Thirteen AM LAW 200 Firms Have Moved into Chicago Since the Start of 2001. Do They Know Something Everyone Else Doesn't?', *The American Lawyer*, July: 102–4.

Fortney, S. S. (2001). 'Soul for Sale: An Empirical Study of Associate Satisfaction, Law Firm Culture, and the Effects of Billable Hour Requirements', *UMKC Law Review*, 69: 239–308.

Freidson, E. (1970). *Professional Dominance*. Chicago, IL: Aldine.

Freshfields Brukhaus Deringer (2001). Annual Report.

Fritz, A. (2002). 'Corporate America Commits to Diversity', *Memphis Lawyer*, August 2002.

Galanter, M. and Palay, T. (1991). *Tournament of Lawyers: The Transformation of the Big Law Firm*. Chicago, IL: The University of Chicago Press.

_____ _____ (1994). 'The Many Futures of the Big Law Firm', *South Carolina Law Review*, 45: 905–28.

Garth, B. (2006). 'Lawyers in their Habitats: Law Firms Contemplating Transnational Mergers Should Start Thinking Like Anthropologists', *Legal Affairs*, January–February: 20.

Gawalt, G. W. (1979). *The Promise of Power: The Emergence of the Legal Profession in Massachusetts' 1760–1840*. Westport, CT: Greenwood Press.

Gellhorn, E. (1968). 'The Law School and the Negro', *Duke Law Journal*, 6: 1069–99.

General Motors Corporation (2003). 'Brief in Support of Respondents', in *Grutter v. Bollinger* and *Gratz v. Bollinger*.

General's Brief (2003). 'Consolidated Brief of Lt. General Julius W. Benton, Jr. et al. in Support of Respondents', in *Grutter v. Bollinger* and *Gratz v. Bollinger*.

Gerson, B. (2005). 'The Limits of Professional Behaviour', *Harvard Business Review*, April: 14–16.

Gill, D. (1992). 'Lawyers of Color: Encouraging Diversity', *Chicago Lawyer*, July: 1.

Gilson, R. and Mnookin, R. H. (1985). 'Sharing Among the Human Capitalists: An Economic Inquiry into the Corporate Law Firm and How Partners Split Profits', *Stanford Law Review*, 37: 313–92.

_____ _____ (1989). 'Coming of Age in a Corporate Law Firm: The Economics of Associate Career Patterns', *Stanford Law Review*, 41: 567–95.

Glaberson, W. B. (1986). 'Megafirms Are Taking Over Corporate Law', *Business Week*, 104–12.

Glazer, A. (1985). 'The Advantages of Being First', *American Economic Review*, 75: 473–80.

Goldhaber, M. D. (2002). 'First in Second City: Chicago Law Firm Mayer Brown and Platt Acquires London Firm', *The American Lawyer*, March: 28.

_____ (2005). 'Here Comes China: The Market Is Booming and Lawyers from Both Sides of the Globe Are Getting in on It', *The American Lawyer*, November: 76–7.

Goode, W. J. (1957). 'Community Within a Community: The Professions', *American Sociological Review*, 22: 194–200.

Granovetter, M. (1985). 'Economic Action and Social Structure: The Problem of Embeddedness', *American Journal of Sociology*, 91(3): 491–510.

Grant, R. (2002). *Contemporary Strategy Analysis*. Malden, MA: Blackwell.

Greenwood, R. and Empson, L. (2003). 'The Professional Partnership: Relic or Exemplary Form of Governance?', *Organization Studies*, 24(6): 909–33.

_____ and Hinings, C. R. (1996). 'Understanding Radical Organizational Change: Bringing Together the Old and New Institutionalism', *Academy of Management Review*, 21: 1022–54.

_____ Hinings, C., and Brown, J. (1990). ' "P²-form" Strategic Management: Corporate Practices in Professional Partnerships', *Academy of Management Journal*, 33: 725–55.

_____ Li, S., and Deephouse, D. (2003). 'A Forgotten Question: Does Type of Ownership Matter for Organizational Performance?', Presented at Clifford Chance Conference on Professional Service Firm Management, Saïd Business School, University of Oxford.

Griffiths, A. (2003). 'It's the Economy, Dummkopf: The Law Firm Names May Have Been Anglicized, But Germany's Legal Culture Is Stronger Now than Ever. And This Is Just the Beginning', *The American Lawyer*, April: 130–2, 140.

Hall, R. (1968). 'Professionalization and Bureaucratization', *American Sociological Review*, 33: 725–55.

Hallman, B. (2005). 'The Color of Change: Wal-Mart Continues its Campaign to Hire Diverse Relationship Partners', *American Lawyer*, December.

Hart, O. and Moore, J. (1990). 'Property Rights and the Nature of the Firm', *Journal of Political Economy*, 98(6): 1119–58.

Harvard Law Review Notes (1972). 'A Critical Analysis of Bar Association Minimum Fee Schedules', *Harvard Law Review*, 85: 971–82.

Heinz, J. P. and Laumann, E. O. (1978). 'The Legal Profession: Client Interests, Professional Roles, and Social Hierarchies', *Michigan Law Review*, 76: 1111–42.

_____ _____ (1982). *Chicago Lawyers: The Social Structure of the Bar*. Chicago, IL: University of Chicago Press.

_____ Nelson, R. L., and Laumann, E. O. (2001). 'The Scale of Justice: Observations on the Transformation of Urban Law Practice', *Annual Review of Sociology*, 27: 337–62.

_____ _____ Sandefur, R. L., and Laumann, E. O. (2005). *Urban Lawyers*. Chicago, IL: University of Chicago Press.

Herring, J. (1992). 'Derailed Over Diversity', *San Francisco Recorder*, November 6: 7.

Heydebrand, W. (1973). 'Autonomy, Complexity, and Non-Bureaucratic Coordination in Professional Organizations', in W. Heydebrand (ed.), *Comparative*

Organizations: The Results of Empirical Research. Englewood Cliffs, NJ: Prentice Hall.

Hinings, C. R., Brown, J. L., and Greenwood, R. (1991). 'Change in an Autonomous Professional Service Firm', *Journal of Management Studies*, 24: 373–95.

Hitt, M. A., Bierman, L., Shimizu, K., and Kochhar, R. (2001). 'Direct and Moderating Effects of Human Capital on Strategy and Performance in Professional Service Firms: A Resource-Based Perspective', *Academy of Management Journal*, 44: 13–28.

Hobbs, M. (2005). 'Wal-Mart Diversity Programs Sweeps in 40 New Relationship Partners', *Fulton County Daily Report*, October 25.

Hunt, M. S. (1972). 'Competition in the Home Appliance Industry', doctoral dissertation, Harvard University.

Jemison, D. B. and Sitkin, S. B. (1986). 'Corporate Acquisitions: A Process Perspective', *Academy of Management Review*, 11: 145–63.

Jensen, M. and Meckling, W. (1976). 'Theory of the Firm: Managerial Behaviour, Agency Costs, and Ownership Structure', in J. Barney and W. Ouchi (eds.), *Organizational Economics*. San Francisco, CA: Jossey-Bass.

Johnson, T. J. (1972). *Professions and Power*. London: MacMillan Press.

Jones, L. (2005). 'Corporate Counsel Focus New Attention on Law Firm Hires', *National Law Journal*, November 22.

Jones, S. W. and Glover, M. B. (1998). 'The Attack on Traditional Billing Practices', *UALR Law Journal*, 20: 293–311.

Kang, J. and Banaji, M. (2006). 'Fair Measures: A Behavioral Realist Revision of Affirmative Action', *California Law Review*, 94: 1063–1118.

King, D. R., Dalton, D. R., Daily, C. M., and Covin, J. G. (2004). 'Meta-Analysis of Post-Acquisition Performance: Indicators of Unidentified Moderators', *Strategic Management Journal*, 25: 187–200.

Koppel, N. (2005). 'The High Priced Spread: Behind Every Firm's Average Compensation Number is a More Textured Tale of Business Strategy and Culture', *The American Lawyer*, July: 98.

Krawiec, K. D. (2003). 'Cosmetic Compliance and the Failure of Negotiated Governance', *Washington University Law Quarterly*, 81: 487.

Kritzer, H. M. (1994). 'Lawyer's Fees and the Holy Grail: Where Should Clients Search for Value?, *Judicature*, 77(4): 187–90.

—— (2002). 'Lawyer Fees and Lawyer Behavior in Litigation: What Does the Empirical Literature Really Say?', *Texas Law Review*, 80: 1943–83.

Kummel, W. (1996). 'A Market Approach to Law Firm Economics: A New Model for Pricing, Billing, Compensation and Ownership in Corporate Legal Services', *Columbia Business Law Review*, 1996: 379–422.

Larson, M. S. (1977). *The Rise of Professionalism: A Sociological Analysis*. Berkeley, CA: University of California Press.

Law Society (2004). *Delivering Equality and Diversity: A Handbook for Solicitors*. London: Law Society.

Leibowitz, A. and Tollison, R. (1980). 'Free-Riding, Shirking, and Team Production in Legal Partnerships', *Economic Inquiry*, 18(3): 380–94.

Levinson, S. (1993). 'Identifying the Jewish Lawyer: Reflections on the Construction of Professional Identity', *Cardozo Law Review*, 14: 1577.

Lieberman, M. B. and Montgomery, D. B. (1988). 'First-Mover Advantages', *Strategic Management Journal*, 9: 41–58.

Lieberman, M. B. and Montgomery, D. B. (1998). 'First-Mover (Dis)Advantages: Retrospective and Link with the Resource-Based View', *Strategic Management Journal*, 19: 1111–25.

Longstreth, A. (2003). 'The French Connection', *The American Lawyer*, January: 30–7.

—— (2005a). 'Handing Over The Keys: Coudert Brothers Gives Up 130,000 Square Feet in Manhattan's Grace Building, for "Fair Market Value"', *The American Lawyer*, November: 20.

—— (2005b). 'Princes of the City: Twenty Years after Arriving in Manhattan, Latham and Watkins Now Plays in the Highest Tier of New York Firms. Is it Too Late for Others? Not if they Can Follow Latham's Four Rules', *The American Lawyer*, June: 92–9.

Lorsch, J. and Mathias, P. (1987). 'When Professionals Have to Manage', *Harvard Business Review*, July: 78.

Lorsch, J. W. and Tierney, T. J. (2002). *Aligning the Stars: How to Succeed When Professionals Drive Results*. Boston, MA: Harvard Business School Press.

Lowendahl, B. (2000). *Strategic Management of Professional Service Firms*. Copenhagen: Handelshojskolens Forlag.

Macaulay, S. (1963). 'Non-Contractual Relations in Business: A Preliminary Study', *American Sociological Review*, 28(1): 55–67.

Macneil, I. (1980). *The New Social Contract: An Inquiry into Modern Contractual Relations*. New Haven, CT: Yale University Press.

Maister, D. H. (1993). *Managing the Professional Service Firm*. New York: Free Press.

—— (1997). *Managing the Professional Service Firm*. New York: Free Press.

March, J. G. (1991). 'Exploration and Exploitation in Organizational Learning', *Organization Science*, 2: 71–87.

Mayson, S. W. (1997). *Making Sense of Law Firms: Strategy, Structure and Ownership*. London: Oxford University Press/Blackstone Press.

McGee, J. and Thomas, H. (1986). 'Strategic Groups: Theory, Research and Taxonomy', *Strategic Management Journal*, 7: 141–60.

Meiksins, P. and Watson, J. (1989). 'Professional Autonomy and Organizational Constraint: The Case of Engineers', *The Sociological Quarterly*, 30(4): 561–85.

Menkel-Meadow, C. (1985). 'Portia in a Different Voice: Speculations on a Women's Lawyering Process', *Berkeley Women's Law Journal*, 1: 39.

—— (1995). 'Portia Redux: Another Look at Gender, Feminism and Legal Ethics', in S. Parker and C. Sampford (eds.), *Legal Ethics and Legal Practice*. Oxford: Clarendon Press.

Middleton, D. (2006). 'Barclays Ups the Ante on Panel Firm Diversity', *The Lawyer*, 13 February.

Minority Law Journal (2003). 'The 2003 Diversity Scorecard', *Minority Law Journal*, Summer: 10–11.

Mintzberg, H. (1993). *Structure in Fives: Designing Effective Organizations*. Englewood Cliffs NJ: Prentice Hall.

Mitchell, S. (2001). 'MCAA Presents its Recent Findings: Law Firm Diversity', *Diversity and the Bar*, December.

Mizruchi, M. (1996). 'What Do Interlocks Do? An Analysis, Critique, and Assessment of Research on Interlocking Directorates', *Annual Review of Sociology*, 22: 271–98.

Moore, D. A., Tetlock, P. E., Tanlu, L., and Bazerman, M. X. (2006). 'Conflicts of Interest and the Case of Auditor Independence: Moral Seduction and Strategic Issue Cycling', *Academy of Management Review*, 31(1): 10–29.

Morgan, L. M. (2002). 'The Nature, Antecedents and Consequences of Social Identity-Based Impression Management: Uncovering the Strategies for Professional Image Construction in Cases of Negative Stereotyping', Unpublished Ph.D. Dissertation, University of Michigan.

Morris, T. and Pinnington, A. (1998). 'Promotion to Partner in Professional Service Firms', *Human Relations*, 51(1): 3–24.

National Association of Law Placement Foundation (1998). *Keeping the Keepers: Strategies for Associate Retention in Times of Attrition*. Washington, DC: NALP Foundation.

Nelson, R. L. (1988). *Partners with Power: The Social Transformation of the Large Law Firm*. Berkeley, CA: University of California Press.

—— and Trubek, D. M. (1992). 'Arenas of Professionalism: The Professional Ideology of Lawyers in Context', in R. L. Nelson, R. Solomon, and D. Trubek (eds.), *Lawyers' Ideals/Lawyers' Practices: Transformations in the American Legal Profession*. Ithaca, NY: Cornell University Press.

Nicholson, N. (1998). 'How Hardwired is Human Behaviour?', *Harvard Business Review*, 76(4): 134–47.

Nicolson, D. (2005). 'Demography, Discrimination and Diversity: A New Dawn for the British Legal Profession?', *International Journal of the Legal Profession*, 12: 201.

Parsons, T. (1954). 'The Professions and Social Structure', in T. Parsons (ed.), *Essays in Sociological Theory*. Glencoe, IL: Free Press, pp. 34–49.

Pearce, H. (1988). 'Letter From GM's General Counsel To Outside Law Firms', in D. B. Wilkins and G. M. Gulati (1996), 'Why are There So Few Black Lawyers in Corporate Law Firms?', *California Law Review*, 84: 493.

Pearlman, L. (2002). 'Keeping Up With the Jones Days: Focused and Nimble, Squire, Sanders Has Made a Big Move Up the Global Ranks', *The American Lawyer*, November: 91–2.

Podolny, J. M. (1993). 'A Status-Based Model of Market Competition', *American Journal of Sociology*, 98(4): 829–72.

—— (1994). 'Market Uncertainty and the Social Character of Economic Exchange', *Administrative Science Quarterly*, 39(3): 458–83.

Porter, M. E. (1979). 'The Structure Within Industries and Companies' Performance', *Review of Economics and Statistics*, 61: 417–27.

Porter, M. E. (1980). *Competitive Strategy: Techniques for Analyzing Industries and Competitors*. New York: The Free Press.

Pound, R. (1953). *The Lawyer From Antiquity to Modern Times*. St. Paul, MN: West Publishing.

Powell, W. W. (1990). 'Neither Market nor Hierarchy: Network Forms of Organization', *Research in Organizational Behavior*, 12: 295–336.

Pratt, S. P., Reilly, R. F., and Schweihs, R. P. (1998). *Valuing Small Businesses and Professional Practices*, 3rd edn. New York: McGraw-Hill.

Raelin, J. A. (1985). *Clash of Cultures: Managers Managing Professionals*. Boston, MA: Harvard Business School Press.

—— (1989). *The Clash of Culture—Managers and Professionals*. Boston, MA: Harvard Business School Press.

Reed, R. C. (1989). *Beyond the Billable Hour: An Anthology of Alternative Billing Methods*. Chicago, IL: American Bar Association.

Rhode, D. L. (1993). 'Missing Questions: Feminist Perspectives on Legal Education', *Stanford Law Review*, 45: 1547.

—— (2000). *In the Interests of Justice: Reforming the Legal Profession*. New York: Oxford University Press.

Ross, W. G. (1996). *The Honest Hour: The Ethics of Time-Based Billing by Attorneys*. Durham, NC: Carolina Academic Press.

Rotunda, R. D. (1999). 'Legal Ethics: Innovative Legal Billing, Alternatives to Billable Hours and Ethical Hurdles', *Journal of the Institute for the Study of Legal Ethics*, 2: 221–53.

Rumelt, R. P. (1984). 'Towards a Strategic Theory of the Firm', in R. B. Lamb (ed.), *Competitive Strategic Management*. Englewood Cliffs, NJ: Prentice-Hall, pp. 556–70.

Rutherglen, G. and Kordana, K. A. (1998). 'Farewell to Tournaments—the Need for an Alternative Explanation of Law Firm Structure and Growth', *Virginia Law Review*, 84: 1695–705.

Samuelson, S. S. (1990). 'The Organizational Structure of Law Firms: Lessons from Management Theory', *Ohio State Law Journal*, 51: 645–73.

—— and Jaffe, L. J. (1990). 'A Statistical Analysis of Law Firm Profitability', *Boston University Law Review*, 70: 185–211.

Schultz, U. and Shaw, G. (2003). *Women in the World's Legal Professions*, Oxford: Hart Publishing.

Scott, W. R. (1965). 'Reactions to Supervision in a Heteronymous Professional Organization', *Administrative Science Quarterly*, 10: 65–81.

Shafer, W., Lowe, D., and Fogarty, T. (2002). 'The Effects of Corporate Ownership on Public Accountants' Professionalism and Ethics', *Accounting Horizons*, 16: 109–25.

Sharma, A. (1997). 'Professional as Agent: Knowledge Asymmetry in Agency Exchange', *Academy of Management Review*, 22(3): 758–98.

Shepherd, G. B. and Cloud, M. (1999). 'Time and Money: Discovery Leads to Hourly Billing', *University of Illinois Law Review*, 91–165.

Sherer, P. D. (1995). 'Leveraging Human Assets in Law Firms: Human Capital Structures and Organizational Capabilities', *Industrial and Labor Relations Review*, 48: 671–91.

—— (2005). 'Acquisition Capabilities in Large Law Firms: Gaining Value Through Lateral Partners', Presented at the Clifford Chance Professional Service Firm Conference, Oxford, UK: Oxford University, July 2005.

Shiner, M. (2000). 'Young, Gifted and Blocked! Entry to the Solicitors' Profession', in P. Thomas (ed.), *Discriminating Lawyers*. London: Cavendish Publishing.

Smigel, E. (1969). *The Wall Street Lawyer: Professional Organizational Man?* New York: Russell Sage.

Sommerlad, H. and Sanderson, P. (1998). *Gender, Choice and Commitment: Women Solicitors in England and Wales and the Struggle for Equal Status*, Aldershot, UK: Dartmouth.

Sorenson, J. and Sorenson, T. (1974). 'The Conflict of Professionals in Bureaucratic Organizations', *Administrative Science Quarterly*, 19(1): 98–106.

Spurr, S. J. and Sueyoshi, G. T. (1994). 'Turnover and Promotion of Lawyers: An Inquiry into Gender Differences', *Journal of Human Resources*, 29(3): 813–42.

Stinchcombe, A. L. (1986). *Stratification and Organization: Selected Papers*. Cambridge: Cambridge University Press.

Suddaby, R. and Greenwood, R. (2001). 'Colonizing Knowledge: Commodification as the Dynamic of Jurisdictional Expansion in Professional Service Firms', *Human Relations*, 54: 933–53.

Sunstein, C. R. (2003). *Why Societies Need Dissent*. Cambridge, MA: Harvard University Press.

Thernstrom, S. and Thernstrom, A. (1997). *America in Black and White: One Nation, Indivisible*. New York: Simon & Schuster.

Thomas, D. and Ely, R. J. (1996). 'Making Difference Matter: A New Paradigm for Managing Diversity', *Harvard Business Review*, September–October: 79.

Thomas, H. and Venkatraman, N. (1988). 'Research On Strategic Groups: Progress and Prognosis', *Journal of Management Studies*, 25: 538–55.

Thomas, P. (ed.) (2000). *Discriminating Lawyers*. London: Cavendish Publishing.

Tolbert, P. (1988). 'Institutional Sources of Organizational Culture in Major Law Firms', in L. Zucker (ed.), *Institutional Patterns and Organizations: Culture and Environment*. Cambridge, MA: Ballinger.

—— and Stern, R. (1991). 'Organizations of Professionals: Governance Structures in Large Law Firms', in P. Tolbert and S. Barley (eds.), *Research in the*

Sociology of Organizations: Vol. 8, Organizations and Professions. London: JAI Press, pp. 97–118.

Tomer, J. F. (1987). *Organizational Capital: The Path to Higher Productivity and Well-being*. New York: Praeger.

Trotter, M. H. (1997). *Profit and the Practice of Law*. Athens, GA: The University of Georgia Press.

Tushman, M. and O'Reilly, C. (2002). *Winning Through Innovation*. Boston, MA: Harvard Business School Press.

Uzzi, B. (1996). 'The Sources and Consequences of Embeddedness for the Economic Performance of Organizations: The Network Effect', *American Sociological Review*, 61(4): 674–98.

—— (1997). 'Social Structure and Competition in Interfirm Networks: The Paradox of Embeddedness', *Administrative Science Quarterly*, 42(1): 35–67.

—— (1999). 'Social Embeddedness in the Creation of Financial Capital', *American Sociological Review*, 64(4): 481–505.

—— and Gillespie, J. (2002). 'Knowledge Spillover in Corporate Financing Networks: Embeddedness and the Firm's Debt Performance', *Strategic Management Journal*, 23(7): 595–618.

—— and Lancaster, R. (2003). 'Relational Embeddedness and Learning: The Case of Bank Loan Managers and Their Clients', *Management Science*, 49(4): 383–99.

—— —— (2004). 'Embeddedness and Price Formation in the Corporate Law Market', *American Sociological Review*, 69(3): 319–44.

Vanderwerf, P. and Mahon, J. F. (1997). 'Meta-Analysis of the Impact of Research Methods on Findings of First-Mover Advantages', *Management Science*, 43: 1510–19.

von Nordenflycht, A. (2003). 'Is Public Ownership Bad for Professional Service Firms? Evidence from Advertising Agencies', Presented at Academy of Management Meeting, Seattle.

Weick, K. (1979). *Social Psychology of Organizing*, 2nd edn. New York: McGraw-Hill.

Wenger, E. (1998). *Communities of Practice*. Cambridge: Cambridge University Press.

—— McDermott, R. A., and Snyder, W. M. (2002). *Cultivating Communities of Practice*. Boston, MA: Harvard Business School Press.

Wernerfelt, B. (1984). 'A Resource-Based View of the Firm', *Strategic Management Journal*, 5: 171–80.

Wilkins, D. B. (1993). 'Two Paths to the Mountaintop? The Role of Legal Education in Shaping the Values of Black Corporate Lawyers', *Stanford Law Review*, 45: 1981.

—— (1998a). 'Do Clients Have Ethical Obligations to Lawyers? Some Lessons from the Diversity Wars', *Georgetown Journal of Legal Ethics*, 11: 855.

—— (1998b). 'Fragmenting Professionalism: Racial Identity and the Ideology of Bleached Out Lawyering', *International Journal of The Legal Profession*, 5: 141.

—— (1999a). 'On Being Good and Black', *Harvard Law Review*, 112: 1924.

—— (1999b) 'Partners Without Power? A Preliminary Look at Black Partners in Corporate Law Firms', *Journal of the Institute for the Study of the Legal Profession*, 2: 15.

—— (2000). 'Why Global Law Firms Should Care About Diversity: Five Lessons from the American Experience', *European Journal of Law Reform*, 2: 15.

—— (2004a). 'From "Separate is Inherently Unequal" to "Diversity is Good for Business": The Rise of Market-Based Diversity Arguments and the Fate of the Black Corporate Bar', *Harvard Law Review*, 117: 1548.

—— (2004b). 'Doing Well by Doing Good? The Role of Public Service in the Careers of Black Corporate Lawyers', *Houston Law Review*, 41: 1.

—— (2005). 'A Systematic Response to Systemic Disadvantage: A Reply to Sander', *Stanford Law Review*, 57: 1915.

—— and Gulati, G. M. (1996). 'Why are There So Few Black Lawyers in Corporate Law Firms?', *California Law Review*, 84: 493.

—— —— (1998). 'Reconceiving the Tournament of Lawyers: Tracking, Seeding, and Information Control in the Internal Labor Markets of Elite Law Firms', *Virginia Law Review*, 84: 1581–620.

Zollo, M. and Singh, H. (2004). 'Deliberate Learning in Corporate Acquisitions. Post-Acquisition Strategies and Integration Capability in US Bank Mergers', *Strategic Management Journal*, 25: 1233–45.

Index

Abbott, A. 186
accountability, and ethics 190
advertising agencies
   billing structures 120
   and capital value 142
affirmative action 42, 44
agency theory, and partnership
      governance 14–15
Agincourt, Battle of, and the partnership
      ethos 22, 29
Aldenderfer, M. S. 168
Allen & Overy 201
alternative dispute resolution movement 58
Altheimer & Gray 163–4, 170, 177–9,
      181
Altman Weil Inc. 132
Alvesson, M. 15
American Bar Association, and billing
      practices 119, 125
American Lawyer Corporate Scorecard 105
American Sociological Review 93
Anand, Narasimhan 5
Angel, Tony 3, 8, 21, 35
apprenticeship model, and
      socialization 22–3
Arthur Andersen 215
associates
   and managerialism 50
   ownership practices 137–8
   and pricing in mega law firms 98, 99, 100,
      101–4, 109, 111–12
attorneys, in mega law firms 98, 99
Australia 142
autonomy
   global law firms and the partnership
      ethos 205, 206, 207–8
   and partnership 13–14, 20–2

Baker & McKenzie xvii, 110, 163, 170, 172,
      174, 177–8, 179, 184, 188, 196
Baker, W. E. 94
Banaji, M. 60

Barclays 42, 46
Barney, J. 168, 184
Barrett, P. 44
Baxter, M. 42
Best Lawyers in America 101, 104
Big Bang (1986) 11
billing practices 6, 117–40
   alternatives for the future 135–8
   complaints about attorney's fees 122
   contingency fees 124–5, 127, 136
   cost-plus pricing 130, 131–2, 134,
      135
   explaining choices made by law
      firms 129–30
   fee schedules 123, 124, 126
   flat fees 136
   and the future of law firms 139–40
   historical evolution of 121–6
   hourly billing 118, 119, 122, 125–6,
      127–8, 129–30, 134, 135, 136, 137,
      139, 190
   professional service firms and the
      exchange of labour 119–21
   and state ethical codes 126–7
black American lawyers
   and the business case for diversity 39
   and cosmetic diversity 52–3, 53–4, 55
   and large law firms 44
   and new markets 45–6, 46–7, 49
   and problem-solving 51
   and public service 58–9
Blashfield, R. K. 168
bleached out professionalism 57–9
board membership, and embedded ties in
      mega law firms 97, 108 10, 114 15,
      116
Boies, David 172
Boies Schiller 172, 179
Bower, Marvin 30
Bower, W. 132
Braverman, P. 181
Brint, S. 191, 192

Britain
  Bar Council 37, 39, 44
  Law Society 37, 39, 44
  see also UK law firms
Brock, D. 178
Brown, C. R. 66
Brown, J. 14
bureaucracy
  and organizational structure 155
  and the traditional law firm model xxiii

Calloway, J. A. 119, 135
capital 6–7, 141–61
  demand for 16
  human capital 6, 60, 143, 149–50,
    151, 152, 153, 156, 157, 158–9,
    161
  income-based perspective 6
  and individual and collective
    interests 146–8
  organizational capital 6–7, 143, 150,
    152–6, 156, 157–60
  and ownership 148–9
  relationships between different forms
    of 156
  social capital 6, 143, 150–2, 153, 156,
    157, 158, 160, 161
  valuation 6, 144–6
    making choices 156–60
Carbado, D. 51
Carroll, John 139
Catch Up practices 70–3, 87
Caves, Richard 164–5, 168
Chandler, Mark 139
Chapman, Chris 18, 25
'Charmed Circle' firms 159
China, US law firms in 180
Chroust, A-H. 124
Cisco Systems 139
Clark, E. T. J. 120, 127
Claudius, Emperor 122, 123
Cleary Gottlieb 163–4, 170, 174, 177, 178,
    179, 182, 184
Clementi Review (2004) 12, 142
client relationships 1, 5, 91–116
  and billing practices 135–6
  changing 91–2
  and new practice development 77
  and pricing 91–116
    embedded model of 94–8
    study of US mega law firms 93,
      98–116
  and social capital 150
clients, and partnership governance 15

Clifford Chance vii, viii, xvii, xx, xxi, 8,
    139, 142, 188, 201
  and diversity 37, 40, 56
Clifford Chance Centre for the Management
    of Professional Service Firms 1–2
Cloud, M. 118, 129
cluster analysis 163
  and global law firms 200–1
  of large US law firms 168–85
Coleman, J. S. 94
collective interests, and partnership
    governance 3–4, 20–2, 25–6, 27, 31,
    33
collegiality, global law firms and the
    partnership ethos 205, 206, 207–8,
    212–14, 217
commercialism, and professionalism 7–8
commodification, and partnership
    governance 16–17
Commons, J. R. 121
compensation systems 6, 117–18, 119–20,
    125, 128, 131
  deferred compensation 130, 132–3, 134,
    137
  and new practice development 89–90
  and strategic positioning of law firms 184
competition, and capital investment 141
competitive advantage
  and capital 143
  and global law firms 202
competitors 7, 162–85
  strategic group analysis 7, 162–8
contingency legal fees 124–5, 127
Cooper, D. J. 190
corporate clients
  and billing practices 128
  and diversity 39–40, 41, 45, 46–9
  in-house legal departments 91–2
corporate law firms
  billing practices 118, 119, 123, 126, 128,
    130–5, 138–40
  growth of xvii, 133–4
  ownership practices 133–5
  trends of 'creeping corporatism' 16
corporate management practices, and
    ethics 8
corporate model xix–xxiii
  routinization and standardization xx
  separation of managerial and producing
    roles xix
  separation of ownership and management
    functions xix–xx
  and specialization by function xix
Corporate Scorecard 100

Coser, Lewis 57
cost-plus pricing 130, 131–2, 134, 135
Cotterman, J. D. 118, 133
Coudert Brothers 163–4, 170, 174, 177, 178, 179, 181, 196
Covaleski, M. 14
Cravath 110, 163, 169, 170, 172, 179, 180, 181, 183
cross-border transactions xvii
cultural alignment and collegiality, global law firms and the partnership ethos 205, 206, 212–14
cultural integration, in US law firms 57
culture, and organizational capital 158
Culvahouse, A. B. Jr. 182
Curtis, D. 119

Davis, L. F. 129
Davis Polk 163, 170, 179, 183
Deephouse, D. 11
deferred compensation 130, 132–3, 134, 137
demographic diversity 51
Dickstein Shapiro 172
Dilg, Joseph 139
Dirsmith, M. 14
diversity in law firms 4, 37–63
   business case for 38–43
      limitations of 43–55
   and changing career patterns 61–2
   dangers of cosmetic 52–5
   demand-side diversity initiatives 48
   ethics of 37–8
   learning from 55–62
   and managerialism 49–50
   and problem-solving 50–2
   serving new markets 45–9
   and the tournament of lawyers 60–1
Doosje, B. 51
Dun and Bradstreet 96
Dunlap, Shannon 5, 15, 150

economic income, and valuation 145–6
Edelman, L. B. 51, 54–5
Edvinsson, L. 158
Ehrlich, C. 138
Ellemers, N. 51
Ely, R. J. 45, 51
embeddedness model of pricing 94–8
   and mega law firms 101, 102, 105–16
Empson, Laura 1, 3, 11, 16, 44, 118, 134, 138, 145, 146, 150, 190, 194, 197
Enron affair 193

ethics 7–8, 186–96
   and approaches to the professions 191–2
   balance between commercial and professional values 186
   and the changing context of law 187–8
      law firm responses to 188–9
   and expert definitions of professionalism 192
   and formal managerial practices 190
   and the internal functioning of law firms 187
   and the law as a profession 186–7
   professional behaviour and socializing agents 193–4
expert definitions of professionalism 192
expertise 1, 2, 4–5
   and mega law firms 98
   move from trusteeship to 194
   and new practice development 69, 71–3, 74, 78, 79–83, 86
expertise-driven firms, and organizational capital 153, 154–5
external social capital 150, 152

Fiegenbaum, A. 166
firm size
   and cluster analysis of US law firms 169, 170–2
   and strategic group analysis 167–8
Fleischer-Black, M. 183
Fortney, S. S. 126
founding partners, and new practice development 67, 77–9
Freidson, E. 186, 191
Freshfields xvii, 8, 42, 201
   and diversity 56, 57, 59
   and new practice development initiatives 5
Fuller, S. R. 51

Gabarro, John J. 1, 3, 10
Galanter, M. 66, 133, 138, 187
Gardner, Heidi 4–5
Garth, B. 57
Gawalt, G. W. 124
General Motors Corporation 44, 45, 47, 49–50
Gerson, B. 29
Gillespie, J. 94, 115
Gilson, R. 66, 118, 132, 158
Glaberson, W. B. 134
global law firms xx
   history of 198–201
   and partnership 8–9, 196–217

global law firms (*cont.*)
  and the partnership ethos 205–17
  as partnerships or corporations 215–17
  strategy and alignment 202–5
  and the UK 196–7
globalization xvii, 197
  and diversity 52
Goldhaber, M. D. 179, 180
Goldman Sachs 11
Goode, W. J. 191
Granovetter, M. 94
Grant, R. 168
Greenberg Traurig 184
Greenwood, Royston 7–8, 11, 14, 15, 16, 66, 70, 134
Gulati, G. M. 51, 56, 60, 133

Hall, R. 66
Harvard Law Review 125
Heian, J. 14
Heinz, J. P. 39, 41, 133
hero myth, of new practice development 67, 88
Hinings, C. R. 14, 66, 70, 189
Hitt, M. A. 66
human capital 6, 60, 143, 149–50, 151, 152, 153, 156, 157, 158–9, 161
  and billing practices 130, 139
  and partnership tournaments 133
human capital quality, in mega law firms 102, 104–5
Hunt, M. S. 165

income 6, 117–40
  see also billing practices; compensation systems
individual and collective interests
  and capital valuation 146–8
  and partnership governance 3–4, 20–2, 25–6, 27, 31, 33
information technology xviii
internal social capital 150, 152, 155
International Bar Association 198
international presence, cluster analysis of US firms with 173, 174–9
internationalization of US law firms 163–4
  and competition 180–1
  first and second movers 181–2
investment banking
  billing structures 120
  and capital value 142
  and partnerships 11, 16, 17
investors, and capital valuation 144

Jemison, D. B. 180
Johnson, T. J. 191
Jones Day xvii, 164, 170, 174, 177, 178, 179
junior professionals
  and new practice development 66
  and the partnership ethos 33

Kang, J. 60
King, D. R. 180
knowledge workers, and global law firms 215–16
Koppel, N. 184
Kordana, K. A. 133
Krawiec, K. D. 52
Kritzer, H. M. 122, 126, 128
Kummel, W. 128, 130, 133, 136, 138

Lancaster, Ryon 5, 15, 93, 94, 115, 150
Larson, M. S. 191
lateral recruitment xviii
  and global law firms 204
  in large US firms 175, 176, 177, 181
  and organizational capital 159, 160
Latham & Watkins 170–2, 178, 179, 183
Laumann, E. O. 39, 133
leadership
  and the corporate model xix
  and partnership governance 27–8
Leblebici, Huseyin 6, 55, 142, 158, 187–8, 190, 191, 192–3
leverage, and cluster analysis of US law firms 169, 171
Levinson, Sanford 57
Li, S. 11
Lieberman, M. B. 181
Linklaters xvii, xx, 3, 8, 197, 199–200, 201, 202
  board structure 211–12
  management structure 208–9
Lipton 169
litigation, and partnership governance 17
LLP (limited liability partnership) status 12, 17, 18
lockstep systems
  and capital value 145
  and compensation practices 132
  and global law firms 204, 205, 216
  and new practice development 90
  and partnership governance 18, 25–6
  and strategic positioning of law firms 184
Longstreth, A. 182
Lorsch, J. 187
Lowe Worldwide 149
Lowendahl, B. 187

Macaulay, S. 98
McDermott, R. A. 154
McGee, J. 162, 167
McKinsey & Company 30
Macneil, I. 98
'Magic Circle' firms 159, 197, 198–9, 200, 201
Mahon, J. F. 181
Maister, D. H. 66, 117, 137
Malone, M. S. 158
management
  and the corporate model xix–xx
  global law firms and the partnership ethos 205, 206, 208–10
  lawyers in management roles 1–2
managerial authority, in partnerships 28–9
managerialism, and diversity in law firms 49–50
Mara-Drita, I. 51
March, J. G. 181
market myth, of new practice development 67, 88
Martindale-Hubbell Directory 101
matrix organization structure, and partnership governance 31–2
Mayer Brown 178, 179, 180, 183
Mayson, S. W. 6–7, 155
mega law firms 187 8
  descriptive statistics on 98, 99
  social factors and pricing 93, 98–116
    and board membership 97, 108–10, 114–15, 116
    and firm quality 102, 104–5
    and status affiliations 110–13, 115
    weighing worth of social ties 113–14
mergers and acquisitions xiii, xvii
  and client relationships 91, 92
  and global law firms 204
  and internationalized US law firms 164, 175, 176–7
  and movement of firms 180
  and organizational capital 159–60, 160
Middleton, D. 42
Milbank Tweed xx
minority lawyers
  and the business case for diversity 41, 42
  and changing career patterns 61–2
  and cosmetic diversity 52–5
  exclusion and alienation from traditional law firm culture 56–60
  and exclusionary practices 43
  and new markets 46, 47, 48–9

and the tournament of lawyers 60–1
  see also black American lawyers; minority lawyers; women lawyers
Mintzberg, H. 155
Mirror of Justices 117
Mizruchi, M. 108
Mnookin, R. H. 66, 118, 132, 158
mobility barriers, and strategic groups 166–7
Model Code of Professional Responsibility 122
Montgomery, D. B. 181
Moore, D. A. 194
Morris, T. 5, 66
movement, across strategic groups of law firms 179–80, 183

National Law Journal (NLJ), surveys on mega law firms 100–1, 108
Nelson, R. L. 137, 187
networks
  and the embeddedness model of pricing 97–8
  and social capital 151, 152
new practice development 64–90
  Catch Up 70, 71, 72, 73, 87
  failures 5, 64–5
  growth and diversification 65–6
  myths about 67–8, 88
  Product Extension 70, 71, 72, 73, 87
  recipe ingredients required 69–74, 88
    expertise 69, 71–3, 74, 78, 81, 82
    support 69, 73, 74, 78, 81, 82
    turf 69, 70–1, 74, 78, 81, 82, 86, 87
  recipes 75–87, 88–90
    expertise-led 79–83
    support-centred 84–7
    turf-driven 75–9, 89
  research study 68–9
  Tweaking 70, 71, 72, 73, 87, 89
  White Space 70, 71, 72, 73, 87, 89
Nicolson, Donald 38, 39–40, 42, 44–5, 54
non-equity partners xviii
non-lawyer COOs xviii

O'Melveny & Myers 172, 182
O'Reilly, C. xxiii
organizational capital 6–7, 143, 150, 152–6, 156, 157–60
  and culture 158
  mergers, laterals and retention 159–60
  and rewards 158–9
  and strategy 169

owners
and capital valuation 144–5
and partnership governance 14–15
ownership
balancing incentives and
risk-taking 137–8
and capital 148–9
external ownership and capital
investment 141, 142, 143
global law firms and the partnership
ethos 205, 206, 211–12
partnership tournaments 130, 133–5

Palay, T. 66, 133, 138, 187
Palmore, Richard 38, 47
Parsons, T. 191
partners
and capital investment 141–2
diverse backgrounds of 34
and the growth in legal markets xviii
newly promoted 65–6
non-equity xviii
partner income and cost-plus
pricing 131–2
and pricing in mega law firms 98, 99,
101–4, 109, 111–12
selecting 34
partnership 3–4, 10–36
dynamics of 19–29
ethos 3–4, 11, 18, 19–22, 23–4, 33–6,
194
and global law firms 197, 205–17
evidence for decline of 11–12
evolution of 33–5
and formal management structures 190
and global law firms 8–9, 196–217
imitating 29–32
pressures on 16–18
research study 10–11, 18–19
and socialization 4, 15, 22–4, 25–6, 34
structures 26–9, 35–6
systems 24–6, 35
under-performing partners 26
why it works 12–15
partnership tournaments 130, 133–5
Pearlman, L. 183
peer pressure, and partnership 26
people see diversity in law firms
percentage international, and cluster
analysis of US law firms 169
personal autonomy, and partnership 13–14,
20–2
physicians, billing structures 120
Pinnington, A. 66

plaintiff litigation work, and movement of
firms 180
Podolny, J. M. 15, 94
Popham, Stuart 1
Porter, Michael 164–5, 166, 167, 168, 174
Pound, R. 122
Powell, M. 189
Powell, W. W. 94
PPP variables, and cluster analysis of US law
firms 169, 171, 172–4, 177, 180, 184
Pratt, S. P. 144
PricewaterhouseCoopers 188
pricing
and client relationships 5, 91–116
embedded model of 94–8
study of US mega law firms 93, 98–116
hourly billing 6
see also billing practices
problem-solving, and diversity in law
firms 50–2
process-driven firms, and organizational
capital 153–4
Proctor & Gamble 45
Product Extension practices 70, 71, 72, 73,
87
productivity
compensation systems based on 133,
137
and organizational capital 152
and valuation 145
professional service firms
capital value of 142, 144
and the corporate model xx–xxi
and the exchange of labour 119–21
new practice development 64–90
study of governance in 18–19, 29–32
professionalism
and commercialism 7–8
and global law firms 8–9
and partnership 11
professionals, and partnership
governance 13–14
profitability
and capital value 143, 144
global law firms and the partnership
ethos 205, 206, 214–15, 216
and social capital 151
property rights theory, and partnership
governance 14
public good, global law firms and the
partnership ethos 205, 206, 214–15
public information, and the embeddedness
model of pricing 96–7
public ownership of law firms 12

public service, and black American
    lawyers 58–9

Quinn Emanuel 172, 179

race-matching, and diversity 53–4
Raelin, J. A. 187
Reed, R. C. 122
Reilly, R. F. 144
reputation 1, 5
  and the embeddedness model of
      pricing 97–8, 110–13
  and partnership governance 15
Resnik, J. 119
rewards, and organizational capital 158–9
Rhode, D. L. 119
Robertson, M. A. 119, 135
Robins, Kaplan, Miller & Ciresi 169, 172
Roman law, and legal fees 122–3
Rosen & Katz (Wachtell) 169
Ross, E. G. 122, 124, 125
Rotunda, R. D. 127
Rowe & Maw 179, 180
Rutherglen, G. 133

salaried partners xviii
  and the partnership ethos 33
Samuelson, S. S. 118
Sanderson, P. 44, 56
Sara Lee Corporation 38, 46
Schulte Roth 172
Schweins, R. P. 144
Scott, W. R. 187
self-actualization, and partnership 13–14
senior professionals, and the partnership
    ethos 33
seniority, compensation systems based
    on 132–3, 137
serendipity myth, of new practice
    development 67, 88
Sharma, A. 15
Shearman & Sterling 163–4, 170, 174, 178,
    179, 182
Shepherd, G. B. 118, 129
Sherer, Peter D. 7, 159, 181, 188, 200
Shiner, M. 56
Sidley Austin Brown & Wood 12, 178, 179,
    180
Simpson Thatcher 183
Singh, H. 180
Sitkin, S. B. 180
Skadden Arps xvii, 110, 164, 174, 177, 178,
    179, 181–2, 183
Smigel, Erwin 43–4, 50

Smith, Adam 121
Snyder, W. M. 154
social capital 6, 143, 150–2, 153, 156, 157,
    158, 160, 161
social trustee model of professionalism 15
socialization, and partnership
    governance 4, 15, 22–4, 25–6, 34
Sommerlad, H. 44, 56
South Africa 142
Spears, R. 51
Spurr, S. J. 133
Squire Sanders 183
stability, in clusters of law firms 179–80
staff attorneys xviii
stakeholders
  and capital valuation 144–5
  and partnership governance 12–15
status, and the embeddedness model of
    pricing 97–8, 110–13, 115
Stinchcombe, A. L. 121
strategic group analysis, of large US law
    firms 7, 162–85
stratified apprenticeship xx, xxi–xxiii
Sueyoshi, G. T. 133
Sullivan & Cromwell 183
support, and new practice development 69,
    73, 74, 78, 81, 82, 84–7
sustainability
  and organizational capital 157, 160
  and social capital 151

teamwork, global law firms and the
    partnership ethos 205, 206, 207–8
Tesco 149
Thomas, D. 45, 51
Thomas, H. 162, 166, 167, 168
Thomas, P. 42
The Three Musketeers, and the partnership
    ethos 22, 29
Tierney, T. J. 187
Tolbert, P. 15
tournament system 60–1, 65–6, 130,
    133–5
Toyota 215
traditional career patterns, and bleached out
    professionalism 57–8
traditional law firm culture, and women and
    minority lawyers 56–60
traditional law firm model xviii, xx–xxiii
  effects of growth, competitiveness and
      change xxii–xxiii
  and ethics 8
  managing scale and complexity xxiii, 3
  organization by practices xx–xxi

traditional law firm model (*cont.*)
  partners as managers and owners xxi
  and stratified apprenticeship xx, xxi–xxiii
Trotter, M. H. 117
trusted advisor roles, in mega law firms
    107
turf, and new practice development 69,
    70–1, 74, 75–9, 81, 82, 86, 87,
    89–90
Tushman, M. xxiii
Tweaking practices 70, 71, 72, 73, 87, 89

UK law firms
  diversity in 37, 56
  exclusionary practices 43
  and globalization 198–201
  'Magic Circle' firms 159, 197, 198–9, 200,
    201
  and partnership 11–12
US law firms
  'Charmed Circle' firms 159
  and cultural integration 57
  diversity in 37–63
  and globalization of UK law firms 200–1
  and homogeneity in large firms 43–4, 52
  internationalization of 163–4, 196
  in major international cities 178–9, 188
  in major US cities 177–8, 182–3
  and partnership 12
  profits per partner (PPP) 7
  revenues 92, 93

strategic group analysis of 7, 162–85
  see also billing practices; mega law firms
Uzzi, Brian 5, 15, 93, 94, 115, 150

Vanderwerf, P. 181
Venkatraman, N. 167, 168
Vietnam War 49
Voge, William 183

Wachtell 169, 170, 172, 179
Wal-Mart 38–9, 41, 46
Weick, Karl xxi
Weil Gotshal xx, xxi–xxiii, 178, 179
Wenger, E. 154
Wernerfelt, B. 168
White & Case 164, 170, 174, 178, 179
White Space practices 70, 71, 72, 73, 87, 89
Wilkins, David B. 4, 34, 51, 52, 56, 60, 133,
    138
women lawyers 4
  and the business case for diversity 41
  and changing career patterns 61–2
  exclusion and alienation from traditional
    law firm culture 56–60
  and exclusionary practices 43
  and managerialism 50
  and new markets 46
  and the tournament of lawyers 60–1
workers, and capital valuation 144

Zollo, M. 180